UNIX® FOR DUMMIES®

3RD EDITION

by John R. Levine
and Margaret Levine Young

IDG Books Worldwide, Inc.
An International Data Group Company

Foster City, CA ♦ Chicago, IL ♦ Indianapolis, IN ♦ Southlake, TX

UNIX® For Dummies®, 3rd Edition

Published by
IDG Books Worldwide, Inc.
An International Data Group Company
919 E. Hillsdale Blvd.
Suite 400
Foster City, CA 94404
www.idgbooks.com (IDG Books Worldwide Web site)
www.dummies.com (Dummies Press Web site)

Library of Congress Catalog Card No.: 97-73295

ISBN: 0-7645-0130-5

Printed in the United States of America

10 9 8 7 6 5 4 3 2

3DD/ST/QZ/ZX/IN

Distributed in the United States by IDG Books Worldwide, Inc.

Distributed by Macmillan Canada for Canada; by Transworld Publishers Limited in the United Kingdom; by IDG Norge Books for Norway; by IDG Sweden Books for Sweden; by Woodslane Pty. Ltd. for Australia; by Woodslane Enterprises Ltd. for New Zealand; by Longman Singapore Publishers Ltd. for Singapore, Malaysia, Thailand, and Indonesia; by Simron Pty. Ltd. for South Africa; by Toppan Company Ltd. for Japan; by Distribuidora Cuspide for Argentina; by Livraria Cultura for Brazil; by Ediciencia S.A. for Ecuador; by Addison-Wesley Publishing Company for Korea; by Ediciones ZETA S.C.R. Ltda. for Peru; by WS Computer Publishing Corporation, Inc., for the Philippines; by Unalis Corporation for Taiwan; by Contemporanea de Ediciones for Venezuela; by Computer Book & Magazine Store for Puerto Rico; by Express Computer Distributors for the Caribbean and West Indies. Authorized Sales Agent: Anthony Rudkin Associates for the Middle East and North Africa.

For general information on IDG Books Worldwide's books in the U.S., please call our Consumer Customer Service department at 800-762-2974. For reseller information, including discounts and premium sales, please call our Reseller Customer Service department at 800-434-3422.

For information on where to purchase IDG Books Worldwide's books outside the U.S., please contact our International Sales department at 415-655-3200 or fax 415-655-3295.

For information on foreign language translations, please contact our Foreign & Subsidiary Rights department at 415-655-3021 or fax 415-655-3281.

For sales inquiries and special prices for bulk quantities, please contact our Sales department at 415-655-3200 or write to the address above.

For information on using IDG Books Worldwide's books in the classroom or for ordering examination copies, please contact our Educational Sales department at 800-434-2086 or fax 817-251-8174.

For press review copies, author interviews, or other publicity information, please contact our Public Relations department at 415-655-3000 or fax 415-655-3299.

For authorization to photocopy items for corporate, personal, or educational use, please contact Copyright Clearance Center, 222 Rosewood Drive, Danvers, MA 01923, or fax 508-750-4470.

is a trademark under exclusive
license to IDG Books Worldwide, Inc.,
from International Data Group, Inc.

About the Authors

Margaret Levine Young and **John R. Levine** were members of a computer club in high school — before high school students, or even high schools, *had* computers. They came in contact with Theodor H. Nelson, author of *Computer Lib* and inventor of hypertext, who fostered the idea that computers should not be taken seriously and that everyone can and should understand and use computers.

Margy has been using small computers since the 1970s. She graduated from UNIX on a PDP/11 to Apple DOS on an Apple II to MS-DOS and UNIX on a variety of machines. She has done all kinds of jobs that involve explaining to people that computers aren't as mysterious as they might think, including managing the use of PCs at Columbia Pictures, teaching scientists and engineers what computers are good for, and writing computer manuals and books, including *Dummies 101: The Internet For Windows 95* and *Dummies 101: Netscape Navigator* (with Hy Bender), *Dummies 101: WordPerfect 7 For Windows 95* and *Dummies 101: WordPerfect 6.1 For Windows* (with Alison Barrows), *Dummies 101: Access 97 For Windows* and *Dummies 101: Access For Windows 95* (with Rodney Lowe), *The Internet For Windows For Dummies Starter Kit, MORE Internet For Dummies, WordPerfect For Windows For Dummies* (with David C. Kay), *The Internet For Dummies Quick Reference, Understanding Javelin PLUS,* and *The Complete Guide to PC-File.* She has a degree in Computer Science from Yale University.

John wrote his first program on an IBM 1130 (a computer roughly as powerful as your typical modern digital wristwatch, only harder to use) in 1967. His first exposure to UNIX was while hanging out with friends in Princeton in 1974. He became an official system administrator of a networked computer at Yale in 1975. He started working part-time for Interactive Systems, the first commercial UNIX company, in 1977 and has been in and out of the computer and network biz ever since. He put his company on Usenet so long ago that it appears in a 1982 *Byte* magazine article, which included a map of Usenet sites. He used to spend most of his time writing software, but now he mostly writes books (including *Internet SECRETS* [with Carol Baroudi], *The Internet For Dummies* [also with Carol Baroudi], *The Internet For Dummies Quick Reference,* and *MORE Internet For Dummies,* all published by IDG Books Worldwide) because it's more fun. He also teaches some computer courses, publishes and edits an incredibly technoid magazine called *The Journal of C Language Translation,* and moderates a Usenet newsgroup. He holds a B.A. and a Ph.D. in Computer Science from Yale University, but please don't hold that against him.

ABOUT IDG BOOKS WORLDWIDE

Welcome to the world of IDG Books Worldwide.

IDG Books Worldwide, Inc., is a subsidiary of International Data Group, the world's largest publisher of computer-related information and the leading global provider of information services on information technology. IDG was founded more than 25 years ago and now employs more than 8,500 people worldwide. IDG publishes more than 275 computer publications in over 75 countries (see listing below). More than 60 million people read one or more IDG publications each month.

Launched in 1990, IDG Books Worldwide is today the #1 publisher of best-selling computer books in the United States. We are proud to have received eight awards from the Computer Press Association in recognition of editorial excellence and three from *Computer Currents'* First Annual Readers' Choice Awards. Our best-selling *...For Dummies®* series has more than 30 million copies in print with translations in 30 languages. IDG Books Worldwide, through a joint venture with IDG's Hi-Tech Beijing, became the first U.S. publisher to publish a computer book in the People's Republic of China. In record time, IDG Books Worldwide has become the first choice for millions of readers around the world who want to learn how to better manage their businesses.

Our mission is simple: Every one of our books is designed to bring extra value and skill-building instructions to the reader. Our books are written by experts who understand and care about our readers. The knowledge base of our editorial staff comes from years of experience in publishing, education, and journalism — experience we use to produce books for the '90s. In short, we care about books, so we attract the best people. We devote special attention to details such as audience, interior design, use of icons, and illustrations. And because we use an efficient process of authoring, editing, and desktop publishing our books electronically, we can spend more time ensuring superior content and spend less time on the technicalities of making books.

You can count on our commitment to deliver high-quality books at competitive prices on topics you want to read about. At IDG Books Worldwide, we continue in the IDG tradition of delivering quality for more than 25 years. You'll find no better book on a subject than one from IDG Books Worldwide.

John Kilcullen
CEO
IDG Books Worldwide, Inc.

Steven Berkowitz
President and Publisher
IDG Books Worldwide, Inc.

Eighth Annual Computer Press Awards ≥ 1992

Ninth Annual Computer Press Awards ≥ 1993

Tenth Annual Computer Press Awards ≥ 1994

Eleventh Annual Computer Press Awards ≥ 1995

Dedication

Margy dedicates this book to Jordan, Meg, and Zac, who make life worth living.

John dedicates this book to Tonia and to Sarah Willow, who doesn't understand why anyone would publish a book that doesn't contain pictures of cute puppies.

Acknowledgments

The authors thank David Guertin for his important contributions to this third edition, particularly the added coverage of Linux. (Experienced readers of acknowledgement pages will know what that means.)

We thank our editors at IDG, particularly project editor Pat O'Brien, for taming the seething mass of our manuscript into the relatively coherent book you hold in your hands. (Any remaining seething remains our responsibility, of course.)

The entire contents of this book was transmitted among the authors and editors using the Internet and the World Wide Web. We thank our Internet providers Finger Lakes Technology Group (Trumansburg NY), Sovernet (Bellows Falls VT), and Lightlink (Ithaca NY.)

Publisher's Acknowledgments

We're proud of this book; please send us your comments about it by using the IDG Books Worldwide Registration Card at the back of the book or by e-mailing us at feedback/dummies@idgbooks.com. Some of the people who helped bring this book to market include the following:

Acquisitions, Development, and Editorial

Project Editor: Pat O'Brien

Acquisitions Editor: Michael Kelly

Copy Editor: Gregory R. Robertson

Technical Editor: Stephen Pedrick

Editorial Manager: Mary C. Corder

Production

Project Coordinator: E. Shawn Aylsworth

Layout and Graphics: Cameron Booker, Linda M. Boyer, Angela F. Hunckler, Brent Savage

Proofreaders: Renee Kelty, Jennifer K. Overmyer, Robert Springer, Karen York

Indexer: Sharon Hilgenberg

General and Administrative

IDG Books Worldwide, Inc.: John Kilcullen, CEO; Steven Berkowitz, President and Publisher

IDG Books Technology Publishing: Brenda McLaughlin, Senior Vice President and Group Publisher

Dummies Technology Press and Dummies Editorial: Diane Graves Steele, Vice President and Associate Publisher; Kristin A. Cocks, Editorial Director; Mary Bednarek, Acquisitions and Product Development Director

Dummies Trade Press: Kathleen A. Welton, Vice President and Publisher

IDG Books Production for Dummies Press: Beth Jenkins, Production Director; Cindy L. Phipps, Manager of Project Coordination, Production Proofreading, and Indexing; Kathie S. Schutte, Supervisor of Page Layout; Shelley Lea, Supervisor of Graphics and Design; Debbie J. Gates, Production Systems Specialist; Robert Springer, Supervisor of Proofreading; Debbie Stailey, Special Projects Coordinator; Tony Augsburger, Supervisor of Reprints and Bluelines; Leslie Popplewell, Media Archive Coordinator

Dummies Packaging and Book Design: Patti Sandez, Packaging Specialist; Lance Kayser, Packaging Assistant; Kavish + Kavish, Cover Design

◆

The publisher would like to give special thanks to Patrick J. McGovern, without whom this book would not have been possible.

◆

Contents at a Glance

Cartoons at a Glance

By Rich Tennant

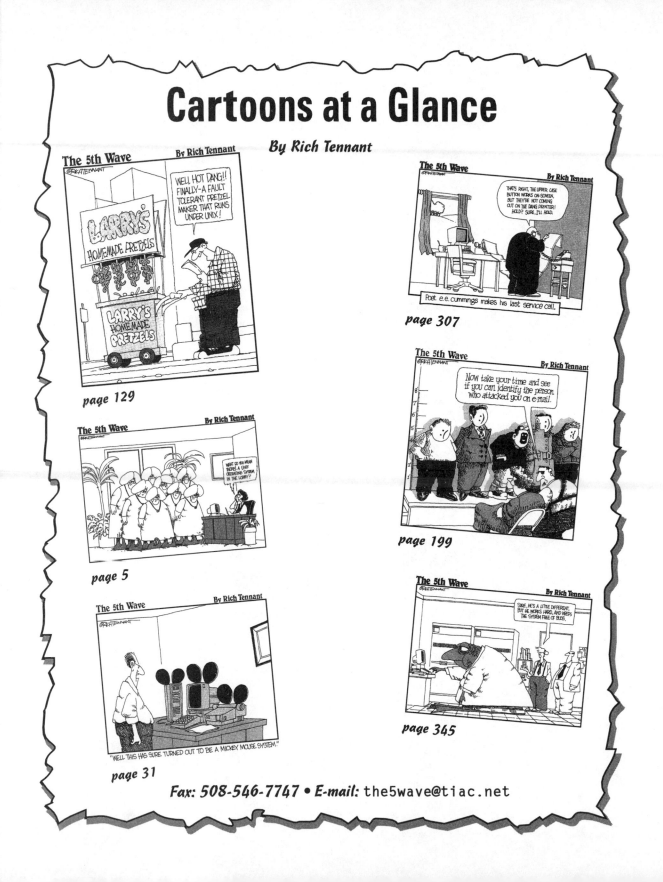

Table of Contents

· ·

IDG Books Worldwide Registration Card .... Back of Book

Introduction

* *

*W*elcome to *UNIX For Dummies,* 3rd Edition! There are lots of good books about UNIX, but most of them assume that you have a degree in computer science, would love to learn every strange and useless command UNIX has to offer (and there are plenty), and enjoy memorizing unpronounceable commands and options. This book is different.

Instead, this book describes what you really do with UNIX — how to get started, what commands you really need, and when to give up and go for help. And we describe it all in plain, ordinary English.

About This Book

This book is designed to be used when you can't figure out what to do next. We don't flatter ourselves that you are interested enough in UNIX to sit down and read the whole thing. When you run into a problem using UNIX ("I thought I typed a command that would copy a file, but it didn't respond with any message . . ."), just dip into the book long enough to solve your problem.

We have included sections about these kinds of things:

- Typing commands
- Copying, renaming, or deleting files
- Printing files
- Finding where your file went
- Using the Internet from UNIX
- UNIX commands for people who know Windows

In this third edition, we've beefed up the information about Linux, a new, widely used version of UNIX, and about the Internet, to which many UNIX computers are connected, including a new chapter on using the World Wide Web from UNIX.

How to Use This Book

Use this book as a reference. (Or use it as a decorative paperweight — whatever works for you.) Look up your topic or command in the table of contents or the index; they refer to the part of the book in which we describe what to do and perhaps define a few terms, if absolutely necessary.

When you have to type something, it appears in the book as follows:

```
cryptic UNIX command to type
```

Type it just as it appears. Use the same capitalization we do — UNIX cares deeply about UPPERCASE and lowercase letters. Then press the Enter or Return key (we call it Enter throughout this book). The book tells you what should happen when you give each command and what your options are. Sometimes part of the command is in *italics;* the italicized stuff is a sample name, and you have to substitute the actual name of the file, computer, or person affected.

Chapter 25 lists error messages you might run into, and Chapter 26 lists common user mistakes. You might want to peruse the latter to avoid these mistakes before they happen.

Who Are You?

In writing this book, we have assumed these things about you:

- You have a UNIX computer or terminal.
- You want to get some work done on it.
- Someone has set it up so that, if you turn it on (in many cases, it's left on all the time), you are talking to UNIX.
- You are not interested in becoming the world's next great UNIX expert.

How This Book Is Organized

This book has six parts. The parts stand on their own — you can begin reading wherever you want. This section lists the parts of the book and what they contain:

Part I: Before the Beginning

This part tells you how to get started with UNIX, including figuring out which kind of UNIX you are using. (You need to know this information later, because commands can differ from one type of UNIX to another.) You learn how to log in, type UNIX commands, and ask for help. For Linux users, we include a short chapter on what's it's all about, why Linux is cool, and how to get more information about Linux.

Part II: Some Basic Stuff

Like most computer systems, UNIX stores information in files. This part explains how to deal with files — creating, copying, and getting rid of them. It also talks about directories so that you can keep your files organized, find files that have somehow gone astray, and print files on paper.

Part III: Getting Things Done

This part talks about getting some work done in UNIX. It gives step-by step instructions for using the four most common text editors to create and change text files, how to run several programs at the same time (to get confused several times as fast), making your Linux system behave, a Rosetta stone to help Windows users figure out how to use UNIX, and directions for a bunch of other useful UNIX commands.

Part IV: UNIX and the Internet

Most UNIX systems are connected to networks, and many are connected to the biggest network of them all: the Internet. This part prepares you for the world of communications, including instructions for sending and receiving electronic mail, for transferring files over the network, for logging in to other computers over the Internet, and for surfing on the World Wide Web.

Part V: Help!

If disaster strikes, check this part of the book. It includes information about what to do if something bad happens, what to do about backups, and a list of common UNIX error messages.

Part VI: The Part of Tens

This part is a random assortment of other tidbits about UNIX, including common mistakes and how to get online help — all organized in convenient ten-item lists, sort of.

Icons Used in This Book

Some particularly nerdy, technoid information is coming up, which you can skip (although, of course, we think it's all interesting).

A nifty little shortcut or time-saver, or a piece of information you can't afford to be without.

Yarrghhh! Don't let this happen to you!

Information that applies only if your computer is on a network. If it is not, you can skip to the next section.

Something presented in an earlier section of the book, or something you need to remember to do.

The friendly penguin tells you there's information specifically about Linux (see Chapter 3 for what Linux is).

What Now?

Whenever you hit a snag in UNIX, just look up the problem in the table of contents or index of this book. Don't feel bad if you look up a number of topics. Most computer users never face anything as daunting as UNIX (remind Windows and Macintosh user friends)!

If you have comments about this book and your computer can send e-mail via the Internet, you can send them to our friendly mail robot (who will write back) at unix3@gurus.com. (We authors will also read your message and write back if time permits.) Also visit our Web site with book info and updates at http://net.gurus.com. For information about the ...*For Dummies* books in general, write to info@idgbooks.com or surf on by http://www.dummies.com.

Part I
Before the Beginning

In this part . . .

Yikes! You have to learn UNIX! Does this mean that you're about to get inducted, kicking and screaming, into a fraternity of hard-bitten, humorless nerds with a religious dedication to a 25-year-old operating system from the phone company? Well, yes and no. We hope we're not humorless.

If you're like most UNIX users, a zealot stopped at your desk, connected your terminal or workstation, gave you five minutes of incomprehensible advice, demonstrated a few bizarre games (like roaches that hide behind the work on your screen) and disappeared. Now you're on your own.

Don't worry. This part of the book explains the absolute minimum you need to to get your UNIX system's attention, persuade it that you are allowed to use it, and maybe even accomplish something useful.

Chapter 1
Start 'Er Up, UNIX!

In This Chapter

▶ Turning your computer on and getting its attention

▶ Persuading your computer to let you use it

▶ Using user names, passwords, and all that

▶ Logging out when you finish

Turning Your Computer On and Off

If you think that turning your computer on and off is easy, you may be wrong. Because UNIX runs on so many almost-but-not-quite-compatible computers — all of which work somewhat differently — you first must figure out which kind of UNIX computer you have before you can turn it on.

A dumb terminal

The simplest way to hook up to a UNIX system is with what's known (sneeringly) as a *dumb terminal.* You can identify a dumb terminal by a complete absence of mice and floppy disks and all that other stuff that causes confusion in a more advanced computer. There's a lot to be said for dumb terminals: They're simple and reliable. With UNIX, you can do hundreds, if not thousands, of things wrong to totally scramble a more advanced machine; these same boo-boos make no difference to a dumb terminal.

Turning on a dumb terminal is easy. You find the power switch (probably on the back) and flip it on. Because there are no pesky disks and stuff, you can turn it on or off whenever you want and not break anything. People make long, sort of theological arguments about whether to leave the picture tube on all the time. Personally, we turn off our terminals overnight and don't worry about them at other times.

After you turn on the terminal, you use it to communicate with the computer that is running UNIX. If it is directly wired to the computer, UNIX asks you to log in before you can do anything else. (See "Hey, UNIX! I Want to Log In," later in this chapter.) If not, you may have to perform some additional steps to call the computer or otherwise connect to it.

The PC masquerade ball

Because PCs are so cheap these days, it is common to press a PC into duty as a terminal. You run a *terminal emulator* program on the PC, and suddenly your mild-mannered PC turns into a super UNIX terminal. (Truthfully, it's more the other way around: You make a perfectly good PC that can run Leisure Suit Larry and other business productivity-type applications act like a dumb terminal that can't do much of anything on its own.)

When you finish with UNIX, you leave the terminal emulator, usually by pressing Ctrl+X or some equally arcane combination of keys. (Consult your local guru: There's no standardization.) Like Cinderella at the stroke of midnight, the terminal-emulating PC turns back into a real PC. To turn it off, you wait for the PC's disks to stop running (carefully scrutinize the front panel until all the little red or green lights go out) and then reach around and turn off the big, red switch. If you don't wait for the lights to go out, you're liable to lose some files.

If you have a network installed, which these days has become so cheap that nearly everyone does, your PC running Windows may have a network connection to your UNIX system. Windows 95 and Mac OS (the Macintosh operating system) have the network stuff built in, but on Windows 3.1, you have to add extra network software with names such as Trumpet or Chameleon.

If you do have a network connection, you can use a program called telnet (described in Chapter 21) to connect to your UNIX system. After telnet is running and connected to your UNIX system, within your telnet program's window, you get a faithful recreation of a 1970s dumb terminal, and you can proceed to log in, as described in the next section.

If a train stops at a train station, what happens at a workstation?

A *workstation* is a computer with a big screen, a mouse, and a keyboard. You may say, "I have a PC with a big screen, a mouse, and a keyboard. Is it really a workstation?" Although UNIX zealots get into long arguments over this question, for our purposes, we'll say that it is.

What you were hoping we wouldn't tell you: The difference between a PC and a workstation

First, you have to understand that this isn't a technical question — it's a theological question. Back in olden days (about 1980), telling the difference was easy. A workstation had a large graphical screen — at least large by the standards of those days — 1,000K of memory, a fast processor chip, and a network connection, and it cost about $10,000. A PC had a lousy little screen, 64K of memory, a slow processor chip, and a floppy or two, and it cost more like $4,000.

Well, these days your typical $1,200 PC has a nice screen (a lot nicer than what the workstation used to have), 16,000K of memory, a fast Pentium processor, a big disk, and a network connection. That's a lot better than what people used to call a workstation. Does that make a PC a workstation? Oh, no. Modern workstations have even better screens, buckets of memory, a turbocharged processor chip . . . you get the idea. What's the difference?

Maybe it's the software that people use: Most workstations are designed to run UNIX (or, in a few cases, proprietary systems similar in

power to UNIX), whereas PCs run DOS or Windows or Macintosh software. But wait, there are perfectly good versions of UNIX that run on PC hardware, and Windows NT runs on a lot of boxes that everyone agrees are workstations. Now what? You can get into esoteric arguments about the speed of the connection between the guts of the computer on the one hand and the disks, screens, and networks on the other hand and argue that workstations have faster connections than PCs, but there are examples that don't fit there, too.

As far as we can tell, if a computer is *designed* to run DOS or Windows or the Mac OS, then it's a PC. If it's *designed* to run UNIX, then it's a workstation. If this sounds to you like a pretty feeble and arbitrary distinction, you understand perfectly. Here at UNIX For Dummies Central, we have a couple of large PCs running UNIX (which makes them look, to our eyes, just like workstations) and a couple of other smaller ones running Windows. Works fine for us.

Turning on a workstation is easy enough: You reach around the back and turn on the switch. Cryptic things that appear on the screen tell you that UNIX is going through the long and not-at-all-interesting process of starting up. Starting up can take anywhere from 10 seconds to 10 minutes, depending on the version of UNIX, number of disks, phase of the moon, and so on. Sooner or later, UNIX demands that you log in. To find out how, skip to the section "Logging In: U(NIX) Can Call Me Al," later in this chapter.

Turning *off* a workstation is a more difficult problem. Workstations are jealous of their prerogatives and *will* punish you if you don't turn them off in exactly the right way. Their favorite punishment is to throw away all the files related to whatever you were just working on. The exact procedure varies from one model of workstation to another, so you have to ask a local guru for advice. Typically, you enter a command along these lines:

```
shutdown +3
```

This command tells the workstation to shut down (in three minutes, in this example). With some versions of UNIX, that would be too easy. The version we use most often uses this command:

```
halt
```

If you use Linux, type this command to shut down the system right away:

```
shutdown -r now
```

The workstation then spends a while putting a program to bed or whatever else it does to make it feel important because it knows that you're waiting there, tapping your feet. Eventually, it tells you that it's finished. At that point, turn it off right away, before it gets any more smart ideas.

An approved method for avoiding the hassle of remembering how to turn off your workstation is never to shut off your computer (although you can turn off the *screen*). That's what we do.

X marks the terminal

An *X terminal* is similar to an extremely stripped-down workstation that can run only one program — the one that makes X Windows work. (See Chapter 4 to find out what X Windows are — or don't. It's all the same to us.) Turning an X terminal on and off is pretty much like turning a regular dumb terminal on and off. Because the X terminal doesn't run programs, turning it off doesn't cause the horrible problems that turning off a workstation can cause.

Hey, UNIX! I Want to Log In

Whether you use a terminal or a workstation, you have to get the attention of UNIX. You can tell when you have its attention because it demands that you identify yourself by logging in. If you use a workstation, when UNIX has finished loading itself, it is immediately ready for you to log in. (Skip ahead to "Logging In: U(NIX) Can Call Me Al.") But you terminal users (X or otherwise) may not be so lucky.

Direct access

If you're lucky, your terminal is attached directly to the main computer, so that it immediately displays a friendly invitation to start work, something like this:

```
ttyS034 login:
```

Well, maybe the invitation isn't that friendly. By the way, the ttyS034 is the name UNIX gives to your terminal. Why doesn't it use something easier to remember, like Fred or Muffy? Beats us!

This catchy phrase tells you that you have UNIX's attention and that it is all ears (metaphorically speaking) and waiting for you to log in. You can skip the next section and go directly to "Logging In: U(NIX) Can Call Me Al."

If your UNIX system displays a terminal name, make a note of it. You don't care what your terminal's name is, but if something gets screwed up and you have to ask an expert for help, we can promise you that the first thing the guru will ask is, "What's your terminal name?" If you don't know, the guru may make a variety of nerd-type disparaging comments. But if you can say, "A-OK, Roger. That's terminal tty125," your guru will assume that you are a with-it kind of user and may even try to help you.

Yo, UNIX! — not-so-direct access

If you're using a PC with a modem, you probably have to tell the modem to call the UNIX system. All terminal emulators have a way to make the call with two or three keystrokes, but all these ways are different, of course. (Are you surprised?) You have to ask your local guru for info.

After your terminal is attached to the computer, turned on, and otherwise completely ready to do some work, UNIX, as often as not, doesn't admit that you're there. It says nothing and appears to ignore you. In this way, UNIX resembles a recalcitrant child — firm but kind discipline is needed here.

The most common ways to get UNIX's attention are as follows:

✔ Press the Return or Enter key. (We'll call it the Enter key in this book, if you don't mind.) Try it two or three times if it doesn't work the first time.

✔ Try other attention-getting keystrokes. Ctrl+C (hold down the Ctrl key, sometimes labeled Control, and press C) is a good one. So is Ctrl+Z.

✔ If you're attached to UNIX through a modem, you may have to do some speed matching (described in a minute). You do this by pressing the Break key a few times. If you're using a terminal emulator, the Break key may be disguised as Alt+B or some other hard-to-find combination.

Two modems can talk to each other in about 17,000 different ways, and they have easy-to-remember names, such as B212, V.32, and V.32bis. (*Bis* is French for "and a half." Really.) After you call the UNIX system's modem with your modem, the two modems know perfectly well which way they're communicating, but UNIX sometimes doesn't know. Every modem made since about 1983 announces the method it's using when it makes the connection. Because the corresponding piece of UNIX code dates from about 1975, though, UNIX ignores the modem's announcement and guesses, probably incorrectly, at what's being used.

If you see something like ~xxx~~r.!" on-screen, you need to try *speed matching.* Every time you press Break (or the terminal emulator's version of Break), UNIX makes a different guess at the way its modem is working. If it guesses correctly, you see the login prompt; if it guesses incorrectly, you see another bunch of ~xxx~~~@(r)!" or you see nothing. If UNIX guessed incorrectly, press Break again. If you overshoot and keep Breaking past your matched speed, keep going, and it'll come around again.

After a while, you will discover exactly how many Returns, Enters, Breaks, and what-nots your terminal needs in order to get UNIX's attention. It will become second nature to type them, and you won't even notice what a nerd you look like while you do it. There's no way around that last part, unfortunately.

Logging In: U (NIX) Can Call Me Al

Every UNIX user has a user name and a password. Your system administrator assigns you a user name and a password. You can and should change your password from time to time, but you're stuck with your user name.

Before you can start work, you must prove your bona fides by logging in — that is, by typing your user name and password. How hard can it be to type two words? Really, now. The problem is this: Because of a peculiarity of human brain wiring, you will find that you can't enter your user name and password without making a typing mistake. It doesn't matter whether your user name is *al* — you will type *Al, la, a;L,* and every other possible combination.

UNIX always considers uppercase and lowercase letters to be different: If your user name (sometimes also called your *login* name) is *egbert,* you must type it exactly that way. Don't type *Egbert, EGBERT,* or anything else. Yes, we know that your name is *Egbert* and not *egbert,* but your computer doesn't know that. UNIX user names almost always are written entirely in lowercase. Pretend that you're a disciple of e. e. cummings.

When you type your user name and password and make a mistake, you may be tempted to backspace over your mistake. If only life were that easy. Guess how you backspace over typing errors when you type your user name and password? You use the # key, of course! (We're sure that it made sense in 1975.) Some — but not all — versions of UNIX have changed so that you can use Backspace or Delete; you may have to experiment. If you want UNIX to ignore everything you have typed, press @, unless your version of UNIX has changed the command key to Ctrl+U (for *untype,* presumably — doubleplusungood). So, Egbert (as you typed your user name), you may have typed something like this:

```
ttyS034 login: Eg#Iegberq#t
```

Finish entering your user name by pressing Enter or Return.

After you type your user name, UNIX asks you to enter your password, which you type the same way and end by pressing Enter (or Return, but we'll call it Enter). Because your password is secret, it doesn't appear on-screen as you type it. How can you tell whether you've typed it correctly? You can't! If UNIX agrees that you've typed your user name and password acceptably, it displays a variety of uninteresting legal notices and a message from your system administrator (usually delete some files, the disk is full) and passes you on to the shell, which you learn about in Chapter 2.

If UNIX did not like either your user name or your password, UNIX says Login incorrect and tells you to start over with your user name.

In the interest of security, UNIX asks you for a password even if you type your user name wrong. This arrangement confuses the bad guys — but not nearly as much as it confuses regular users. So if UNIX rejects your password, maybe you typed your user name incorrectly.

Password Smarts

Like every UNIX user, you should have a password. You can get along without a password only under these circumstances:

✔ You keep the computer in a locked room to which you have the only key, and it's not connected to any network.

✔ You don't mind whether unruly 14-year-olds borrow your account and randomly insert dirty knock-knock jokes in your reports.

You want a password easy for you to remember but difficult for other people to guess. Here are some bad choices for passwords: single letters or digits, your name, the name of your spouse or significant other, your kid's name, your cat's name, or anything fewer than eight characters long. (Bad guys can try every possible seven-letter password in less than a day.)

Good choices include things such as your college roommate's name misspelled and backwards. Throw in a digit or two, or some punctuation, and capitalize a few letters to add confusion, so that you end up with something like *yeLLas12*. Another good idea is to use a pair of words, like *fat;Head*.

You can change your password whenever you're logged in, by using the passwd program. It asks you to enter your old password to prove that you're still who you were when you logged in. Then the passwd program asks you to enter your new password twice, to make sure that you type it consistently. None of the three passwords you type appears on-screen.

Some system administrators do something called *password aging;* this strategy makes you change your password every once in a while. Some administrators put rules in the passwd program that try to enforce which passwords are permissible, and some even assign passwords chosen randomly. The latter idea is terrible, because the only way you can remember a password you didn't choose is to write it on your terminal.

Be sure that no one but you knows your password. Change your password whenever you think that someone else might know it. If you forget your password, the administrator can give you a new one, but she can't tell you what your old one was.

If you're paranoid about passwords, don't use a password that appears in dictionaries. System breakers may use UNIX's password-encryption program to encrypt every last word in a dictionary, and then compare each of the encrypted words to your password.

Ciao, UNIX!

Logging out is easy. You usually can type logout. Depending on which shell you're using, you might have to type exit instead. In many cases, you can press Ctrl+D. UNIX either invites the next sucker to log in, hangs up the phone, or, if you're connected by telnet, disconnects from your telnet program.

Chapter 2
What Is UNIX, Anyway?

*T*his entire chapter tells you how to figure out which kind of UNIX system you have gotten involved with. If you *really* don't think that you care, skip this chapter. As you read the rest of this book and run into places where you need to know which kind of UNIX or shell you are using, you can always come back here.

Why Do We Ask Such Dumb Questions?

"What is UNIX?" UNIX is UNIX, right? Not entirely. UNIX has been evolving feverishly for close to 30 years, sort of like bacteria in a cesspool — only not so attractive. As a result, there have been many different varieties of UNIX along the way. They all share numerous characteristics, but (we bet this doesn't surprise you) they differ just enough that even experienced users are tripped up by the differences between versions.

May a thousand UNIXes flower

Indulge us while we tell a historical parable. Imagine that UNIX is a kind of automobile rather than a computer system. In the early days, every UNIX system was distributed with a complete set of source code and development tools. If UNIX had been a car, this distribution method would have been the same as every car being supplied with a complete set of blueprints, wrenches, arc-welders, and other car-building tools. Now imagine that nearly all these cars were sold to engineering schools. You might expect that the students would get to work on their cars and that soon, no two cars would be the same. That's pretty much what happened to UNIX.

Bell Labs released the earliest editions of UNIX only to colleges and universities. (Because Bell Labs was The Phone Company at that time, it wasn't supposed to be in the software business.) From that seed, a variety of more-or-less scruffy mutants sprang up, and different people modified and extended different versions of UNIX.

Although about 75 percent of the important stuff is the same on all UNIX systems, it helps to know which kind of UNIX you're using, for two reasons. First, you can tell which of several alternatives applies to you. Second, you can impress your friends by saying things like "HP-UX is a pretty good implementation of BSD, although it's not as featureful as SunOS." It doesn't matter whether you know what it means — your friends will be amazed and speechless.

Throughout this book, we note when a command or feature being discussed differs among the major versions of UNIX. And when we talk about the popular new Linux system, you'll see our cute Linux icon in the margin. We don't waste your time with a family tree of UNIX systems. The following sections describe the most common kinds of UNIX systems.

The two main versions of UNIX are BSD UNIX and System V. Although they differ in lots of little ways, the easiest way to tell which one you're using is to see how you print something. If the printing command is `lp`, you have System V; if it's `lpr`, you have BSD. (If the command is `print`, you cannot be using UNIX; nothing in UNIX is that easy.)

Here are the major types of UNIX that you're likely to run into:

- **Berkeley UNIX:** One of the schools that received an early copy of UNIX was the University of California at Berkeley. No student's career was complete without adding a small feature to Berkeley UNIX, so you can still see on every part of BSD UNIX the greasy fingerprints of a generation of students, particularly a guy named Bill, about whom you can hear more later.

  The Berkeley people made official Berkeley Software Distributions of their code (named BSD UNIX) and gave numbers to its versions. The most widely used versions of BSD UNIX are versions 4.3 and 4.4. Berkeley graduates fanned out across the country, working for and even starting new companies that sell descendants of BSD UNIX, including Sun Microsystems (which markets SunOS and Solaris), Hewlett-Packard (HP-UX), Digital Equipment (Ultrix), and IBM (AIX). Most workstations run some version of BSD UNIX.

- **Post-Berkeley BSDs:** Shortly before 4.4BSD came out, the folks at Berkeley realized that they had made so many changes to BSD over the years that practically none of the original Bell Labs code was left. Several groups quickly rewrote the missing 1 percent, adapted the BSD code for 386 and newer PC-compatible machines, and made all the code available over the Internet. Three projects, called FreeBSD, OpenBSD, and NetBSD, continued to improve and update the freely available BSD, while a company called Berkeley Software Design offers a commercially supported version of BSD/OS.

✔ **System V:** Meanwhile, back at The Phone Company, legions of programmers were making different changes to UNIX. They gave their versions of UNIX Roman numerals — which are classier than plain ol' digits. Their current version of UNIX is known as System V. The many subversions of System V are known as System V Release 1 — or SVR1 — and SVR2, SVR3, and SVR4. Most nonworkstation versions of UNIX are based on System V or, occasionally, its predecessor, System III. (What happened to System IV? Not ready for prime time, we guess.)

Sun Microsystems, from the BSD camp, and AT&T, of the System V camp, decided to bury the hatchet and combine all the features of BSD and System V into the final incarnation of System V, SVR4. SVR4 has so many goodies that it's only slightly smaller than a blimp. If your system runs SVR4 or its descendants, you have to pay attention to the hints about both BSD *and* System V. The last version of SVR4 was SVR4.2. (Where *do* they get these numbers?) System V was eventually sold to Novell (the NetWare people), who retitled it UNIXWare.

Helpful advice to Sun users: Although Sun changed the name of its software from SunOS to Solaris, it didn't change the way it worked (at least in Solaris 1.0, which is still a BSD-flavored UNIX). So if you use Solaris 1.0, follow instructions for BSD UNIX. Solaris 2.0 is based on SVR4, however, so you have to worry about both BSD and System V. Is this clear? We're still confused about it.

✔ **OSF/1:** When System V and BSD UNIX merged to form SVR4, many UNIX vendors were concerned that, with only one version of UNIX, there would be insufficient market confusion. They started the Open Software Foundation, which makes yet another kind of UNIX: OSF/1. OSF/1 is mostly BSD, but it is also a goulash of some System V and a lot of other miscellaneous eyes of newts and toes of frogs.

OSF/1 has largely disappeared, but if you use OSF/1, pay attention to the BSD advice in this book, and you should be okay.

✔ **Linux:** Without a doubt, the most surprising UNIX development in recent years has been the appearance — seemingly from nowhere (but actually from Finland) — of Linux, a rather nice, freely available version of UNIX. Linux is such a big deal that we devote an entire chapter to it (the next one, in fact). Chapter 14 also has stuff about Linux for those brave souls who run their own Linux systems.

Linux resembles SVR4 as much as it resembles any other version of UNIX.

✔ **XENIX:** A few older versions of UNIX just won't die. The most notable version is XENIX, originally from Microsoft Corporation and later sold by the Santa Cruz Organization (SCO), a Microsoft affiliate. XENIX is considered hopelessly obsolete. On one hand, it occupies much less disk space than do more modern versions of UNIX, but on the other hand, it runs much faster. (To be fair, it's missing some of the more modern versions' zoomy features, but not many you'd likely notice.) Because XENIX is based on one of the ancestors of System V, most System V advice applies to XENIX. SCO has now moved most of its XENIX customers to SCO UNIX, which is based on System V.

What's GNU?

No tour of UNIX versions is complete without a visit to the Free Software Foundation in Cambridge, Massachusetts (not to be confused with the OSF, Open Software Foundation, which is about six blocks down the street). The FSF was founded by a brilliant but quirky programmer named Richard Stallman, who came from MIT, where people wrote lots and lots of software and gave it all away. He firmly (some would say fanatically) believes that all software should be free, and he set up the FSF to produce lots of high-quality free software, culminating in a complete, free version of UNIX. Despite quite a lot of initial skepticism, the FSF has raised enough money and been given and lent enough equipment to do just that. The FSF's project GNU (for *GNU's Not U*NIX) has so far produced versions of most of the UNIX user-level software. The best known and most widely used pieces are the text editor GNU Emacs (which we discuss in Chapter 10), most of the other basic UNIX utilities, and the GNU C compiler (GCC), which is now used on all the free versions of UNIX, including Linux, as well as on a few commercial ones.

The GNU crowd continues to work on new stuff, including their *pièce de résistance,* the GNU Hurd, a complete working version of the guts of the UNIX system. Early on, fans of free software awaited the GNU Hurd with great eagerness, but now that Linux and the freely available BSD versions have arrived, the eagerness has abated somewhat. But Hurd or no Hurd, GNU Emacs, GCC, and the GNU utilities are here to stay.

What the FSF means by "free" software is a little different from what you might expect: It means freely available, not necessarily available for free. That means that if you can find someone willing to pay you a million bucks for some GNU software, that's perfectly okay. But that person, and anyone else to whom you give or sell GNU software, has to be free to give or sell it, in turn, to other people without restriction. The intention is that people can make money by supporting and customizing software, not by hoarding it. Opinions vary on the long-term practicality of this plan, but for now, the FSF sure has written some popular software, and there is at least one company, named Cygnus Support, that makes a pretty good business supporting it.

How Can You Tell?

When you log in to your UNIX system, a variety of copyright notices usually flash by, with an identification of the kind of UNIX you are accessing. Carefully scrutinize the information on the screen, and you may be able to tell which version you have.

Another approach is to type the command uname and press Enter. Sometimes this command displays the name of your computer (such as aardvark or acctg3). Sometimes, however, the command displays the version of UNIX you are running. On Linux systems, it says Linux.

If you can't tell which UNIX version you have, break down, grovel, and ask your local UNIX expert. When you figure out which kind of UNIX you are running, write it down on the Cheat Sheet in the front of this book. You never know when you might need to know this stuff.

If you're using a dumb terminal or an X terminal (or a PC acting like a dumb terminal or connected to your UNIX system by means of a network), the kind of UNIX you're using depends on the maker of the main computer you're attached to — not on the maker of the terminal. Generally, you see the identification of the main computer in a message it sends to the terminal just before or just after you log in.

Cracking the Shell

Now that you have figured out which general variety of UNIX you have, you must figure out one other vital consideration: which shell you're using.

The guts of UNIX are buried deep in the bowels of the computer. They don't deign to deal with such insignificant details as determining what users might want to do. That nasty business is delegated to a category of programs known as shells. A *shell* is a program that waits for you to type a command and then executes it. From the UNIX point of view, a shell is nothing special, other than the first program UNIX runs after you log in. About a dozen UNIX shells are floating around, all slightly incompatible with each other. (You probably guessed that.)

Fortunately, all the popular shells fall into two groups: the Bourne (or Korn or BASH) shell and the C shell. If you can figure out which of the two categories your shell is in, you can get some work done. (There is also a C programming language that is popular for UNIX programs. You don't need to know the C language to use UNIX or the C shell.)

You can disregard this discussion about the true nature of shells

What UNIX calls a shell, many other people — especially DOS users — call a *command processor*. What DOS users call a shell is a fancy graphical program that is supposed to make the computer easier to use by displaying cute little icons for programs and files and other such user-friendly goodies.

The people who wrote UNIX didn't go for all this wimpy, fru-fru, hand-holding stuff, so their idea of a shell was a program in which you

could type zq to run a program called zq. (These guys were notoriously lazy typists.) User-friendly shells are available for UNIX, but they're not widely used, and we don't mention them again in this book.

If a Windows or Macintosh fanatic says rude things about the UNIX shell, you can respond that, although UNIX might be somewhat challenging to use, as a UNIX user, at least you're not a wimp.

You can easily tell which kind of shell you're using. If UNIX displays a $ after you log in, you have a Bourne-style shell; if UNIX displays a %, you're using the C shell. Traditionally, System V systems use the Bourne shell, and BSD systems use the C shell. These days, however, because all versions of UNIX come with both shells, you get whichever one your system administrator likes better. Preferences in command languages are similar to preferences in underwear: People like what they like, so you get what you get, but these days most of the people we know like BASH, a very souped-up Bourne-style shell.

Linux systems usually come with the BASH shell, a Bourne-style shell.

After you have determined whether you have a Bourne-style shell ($) or a C shell (%), note this fact on your Cheat Sheet in the front of this book.

If you use a GUI (see Chapter 4), you see windows and icons after you log in, not a boring little UNIX prompt. But you still need to use a UNIX shell from time to time, usually to perform housekeeping tasks.

The Bourne and Bourne-again shells

The most widely used UNIX shell is the Bourne shell, named after Steve Bourne, who originally wrote it. The Bourne shell is on all UNIX systems. It prompts you with $, after which you type a command and press Enter. Like all UNIX programs, the Bourne shell itself is a program, and its program name is sh. Clever, eh?

There are a few alternative versions of the original Bourne shell, most notably the Bourne-again shell (or BASH, whose program name is `bash`) from the GNU crowd. This version of the Bourne shell is used in many places because of its price — it's free. Some people claim that it's still overpriced, but we don't get into that. BASH is enough like the original Bourne shell that anything we say about the Bourne shell applies also to BASH. The most notable advantage of BASH is that it has "command editing," a fancy way of saying that you can use the arrow keys on your keyboard to correct your commands as you're typing them, just as you can with DOS. (Oops, better not say that when any UNIX fans are listening.)

The Korn-on-the-cob shell

After the Bourne shell was in common use for a couple of years, it became apparent to many people that it was so simple and coherent that a single person could understand all its features and use them all effectively. Fortunately, this shameful situation was remedied by a guy named Dave Korn, who added about a thousand new features to the Bourne shell and ended up with the Korn shell (called `ksh`). Most of the new features are of interest only to people who write *shell scripts* (sequences of shell commands saved in a file), so you can consider the Korn shell the same as the Bourne shell. Most versions of the Korn shell also have command editing.

She sells C shells

No, the C shell wasn't written by someone named C. It was written by Bill, the guy we mention earlier. (He sells C shells by the C shore? Probably.) We would discuss our opinion of the C shell at length, except that Bill is 6'4", is in excellent physical shape, and knows where we live. The C shell's program name is `csh`.

The most notable difference between the C shell and the other leading shell brands is that the C shell has many more magic characters (characters that do something special when you type them). Fortunately, unless you use a lot of commands with names like `ed!3x`, this isn't a problem.

There are many versions of the C shell; most of them differ in which bugs are fixed and which are still there. You might run into a program called `tcsh`, a slightly extended C shell with command editing.

Who says the C shell isn't user-friendly?

If you use the C shell, be aware that some punctuation characters do special and fairly useful things.

An exclamation point (a *bang* — !) tells the C shell to do a command again. Two of them (!!) means to repeat the last command you typed. One of them followed by the first few characters of a command means to repeat the last command that started with those characters. For example, type this:

    !cp

to repeat the last cp command you gave. This is great for lazy typists.

You can also use carets (^) to tell the C shell to repeat a command with some change. If you type this:

    ^old^new

the C shell repeats the last command, substituting "new" for "old" wherever it appears in what you typed. You can use slashes (/) in a similar way, but carets are easier. The C shell also uses colons (:) to perform truly confusing editing of previous commands, which we don't get into.

In Chapter 7, the "UNIX Is History!" section tells you more about reissuing shell commands.

Are Any Good Programs On?

You may be wondering why we refer sometimes to commands and sometimes to programs. What's the difference?

A *command* is something you type that tells UNIX (or actually the shell) what to do. A *program* is a file that contains executable code. The confusion comes because in UNIX, to run a program, you just type its name. (In old-fashioned operating systems, you usually typed something like "RUN BUDGET_ANALYSIS" to run a program called BUDGET_ANALYSIS.)

When you type a command, such as ls or cp or emacs (a text editor we talk about in Chapter 13), the shell looks at it carefully. The shell knows how to do a few commands all by itself, including cd and exit. If the command isn't one that the shell can do by itself, it looks around for a program stored in a file by the same name.

DOS users may recognize the way this works — commands DOS can do itself are called *internal commands,* and commands that require running another program are called *external commands.* Internal commands are also called *built-in commands.*

Finally! You're Ready to Work

We wrap up this chapter with a little advice about hand-to-hand combat with the shell. There are many commands you can give to your shell. Every shell has about a dozen built-in commands, most of which aren't very useful on a day-to-day basis. All the other commands are the names of other programs. The fact that every UNIX system has hundreds of programs lying around translates into hundreds of possible shell commands.

One nice thing about UNIX shells is that, within a given shell, the way you type commands is completely consistent. If you want to edit a file called `my-calendar`, for example, and use an editor called e, you type this line:

```
$ e my-calendar
```

As always, press Enter at the end of the line to tell the shell that you have finished. The shell runs the e editor, which does whatever it does. When you finish, you return to the shell, where you can issue another command.

Whenever you see a UNIX prompt (either $ or %), a shell is running, waiting to do your bidding. Throughout this book, we usually refer to the entire package — UNIX plus shell — as UNIX. We say, "Use the `ls` command to get UNIX to display a list of files" rather than "Use the `ls` command to get the shell to get UNIX to display a list of files." Okay?

Now you know which kind of UNIX you are using, which shell you are using, and why you care. Let's look at a few UNIX (or shell) commands you can use to begin getting something done.

We could tell you the password, but then we'd have to kill you

When you logged in, you probably hated your password because someone else picked it. Hating your password is a good reason to change it. Another reason you might want to change it is that, to get this far, you enlisted the aid of some sort of expert and had to reveal your password. This section shows how to change your password: Use the `passwd` command.

This is easy stuff. Just type the following line:

```
passwd
```

Ending command lines without hard feelings

Remember to end every command line by pressing Enter. UNIX is pretty dumb; in most cases, your pressing Enter is the only way UNIX can tell that you have finished doing something.

With a few programs, notably the text editors vi, pico, and emacs, you don't need to press Enter anywhere; we point out those exceptions. Everywhere else, remember to press the Enter key at the end of every line.

As always, press Enter after typing the command. The passwd command asks you to type your current password to make sure that you are really you. (If it didn't do this, whenever you wandered off to get some more coffee, someone could sneak over to your desk and change your password. Not good.) Type your current password and press Enter. The password doesn't appear as you type, in case someone is watching you.

Then passwd asks for your new password. (Chapter 1 has lots of sage advice about how to choose a password.) You have to type the new password twice so that passwd is sure that you typed it correctly. Assuming that you type the new password twice in the same way, passwd changes your password. The next time you log in, you are expected to know it.

If you forget your password, there is no way to retrieve it; not even your system administrator can tell you what it is. The administrator can assign you a new one and you can change it again.

What's my file?

This section discusses a command you use a lot: the ls command, which lists your files. Chapters 5 and 6 talk more about files, directories, and other stuff that ls helps you with; for now, here's ls Lesson 1. Type the following line (we're not telling you to press Enter anymore, because we know that you have the hang of it):

```
ls
```

The ls command lists the names of the files in the current directory. (Chapter 6 talks about directories.)

Oops!

If you make thousands of typos a day, as we do, pay close attention. If you type something wrong, you can probably press the Backspace key to back up and retype it. If that doesn't work, all is not lost. Try the Delete key, the # key (Shift+3), or Ctrl+H. One should back you up.

To start the line over (not usually necessary with nice, short commands, such as 1s), press Ctrl+U. If that doesn't work, press the @ key (Shift+2).

Play it again, Sam

Sometimes, you may want to issue the same command again (because it was so much fun the first time). If you use the C shell, type the following:

```
!!
```

If you use the BASH shell, press the up-arrow key to see the last command you typed and then press Enter.

In the Korn shell, you can type this line to reissue a command:

```
r
```

If you use the Bourne shell, type your command again.

Everything you wanted to know about typing commands — but were afraid to ask

This list shows a wrap-up of what to do when UNIX displays a prompt (either $ or %) and you want to type a command:

  ✔ As you type, a cursor moves along to indicate where you are. The cursor looks like an underline or a box.

Don't turn off the computer if you make a typo!

PC users get used to just turning the darned thing off if things aren't going well, but UNIX computers don't respond well to this approach.

To stop a UNIX command, press Ctrl+C, or, on some systems, the Break key or the Delete key.

If the situation is out of control, you can use some Advanced and Obscure Techniques to wrestle extremely recalcitrant programs into line. See Chapter 22 if you're desperate.

The UNIX cast of special characters

One of the more exciting aspects of typing shell commands is that many characters are special. They have special meanings to UNIX; the next few chapters discuss some of them. Special characters include the ones in this list:

```
< >     '       "       *
{ }     ^       !       \
[ ]     #       |       &
( )     $       ?       ~
```

Spaces also are considered special, because they separate words in a command. If you want to put special characters in a command, you must *quote* them. You quote something by putting quotation marks around it. Suppose that you have a file called c* (not a great idea, but sometimes you get these things by mistake). You can edit it by typing the following line:

```
e "c*"
```

You can use either single or double quotation marks, as long as you're consistent. You can even quote single quotation marks with double quotation marks, and quote double quotation marks with single quotation marks. Is that clear? Never mind.

- ✔ If you make a typing mistake, press Backspace (or Delete, #, or Ctrl+H).

- ✔ To cancel the entire command before you press Enter, press Ctrl+U (or try @).

- ✔ When you finish typing a command, press Enter.

- ✔ If you issue a command that UNIX (actually, the shell) doesn't know, you see a message like the following:

      ```
      blurfle: Command not found.
      ```

  This means that you typed the command wrong, that you typed a command that UNIX doesn't know (maybe a DOS command crept in), or that someone hasn't told UNIX the right places to look for programs.

- ✔ Don't stick extra spaces in the middle of commands, as in pass wd. Type the command exactly as we show it. On the other hand, *do* type a space after the name of the command but before any additional information you have to type on the line (more about that subject in Chapter 5). Also, do not capitalize except where you know the command has a capital letter.

- ✔ You know that a command resembles a sentence, but you don't end it with a period. UNIX doesn't like the period, and UNIX is unforgiving.

Chapter 3

A Few Lines on Linux

- -

In This Chapter

▶ What is Linux?

▶ Why should you care?

- -

 *L*inux is the hottest thing to arrive in UNIX-land in years: a wildly popular, completely free version of UNIX. It is (quite deliberately) similar to other versions of UNIX; for the most part, then, everything in this book that applies to other versions of UNIX also applies to Linux.

Out of the Frozen North

In 1992, a guy in Finland named Linus Torvalds took a then-popular small educational version of UNIX called Minix, decided it wasn't quite what he wanted, and proceeded to rewrite and extend it so that it was more to his taste. Lots of enthusiastic programmers have started projects like that, but to everyone's astonishment, Linus *actually finished* his. By mid-1993, his system had long since left its Minix roots and was becoming a genuinely usable version of UNIX. Linus's system was picked up with great enthusiasm by programmers, and later by users, all over the Internet. It spread like crazy, to become the fastest growing part of UNIX-dom.

Linux is popular for three reasons:

✔ It works well, even on a small, cheap PC. A 386 PC with 4MB of random-access memory (RAM) and a 40MB hard disk can run Linux — barely. (John bought a computer like that for less than $500, new, from a dealer who had ordered more than he needed.) On a top-of-the-line Pentium Pro PC, its performance approaches that of a full-blown traditional UNIX workstation.

   ✔ Lots of enthusiastic people are working on Linux, with wonderful new features and additions available every day. Many of them even work.

   ✔ It's free!

Linux's many developers proudly describe it as a "hacker's system," one written by and for enthusiastic programmers. (This is the classic meaning of *hacker* and is not to be confused with the other, media-debased "computer vandal" definition.) These programmers keep up the development of Linux at a brisk pace, and a new "development" version is made available on the Internet every few days. Every once in a while, the developers decide that they have gotten enough bugs out of their recent developments, and they release a "stable" version, which stays constant for months rather than days. Most normal people use the stable version rather than a development version. Using a development version of Linux is sort of like living in a house inhabited by a large family of carpenters and architects: Every morning when you wake up, the house is a little different. Maybe there's a new turret, or some walls have moved. Or perhaps someone has temporarily removed the floor under your bed. (Oops, sorry about that.)

How free is free?

Linux is *free software*. In the UNIX software biz, "free" has a very concrete meaning that is different from public domain and different from shareware.

Linux is made available under the GNU General Public License (GPL), Version 2, the same license that the Free Software Foundation uses for most of its programs. It has seven pages of legalese, much of which is about where copyright notices have to appear and stuff like that, but the basic plan is simple. In short, it says

   ✔ You can copy and distribute Linux and other GPL software, and you can charge for it.

   ✔ BUT, anyone to whom you distribute it has the right to give copies away for free,

   ✔ AND you must include the source code (or make it available for no more than a reproduction fee) in the distribution.

The idea is that people are permitted, even encouraged, to distribute copies of GPL software and to sell maintenance service, so long as the software itself remains freely available.

Don't confuse free software with *shareware*, which is software for which you are supposed to pay the original author if you use it, or with *public domain* software, with which you can do anything you want.

The GPL was subject to considerable debate and a fair amount of ridicule when it first came out in about 1990, but it's worked pretty much the way its authors intended — GPL software (including Linux) is very widely available, and people do indeed constantly work on and improve it.

Linux started life as the operating system of choice for students and other cheapskates . . . er . . . users who wanted a UNIX system of their own but couldn't afford a traditional UNIX workstation. As Linux has matured into a stable, reliable UNIX system, this base has expanded to include companies and institutions who *could* afford traditional UNIX workstations but found that Linux enabled them to add PC-based workstations at a fraction of the cost. In fact, Linux is now estimated to have more than 6 million users, making it the third most popular operating system in the world (behind Windows and the Macintosh operating system).

What's Old, What's New

The original guts of Linux was written from scratch by Linus Torvalds and has since been greatly changed and extended by other people. He more or less based it on System V (*descriptions* of System V; there's no code from System V). Most of the programs that people actually use (the shells and other commands) come from the GNU project, which modeled most of them after the Berkeley UNIX versions, so most of the commands are BSD-ish. The networking programs are adapted from the Berkeley ones, so they also are all BSD-ish.

Technically speaking, Linux refers only to the operating system "kernel." When most people refer to a Linux system, though, they usually mean the whole package: operating system plus the GNU programs that come with it. Like all UNIX systems, Linux systems can run various shells, various editors, and various other software. Most versions of Linux use BASH as the default shell, because it's also new and snazzy.

Do keep in mind that Linux is a moving target, with frequent improvements to the programs, so the version of Linux you use is probably not exactly the same as the version described in any book, including this one. When we wrote this book, the latest stable version of Linux was 2.0.30, but even if you have a more recent version, the basic structure is the same.

In Chapter 27, we describe a number of ways you can get additional information about Linux, including reading one of a number of Usenet newsgroups about Linux or subscribing to a Linux magazine.

You say tomAto, I say tomahto

A frequent concern of newcomers to Linux is how to pronounce it correctly, in order not to sound uninformed. It's simple: However you pronounce it will be wrong – or right, depending on your audience. Among English speakers in the U.S, at least, the opinions seem to be divided about evenly between "Line-ucks" and "Linn-ucks."

The name Linux is derived from the first name of its creator, Linus Torvalds. The "Line-ucks" group holds that it's based on the usual English pronunciation of Linus. Linus Torvalds himself, though, a Swedish-speaking Finn, has

helpfully provided an audio file to the Internet in which he provides the definitive answer in both English and Swedish. (The files can be found at the URL `http://sunsite.unc.edu/LDP/links.html` way down at the end of the page. See Chapter 18 for help on what this means.) In it, he says, "Hello, this is Lee-noos Torvalds, and I pronounce Lee-nooks as Lee-nooks." It's up to you whether you want to say "Linux" with a Swedish accent, but to our ears, his reading sounds much closer to the Anglicized "Linn-ucks," so that's what we use.

Where's Linux?

Linux development mostly happens on the Internet, and if you have an Internet connection, you can download the entire system at no charge. You *do* need either a fast connection or great patience, because it's about 50 diskettes full of data. A typical 14.4 Kbps online connection would take about 15 hours to download Linux. Quite a few bulletin board systems around the world make Linux code available. A more practical approach is to buy or borrow a CD-ROM version of Linux, which you can install in an hour or so.

Sounds great, doesn't it? You can install a version of UNIX on your very own computer! But there's one tiny little snag — that makes *you* the system administrator. You have to learn how to create user accounts, deal with disks that fill up, and install and configure software. It's not impossible (far from it — John has done it for years), but you have a lot to learn.

The details of installing and setting up Linux are way beyond the scope of this book. In Chapter 14, we barely touch on a few basics of administering a Linux system. For more details, take a look at *Linux SECRETS,* by Naba Barkakati (IDG Books Worldwide, Inc.), and *Running Linux,* by Welsh and Kaufman (O'Reilly & Associates).

Part II
Some Basic Stuff

The 5th Wave — By Rich Tennant

"WELL THIS HAS SURE TURNED OUT TO BE A MICKEY MOUSE SYSTEM."

In this part . . .

UNIX, like other computer systems, keeps your information in things called *files*. When you work with UNIX, you frequently need to make new files, rename files, make copies of particularly interesting files, get rid of files that have outlived their usefulness, find a file that you have temporarily mislaid, or print what's in a file.

This section also talks about *graphical user interfaces* (GUIs), which let you use a mouse to point at things on the screen. Most people find GUIs a big improvement over typing commands, but you have to know what to point at and click on. You're about to find out!

Chapter 4
Of Mice and Computers

● ●

In This Chapter

▶ What's a GUI — and should you care?

▶ Basic mouse skills for GUI survival

▶ Working with windows

▶ How to tell which windowing theology you subscribe to

▶ Window-wrangling skills

▶ How to use the Motif Window Manager

▶ How to log out

▶ Far too many Motif widgets

● ●

To answer your first question, GUI stands for *graphical user interface* and really *is* pronounced "gooey." We prefer the term WIMP, which stands for *windows, icons,* and *mouse pointing,* but for some reason, the term never caught on. Fast-track executives would rather be gooey than wimps, we suppose.

A GUI is a combination of a graphics screen (one that can show pictures in addition to text), a mouse (or something like it), and a system that divides the screen into several windows that can show different things at the same time. All GUIs work in more or less the same way, because they're all based on the same original work done at Xerox about 20 years ago. The details differ enough, though, to make you want to tear your hair out.

The Big GUIs (The Big Gooey Whats?)

The earliest UNIX systems didn't have fancy, screen-oriented windowing systems. They didn't have screens at all, in fact — they used loud, rattling terminals that printed on actual paper. (The historically minded can find these types of terminals in the Computer Museum in Boston and the Smithsonian Institution in Washington, D.C. Yes, really.) As the years went on, UNIX appeared on computers that did have screens (most notably Sun workstations), and various windowing systems appeared.

One thing about the UNIX community you've probably come to appreciate by now is that you can't get everyone to agree on anything, except, of course, that UNIX is better than every other kind of system and that anyone who thinks otherwise is silly. So, not surprisingly, a variety of incompatible windowing systems arose, each different from the other in various, not particularly interesting, ways. Nearly all the windowing systems were *proprietary* (they belonged to one system vendor or another), and, of course, no vendor would dream of admitting that someone else's window system was better than theirs.

There were also a bunch of window system projects at universities. One of the more successful was the X Window project at MIT (alleged to be a successor to the W Window project at Stanford — as far as we know, there wasn't a V Window project). The X Window System had many virtues, not the least of which were that it worked adequately well and that it was available for free to anyone who wanted it. So X became the window system everyone used.

Today, almost all UNIX systems that have any sort of GUI use one based on the X Window System (frequently abbreviated to just "X Windows," which has been known to drive UNIX purists crazy because it sounds too much like that *other* famous operating system from Redmond, Washington). Old Sun workstations used systems called SunView or NeWS; NeXT machines use NeXTStep (are tHoSE wOrDS cAPiTaLIzed corREctlY?); other than those exceptions, however, you almost certainly will get X Windows.

X (which is an even shorter abbreviation for X Window System) has many advantages as a windowing system, namely, the following:

- ✔ It runs on all sorts of computers, not just those that run UNIX.

- ✔ It is *policy independent:* A program can make the screen look any way it wants; the screen is not constrained to a single style, as it is on the Macintosh or with Microsoft Windows. (As you might imagine, this capability is not an unmitigated blessing. More about this subject later.)

- ✔ It uses a networked client-server architecture (love those buzzwords). You can run X on one computer, but the programs that display stuff on-screen can be on entirely different computers connected by a network.

- ✔ MIT gives it away for free.

You can imagine which of these important advantages is the one that really made all the computer makers choose X. Even though MIT gives away the base version of X, unless you happen to be using the exact same kind of computer the guys at MIT use (or you feel like compiling and debugging a gazillion lines of C code), you don't get it for free. You must buy a version tailored for the particular kind of screen and adapter on your computer. An exception to this is XFree86, a free version of X used by PC-based UNIX systems, such as Linux (see Chapter 3).

How your screen looks depends on which GUI you use. The first part of this chapter talks about things that are the same for all GUIs. Later on, we talk about how to tell which GUI you are using, and how to do things that work differently for each GUI.

A few cool X programs

Because MIT gives away X Windows for free, X quickly became the standard window system at hundreds of colleges and universities around the world. Students, who have a sincere dedication to doing something other than what they are supposed to be doing (not like the rest of us — no way), quickly wrote all sorts of silly programs — nominally to test either X or their understanding of it, and generally to have fun. Assuming that these programs are installed on your computer, you have only to type their names in a window containing a UNIX shell to run them (more about this subject in the next chapter). A few of the better-known fun X programs appear in the following list:

✔ **xeyes.** Pops up a large pair of eyeballs that watch the mouse cursor as you move it around the screen. According to the manual, it checks up on you and reports back to the boss. Hmmm.

✔ **xsnow.** Puts a snowstorm on the screen background. Snowflakes fall down the screen and pile up on top of your windows. The santa option makes an occasional reindeer-drawn sleigh fly across your screen. Ho ho ho.

✔ **xsol.** Plays a game of Klondike solitaire against you. You click on the deck to turn over the next card and drag cards to move them around. It's as good a way as any to learn how to handle the mouse, or at least that's the excuse you can use when the boss comes by. Because the computer controls the card deck, you can't cheat, which means that it's practically

impossible to win in one trip through the deck. We've won honestly once in about two years of play. The program enables you to turn over the deck and try again, which enables you to win nearly half the time, albeit without honor.

✔ **xphoon.** Displays in the background of your screen a detailed, full-screen picture of the moon as it appears today. In a classic display of dedicated geek programming, it correctly computes the relative angular positions of the earth, moon, and sun based on the current time and date, and shows the moon's current phase (full, quarter, half, or whatever). Useful for people who work in windowless offices in cities and have forgotten what the sky looks like.

✔ **xmille.** Plays the Parker Brothers game Mille Bornes against you. It keeps a running score and plays a mean game. Click on the deck with the first mouse button to draw a card, click on a card in your hand to play it, and click on a card with the second button to discard it. During the past year or so, we have won 34 games and lost 42, with each game consisting of about five hands.

✔ **xroach.** Lots of yucky roaches scurry around the screen and hide under the windows, just like in real life. If you run it with the -squish option, you can squish the roaches by clicking on them, leaving an authentic smudge of roach guts on your screen. (UNIX geeks consider this to be humor at its finest.)

I'm Not Just a Server — I'm Also a Client!

X was designed from the beginning to work with computer networks. It makes a clear distinction between the *server* program, which handles the screen, keyboard, and mouse, and the *client* program, which does the actual computing. Although more often than not, the two programs are running on the same computer, but they don't have to be. (Readers who saw John on "The Internet Show" on public TV a few years ago may recall one demonstration of an online subway map of Paris. That was an X application, with the X server running on a PC in the TV studio in Texas and the client program on a computer in France, connected by way of the Internet.)

X's networkability (is that a word?) is most useful in two ways. One way is that you can be sitting at an X workstation attached to a local network and have windows attached to client programs running on computers all over the network, often on computers considerably more powerful than yours. The other is that there are *X terminals,* which are specialized computers with screens, keyboards, mice, and network connections that run only a single program: an X server. The idea of an X terminal is that it's considerably cheaper than a workstation, so you can have a few workstations or larger computers with a flock of inexpensive X terminals attached, getting nearly workstation performance for the X terminal users, but at a considerably lower price.

X terminals should be a passing fad, because these days, a standard PC that runs UNIX, including an X server program, costs about the same as an X terminal and offers more flexibility. (This is the same reason we don't think much of "network computers.") Fortunately, X terminals and workstations running an X server look and work almost exactly the same, so we don't belabor the difference any longer.

Basic Mouse Skills

As an X user, you have a mouse, or a mouse-like thing, such as a trackball or a finger pad. Mice have a way to tell when you have moved them and some buttons you can push to tell the computer you want to do something. The first button, by the way, is the one on the left, unless someone has configured your mouse to be left-handed, and then the first button is the one on the right. (A *trackball* is like a mouse lying on its back. A finger pad is like a trackball without a ball.)

You have to know how to use a mouse to get anything done under X. Fortunately, mouse wrangling is pretty easy.

About your mouse

Your mouse (or mouse-like thing) has some buttons on it. Take a moment to count the buttons. Finished counting? (How long could it have taken?) We hope that you found three buttons. If you found only two buttons, you have a problem, because most X programs were written with three-button mice in mind and don't work well with two-button mice. It is possible to configure some X servers to enable you to get to all of X's features by using only two buttons, but it's much easier to get a three-button mouse. We've found some perfectly usable ones at our local computer store for $10 or less.

When you move the mouse on the pad or on your desk, a *cursor* (a little doohickey on-screen) moves along with it. You can pick up the mouse and put it back down somewhere else on the pad or desk without moving the cursor. This capability comes in handy when you find that you have moved the mouse to the edge of the pad and that the cursor is still in the middle of the screen: Just pick up the mouse and move it to a more convenient part of your desk. If your mouse lives on a mouse pad printed with a grid of lines, it works only when you move it on the pad.

When you move the mouse, try to keep it square to the desk, with the cord (or the tail, depending on whether you're willing to put up with another cute term) pointing away from you. Particularly when the mouse is off to the side of your desk, it's easy to turn the mouse at an angle. Because the computer can't tell that you have done that, you find that you move the mouse down and to the right but that the cursor moves up because the mouse is twisted around. Fortunately, you become accustomed to mousing pretty quickly and all this becomes second nature.

With a click-click here

The two key mouse skills are clicking and dragging. Clicking is easy: You move the mouse until the cursor is on a screen item you want to activate and then you quickly press and release one of the mouse buttons, generally the first (the left) button. In window-ese, this process is called *selecting* the screen item; it means that you want to do something with the item you just clicked on.

Sometimes you need to *double-click* (click the same button twice quickly) to tell the screen item to do something particularly important. It can take some practice to train your finger to click the button quickly enough for the computer to recognize it as a double-click rather than one click and a second click, made when the nerve impulses finally get back to your finger. If you had practiced the piano when you were a kid, as your mother told you to, you would have the finger dexterity to do this the first time. (Really.) To keep your children from being at a disadvantage in the highly computerized land of the future, be sure that they take piano lessons and practice. Or maybe saxophone lessons would do as well and offer more upward political mobility. But we digress. Back to mouse skills.

And a drag-drag there

Dragging the mouse is a slightly more complicated procedure. You move to a point of interest, press a mouse button, *hold it down,* move the mouse as you hold the button, and then let go of the button.

You use dragging in two main ways. The first is for *pop-up menus.* When you press one of the mouse buttons, a menu appears with a list of possible things to do. While you are holding down the button, drag the cursor to the item on the menu you want and then let the button go. If you change your mind and don't want to do any of the things on the menu, drag the cursor entirely off the menu before letting go of the button.

The second way to use the drag technique is to outline some part of a window. You move to one corner of an area you want to select, press a mouse button, drag to the opposite corner of the area, and let go; at this point, a box on-screen shows the area you outlined.

A quick mouse refresher

You probably know all about how to use your mouse. But in the unlikely event that you're a little rusty on the terminology, here are a few basic terms:

Cursor: The cursor is the little doozit (a highly technical term) on the screen that shows where the mouse is pointing. The cursor often changes shape as you move it from one window to another to give you a hint of what's going on in a window. The most common cursor shapes are a black X (when you're not in any window), a little arrow (in windows with graphics), and a little vertical hairline (in windows of text.)

Click: To click something, move the cursor to the thing to be clicked and then press and release the mouse button. Unless otherwise directed, use the left-most mouse button.

Drag: To drag something, move the cursor to the drag-ee, press down the mouse button, move the mouse while holding down the button, and then let go of the button when you get to where you want the drag-ee to be. Most non-Motif programs use the left button to drag stuff, but Motif programs use the middle button.

We Don't Need No Stinkin' Policy

Most windowing systems on most kinds of computers make programs use a consistent style. All Macintosh programs, for example, look pretty much the same: They all use the same menu, the same little window when you want to select a file, similar windows to turn options on and off, and so forth. One Microsoft Windows program looks a lot like all the others: They all use similar sets of windows.

But do all X Windows programs have a consistent look? Of course not — that would be too easy. This is what the X crowd means by *policy independence:* X is utterly agnostic about what windows should look like on the screen, how keystrokes and mouse clicks should be interpreted, and pretty much anything else that affects a user. This lack of policy was part of the original appeal of X, because no matter which window system you were used to, you could make X look just like that system. So the good news is that X offers great flexibility. The bad news is that the word *inconsistent* barely scratches the surface of what you will run into.

How did we manage without this?

One of the ways in which X avoids having any policy built in is that it foists much of the general window-management jobs onto a program called a *window manager.* (Catchy name, huh?) The window manager handles jobs such as creating the borders around each application's main windows; controlling how you move, resize, switch among, and iconify windows; and most of the other tasks that aren't part of any particular application. It's possible to run X without any window manager, but it's rather unpleasant, because without one, there's no way to do some things, such as move a window.

What have I got?

A bunch of competing window "looks" are on the UNIX market. To tell which one you're stuck with . . . er, have the pleasure to use, look at the border around the windows on your screen. If they have 3-D–style borders with sharp corners, as shown in Figure 4-1, you're using the Motif Window Manager (MWM) or its free lookalike counterpart, FVWM. If the borders have rounded corners, as shown in Figure 4-2, you're using OPENLOOK. If they have a thin border around the sides and bottom and their top borders look like those shown in Figure 4-3, you're using a program called TWM, which comes with the base version of X and is still sometimes used because it is simple and small.

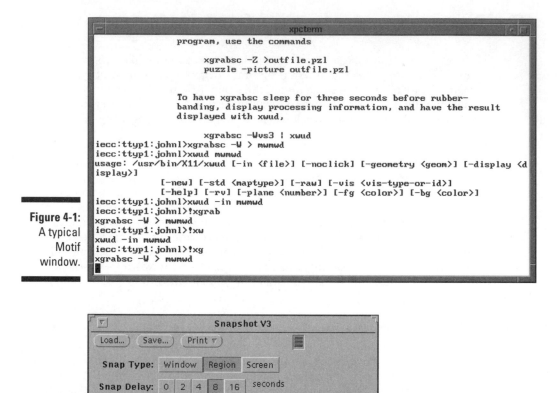

```
                                        xpcterm
              program, use the commands

                   xgrabsc -Z >outfile.pzl
                   puzzle -picture outfile.pzl


              To have xgrabsc sleep for three seconds before rubber-
              banding, display processing information, and have the result
              displayed with xwud,

                   xgrabsc -Wvs3 ¦ xwud
iecc:ttyp1:johnl>xgrabsc -W > mwmwd
iecc:ttyp1:johnl>xwud mwmwd
usage: /usr/bin/X11/xwud [-in <file>] [-noclick] [-geometry <geom>] [-display <d
isplay>]
              [-new] [-std <maptype>] [-raw] [-vis <vis-type-or-id>]
              [-help] [-rv] [-plane <number>] [-fg <color>] [-bg <color>]
iecc:ttyp1:johnl>xwud -in mwmwd
iecc:ttyp1:johnl>!xgrab
xgrabsc -W > mwmwd
iecc:ttyp1:johnl>!xw
xwud -in mwmwd
iecc:ttyp1:johnl>!xg
xgrabsc -W > mwmwd
```

Figure 4-1:
A typical
Motif
window.

Snapshot V3

Load...   Save...   Print ▽

Snap Type: Window   Region   Screen

Snap Delay: 0   2   4   8   16   seconds

✔ Beep During Countdown

☐ Hide Window During Capture

Snap   View

SELECT—Position Rectangle. ADJUST—Snap Image. MENU—Cancel.

Figure 4-2:
A typical
OPENLOOK
window.

There are lots of other window managers, but these are the most common ones. After several years of window system warfare, Motif and its clone FVWM have emerged as the clear favorite window systems, so that's what we concentrate on here.

```
☒ xpcterm                                                                              ⊡
iecc:ttyp1:johnl>who -a       Dec 12 12:32
     .         system boot   Dec 12 12:32
     .         run-level 2   Dec 12 12:32    2      0      S
bcheckrc        .            Dec 12 12:33   0:20         5   id=bchk term=0    exit=77
brc             .            Dec 12 12:33   0:20        15   id= brc term=0    exit=0
brc             .            Dec 12 12:33   0:20        19   id=  mt term=0    exit=0
rc2             .            Dec 12 12:49   0:20        23   id=  r2 term=0    exit=0
root           console       Dec 29 20:16   0:01     17956
sleep           .            Dec 12 12:49   0:20       130   id=  wt term=0    exit=0
johnl          vt01          Dec 21 15:19   0:01      5938
LOGIN          vt02          Dec 29 20:16  20:48     17955
LOGIN          ttyd1         Dec 30 16:24   0:52      2827   492-3869
faxserve        .            Dec 26 11:45   0:20     24871   id=  F2
johnl          ttyp2         Dec 30 17:16    .        3053   id=  p2 term=112 exit=2
johnl          ttyp1         Dec 30 16:55    .        3054
johnl          ttyp0         Dec 30 16:55   0:15      3055
johnl          ttyp3         Dec 30 16:56   0:20      3086   id=  p3 term=112 exit=2
johnl          ttyp4         Dec 30 16:12   1:04     19342   id=  p4 term=112 exit=2
johnl          ttyp5         Dec 23 18:41   old      11186   id=  p5 term=112 exit=2
LOGIN           .            Dec 15 15:28   0:20     25517
LOGIN           .            Dec 15 15:30   0:20     25532
LOGIN          ttyd2         Dec 17 18:55   old       5561   id=  02 term=15  exit=0
iecc:ttyp1:john
iecc:ttyp1:johnl>xgrabsc -W > twmwd
█
```

Figure 4-3:
A typical
TWM
window.

Considerably more than you want to know about window managers, toolkits, and X

The X Window System divides the work of controlling what's on-screen among three separate kinds of programs:

✔ **The X server:** the program that draws the pictures on-screen and reads user input from the keyboard and mouse

✔ **The window manager:** the program that controls where windows appear on-screen, draws borders around windows, and handles basic window operations, such as moving windows, shrinking windows to an *icon* (a little box representing that window), and expanding icons to windows

✔ **Clients:** programs that do some real work

For any particular screen, there is one X server, usually (but not always) one window manager, and a bunch of clients. Every client communicates with the server to tell it what to draw and to find out what you did; the server communicates with the window manager when the user asks for a window-management operation, such as changing the size of a window. Although the server, the window manager, and clients usually run on the same computer, X Windows enables them to exist on separate machines connected by a network. It is not unusual to have a setup in which the server runs in an X terminal, the window manager runs in a nearby workstation, and the clients are on various machines scattered around the network.

The window manager is usually (except on a few X terminals) a regular UNIX program. You can stop one window manager and start another if you decide that you don't like the way your windows look. Client programs can ask

(continued)

(continued)

the X server to ask the window manager to do some specialized operations. A terminal program, for example, can ask the window manager to enable the user to change the size of the window only to a size that is a whole number of lines of text. (This kind of communication starts to resemble that in the ancient Roman Empire, in which proconsuls could officially speak only to procurators, who could speak to senators, and so forth. But computers are like that.) If there isn't a window manager, there aren't any window-management operations available.

Writing an X program is a lot of work. To make life easier for programmers, a programmer can build on *toolkits* of program code that are already written. MIT sends out X Toolkit (immediately called Xt by the usual lazy typists). This toolkit provides a set of basic window functions that most programs use. Starting with Xt, different people have produced libraries of *widgets,* or screen elements a program can use. A menu or a file-selection panel is a widget, for example. There is a Motif widget set for programs that want to look like Motif, a set of Athena widgets from MIT's Project Athena that aren't particularly attractive but that many programs use because (where have we heard this before?) they're

available for free, and other toolkits for other, less commonly used window systems.

What all this means is that any particular X client uses one of the widget sets to control what that client's window looks like. A program that uses the Motif toolkit, for example, is a Motif program. But because clients are separate from window managers, the Motif window manager (named mwm — the lazy typists strike again) can be running and draw a Motif border around the windows of clients using other toolkits.

Because of the constant danger that GUI systems could begin to make sense to users, UNIX people have learned to obfuscate things by using "Motif" to refer to both the Motif window manager and the Motif toolkit, which are, of course, completely separate entities. So, when people refer to "Motif," they might be referring to the window manager, or maybe the toolkit. Or both. Often it's difficult to tell. This confusion is all just part of the proud legacy of UNIX evolution.

One school of thought says we all would be better off if X Windows had picked a window style and stuck with it so that we would have a single window manager and a single set of widgets — as every other window system does — but it's far too late now for that.

Motif and Other Schools of Windowing Theology

The Open Software Foundation, the same people who provide the OSF/1 version of UNIX, created Motif, based on some work done by their members Hewlett-Packard and Digital Equipment. Motif is much more complete than the competition (it has a provision for handling languages other than English, for example), and DEC made it cheap for software vendors to use, so it has become the primary X Window manager in use today.

Déjà vu déjà vu

Readers familiar with Microsoft Windows 95 or NT may find the Motif window manager to be strangely familiar. Its windows don't look all that much like Windows windows, but the mouse and keyboard techniques are extremely similar. That turns out to be no coincidence. Hewlett-Packard has a super-duper application environment that it sells for both Windows and X, so it deliberately made its X package (from which much of Motif is derived) as similar to Windows as possible.

For users who switch back and forth between Windows and Motif (we authors, for example), this capability is a blessing, because the mouse moves and keystrokes our fingers have memorized for one system work by and large in the same way in the other. This practically unprecedented level of compatibility exists between UNIX and something else, so we figure that, deep down, it must have been an oversight.

How do I start Motif, anyway?

You might think that this question would be a simple one to answer, but because UNIX is involved, it's not. The short answer is "Run mwm" (the Motif Window Manager), but that technique is not useful, because you have to run mwm at the right time and place.

If you're lucky, your system manager will have set up everything for you automatically. If you're on an X terminal or a workstation running xdm (the X Display Manager), X will be running already when you sit down and will wait for you to enter your user name and password, and Motif will start as soon as you log in.

The next best thing is that you're at a workstation that has been set up to run X after you log in, so that X and Motif start automatically when you log in.

Failing that, you have to start them yourself after you log in to UNIX. The two most common start-up commands are startx and xinit. If you're not sure which one to use, try them and see what happens. What should happen is that your screen will go *kerflooie!* for a few seconds when it switches from old, dumb, terminal mode to new, cool, graphical X mode; a few windows will appear, running xterm (the dumb terminal emulator that runs under X); and Motif starts and draws attractive borders around all the windows.

If none of those things works, we've run out of ideas, and you will have to ask your local expert how to start X and Motif on your computer or X terminal.

How do I leave Motif, anyway?

This question is only slightly less complicated than starting Motif. As usual, we are the victim of a blizzard of options. Here are some likely possibilities:

🖛 Log out by leaving the Motif Window Manager. In this case, move the mouse cursor outside of any windows, click and hold the right mouse button to get to the Motif root menu, slide the cursor down to Quit, and release the button. Motif displays an incredulous little box asking whether you really want to leave mwm. Click OK.

🖛 Log out by closing the main xterm window. The trick is to figure out which

window is the main one. If one of them is labeled Login or Console, that's it. Switch to that window by moving the mouse to that window and clicking the left mouse button. Then type exit to the shell in that window.

When X and Motif exit, the screen usually *kerflooies!* again when it goes back to dumb terminal mode. (If your system uses the X Display Manager, it may immediately go back to the login screen, in which case you're finished.) If you end up back at a shell prompt in dumb terminal mode, you then have to exit from that as well by typing exit to that shell.

Opening a new window

When you run a new X program, generally speaking, it opens a new window. In some cases, you want to tell a program that's already running to open another window (another file for a word processor, for example), but the way that you do that is specific to each program. You have to read the manual (gasp!) for the program.

You usually have at least one terminal window running. A *terminal window* isn't as sinister as it sounds: It's a window that acts like a terminal. The usual program is called xterm; it acts much like a DEC VT-100 terminal. Most systems also have a modified terminal program that acts like the computer maker's favorite terminal. Hewlett-Packard systems have hpterm, for example, which acts like an HP terminal, and some PC UNIX systems have xpcterm, which acts like a PC console. For most purposes, all these terminal programs act the same. They start up running a UNIX shell, and you type commands just as we describe in this book.

There are two ways to start a new program that opens a new window: the GUI-oriented, user-friendly way and the easy way.

LINUX

FVWM: The chameleon of window managers

Because Motif isn't free, it isn't included with most Linux systems. (Nothing would prevent you from running Motif under Linux, but most people aren't prepared to pay more for a window manager than they did for the whole operating system and included software.) Instead, with Linux, you usually find the window manager called FVWM.

The origins of the name FVWM are forever lost in the mists of history. The *VWM* part stands for *virtual window manager.* The *F* part is a mystery, though. *Fine* and *feeble* are two frequently offered possibilities.

The "virtual" part of this window manager is one of FVWM's best-loved features. Instead of having just a single desktop, you can have any number of virtual desktops, each with its own independent set of windows open. Each desktop is the size of the screen, so this enables you to think of your screen as a porthole looking at part of a much larger screen behind it.

FVWM usually displays a little map of all the virtual desktops at your disposal; most systems have either four or nine, but theoretically, you can have as many or as few as you want. You move around among all your desktops by pressing the Ctrl key and then the arrow key for the direction of the next desktop according to the little map. Is your desktop getting too crowded with windows? No need to close some of them; just pop on over to another desktop. You can have dozens of programs open without getting too crowded; never has slowing your system down to a crawl been easier!

FVWM is almost infinitely configurable. You can make it look like practically anything, but its default look is nearly identical to Motif. There is a version of FVWM, known as FVWM95, that looks remarkably similar to — you guessed it — Windows 95. (Whether this is a Good Thing is a favorite point of religious arguments among many Linux users.) Not only do the window borders mimic Windows 95, but it even features a Start button with pull-up menus. FVWM95 is found by default on recent releases of Red Hat Linux (see Chapter 14 for a discussion of what Red Hat Linux is). Another popular mutation of FVWM is called AfterStep, which looks just like the NeXTStep window system.

FVWM has become enormously popular not only on Linux, but also on other free UNIX versions. You can even find it on some large commercial systems.

Follow these steps for the GUI-oriented, user-friendly way:

1. **Move the cursor so that it's not in any of your current windows.**

2. **Click the Menu mouse button.**

   This button is the last one (the right-most button, unless you have a left-handed mouse) in OPENLOOK and the first button otherwise.

3. **Drag the mouse up and down the menu that pops up until you find the program you want.**

4. **Let go of the button.**

   Sometimes you have nested menus: When you pick an item from the first menu, a second menu pops up, and you must pick an item there, too.

The easy way to start a program has only one step:

1. **Go to a terminal window and type the name of the program you want to run.**

This approach is the same one you use to run any other program or to give a command. To display another terminal window, type **xterm** or the name of the terminal program you use.

Then there's the issue of where on-screen the new window appears. Some programs and window managers have strong opinions of their own, and the new window appears wherever the program or window manager thinks that it should. With other, less-opinionated programs, you make the call: A ghostly window that appears floats near the middle of the screen. You move the ghost around with the mouse and click when the window is where you want it. At that point, the ghost materializes into the regular window. This latter scheme is usually more convenient, because the locations the opinionated programs choose for window placement are rarely where you want them. Beware of one thing, though, while the ghost is on-screen: All other windows are frozen. If you leave the ghost on-screen for a long time (while you're at lunch or overnight), all the others can become rather constipated waiting for the screen to unfreeze so that they can update their windows. If you're using Motif, your local guru can switch your system between opinionated mode and floating ghost mode.

Some systems have desktop manager programs (unrelated to window manager programs) that attempt to make it easier to handle programs and files. Desktop managers have sets of icons you click on to start common programs. They enable you to click on filenames to edit the file, and so forth — sort of like the Macintosh Desktop. Opinions vary on how useful these desktop managers are. We haven't been crazy about them, but it's worth trying them for a few minutes, because some people find them much easier to use than menus and shell commands.

Icon do this with a picture

GUIs are crazy about pictures (they're graphical, after all), especially cute, little ones. The cutest, littlest ones you run into are called icons. An *icon* is a little picture in a little box on-screen that represents a window. When you tell X Windows to "iconify" a window, the window disappears and an icon remains. When you double-click (or single-click if you're not using Motif) on the icon, the window comes back just as it was before. Being able to reduce windows to icons enables you to shove programs out of the way and not lose what you were doing — one of the best things about window systems. Figure 4-4 shows a pair of icons: one for an e-mail program, and one for a terminal program. If new mail arrives, the little flag on the mail icon flips up, which is almost useful enough to make up for its X-treme cuteness.

Figure 4-4:
Icons are
windows in
a miniature
disguise.

Dressing Your Motif-Style Windows

Motif (or, more particularly, the Motif window manager) draws a border around every window on your screen, as shown in Figure 4-5. The border gives you considerable control over the window, enabling you to move it, hide it, change its size, and so on.

The borders of some windows will be missing some or all of the buttons we discuss in this section. That's because not all windows allow all functions. If the button's not there, you can't do what it would have done anyway.

You frequently will find that you don't like the way the windows on your screen are arranged. You can do lots of things to alleviate this problem and simultaneously waste lots of time. In fact, we have found that, by giving your dedicated attention to window management, you can spend the entire day at the computer apparently working but not accomplishing anything. A little rearrangement is inevitable, so the following sections are thumbnail sketches of what you can do and how to do it with Motif:

Window menu   Title area   Iconify
                                                  Maximize

MotifBurger

File   Edit   Order

5 Medium Pickle Hamburgers
1 Medium Fries
1 Cola Drinks
8 Rare Ketchup Mustard Hamburgers
8 Rare Ketchup Mustard Hamburgers
2 Huge Fries
8 Apple Juice Drinks
2 Well Done Ketchup Mustard Onion Pickle Hamburgers
2 Tiny Fries
4 Coffee Drinks
2 Well Done Ketchup Mustard Onion Pickle Hamburgers
2 Tiny Fries
4 Coffee Drinks

Border

Figure 4-5:
A typical
Motif
window.

✔ **Change the layering.** Change which windows are in front of other windows, much like shuffling the papers in the pile on your desk. Unless you're a masochist, you want the active window (the window you're using) to be the one in front.

✔ **Move windows around the screen.** This is even more similar to shuffling the papers on your desk.

✔ **Turn windows into icons and vice versa.**

✔ **Change the size of windows.** Create larger areas for long files you're editing, for example.

Switching and layering your windows

Suppose that you have two or three windows on your screen. How do you tell UNIX which window you want to use? The answer is (wait, no — how did you know this was coming?) *it depends.* In line with X's standard rule of never making up its mind about anything, there are two different ways you switch windows, as follows:

✔ **Click-to-type, or explicit focus:** Move the mouse cursor to the window you want to use, and click the mouse in it somewhere. The window moves to the front (that is, any overlapping windows drop behind it so that you can see the entire window).

✔ **Move-to-type, or pointer focus:** Move the mouse cursor into the window you want to use. Even though it may be partially obscured by other windows, the window becomes active. You can tell when a window is *active* because the border around it changes color. Click the window's title bar if you want to move it to the front as well. Motif also enables you to move a window up front like this: Move the cursor into the window, hold down the Alt or Meta key, and press F1.

If you have to "click to type" and really hate it — or don't and really want to — a guru skilled in the ways of X (naturally called an X-pert) can change some parameters and turn "click to type" on or off. We recommend that you live with whatever you have. There are so many changeable parameters that, after you begin fiddling with them, it can become X-asperating to figure out X-actly how your X-pert left them, and you will utter an X-cess of X-pletives.

You can tell which is the active window because the Motif window manager changes the color of its border to a distinctive darker color. Motif's standard window-switching rule is click-to-type.

Where, oh where, has my window gone?

In Motif, put the cursor in the title bar, press the first mouse button, and drag the window to where you want it (that is, move the window as you hold down the mouse button). This action also brings the window to the front, because you use the same button to do that.

You can move windows so that they are partially off the edge of the screen, sort of like pushing papers to the side of your desk so that they hang over the edge (except that windows are less likely to fall on the floor). This capability is sometimes useful if the interesting stuff in the window is all at the top or all on one side.

Stashing your windows

The title bar of the window has on it little buttons you can click. Near the right of the title bar is a little box that contains a small dot; when you click on it, you *iconify* the window — that is, the window turns into an icon.

To get the window back, double-click on the icon with the first mouse button.

Icons normally appear in the lower-left corner of your screen, but you can move them around by dragging the icon around with the mouse. After you've moved an icon, if you restore the window and then re-iconify it, the icon reappears where you left it. You can lay out the icons to your taste by iconifying every window on the screen, moving the icons to tasteful positions, and then restoring the ones you want to use.

Curiouser and curiouser: Changing window sizes

The last little bit of window magic involves changing window sizes. Motif has gone to a lot of trouble to let you change the size of your windows, which tells us that they gave up trying to make them the right size in the first place. Oh, well. Little "grab bars" are in each corner of most windows. (The few windows you can't resize don't have the grab bars.) You move the cursor to one of the grab bars, click the first mouse button, drag the corner to where you want it (make the window larger or smaller), and release the button. Then do it again two or three times, because you never get it right on the first try. Motif also has grab bars on the top, bottom, and sides of every window, which enable you to change the height of a window without changing the width or vice versa.

Some programs have strong feelings about how big their windows should be. In some cases, they don't let you shrink the window to less than a minimum size. In other cases, you can't change the size at all. For these programs, attempts to resize just don't work. You can click and drag the borders all you want, but nothing moves.

Motif has a shortcut to enable you to expand a window to fill the entire screen. Click on the little box-in-a-box at the right end of the title bar. If you do the same thing again, the window shrinks back to normal size.

In practice, we rarely blow windows up to the full screen, because few UNIX programs take advantage of the entire screen. The full-screen option was a lot more important when screens were smaller.

Getting Rid of Windows

Your screen often becomes cluttered with windows you no longer need. You already know how to turn them into icons to get most of the screen space back, but sometimes you just want to make the program go away.

Remember that, if 57 different programs are running, even if most of them are snoozing behind their icons, it can put enough of a load on your computer to slow down the ones you want to use.

Most programs have a natural way to exit. In terminal windows, you log out from the shell by typing **exit** or **logout** in the terminal window. Real windows-oriented programs usually have menus of their own with a Quit or Exit option that cleans up and makes the program stop. Because some programs just won't die, however, you have to take drastic measures.

In Motif, click on the little bar in the box at the left end of the title bar; a menu of window operations pops up, as shown in Figure 4-6. The Restore, Move, Size, Minimize, and Maximize choices are equivalent to the border-clicking techniques we just discussed. (Minimize is Motif-ese for "iconify.") The two remaining entries can be useful, though. Lower means to push the window behind all the rest so that it doesn't obscure any other windows. That entry is useful when you want to work on something else for a while. Close closes the window and usually also ends the program that started it. This entry can be handy for programs that get stuck or don't have any normal way to exit.

Figure 4-6:
The Motif
window
menu.

Motif offers a set of keyboard equivalents for mouse-haters. To display the window menu, press Shift+Esc or Alt+spacebar. Then either press the cursor keys and Enter to choose one of the entries, or press the underlined letter in the entry you want. For Move and Size, you press the cursor keys to move or resize the window and then press Enter when you're finished.

You can also use the Alt+key equivalents in the menu, such as Alt+F9 for minimize. If your keyboard has two Alt keys (as most PC keyboards do), you may find that the two Alt keys work differently. On our system, the left Alt key is recognized by individual programs, and the right Alt key is the one the Motif Window Manager recognizes.

Motif uses confusing and inconsistent names in the window-operations menu. Close means to destroy the window and the program, and Minimize turns the window into an icon.

More Stupid Window Manager Tricks

The window manager has a *root menu* that appears when you click the right mouse button (the right mouse button, not the left) outside any window. It looks like Figure 4-7.

Root Menu

New Window

Shuffle Up

Shuffle Down

Refresh

Pack Icons

Toggle Behavior...

Restart...

Quit...

Figure 4-7:
The Motif
root menu.

Like most other features related to X, the contents of the root menu are infinitely configurable, but Table 4-1 shows you the typical entries.

Table 4-1	Window Manager Root Menu Options
Entry	*What It Does*
New Window	Starts a new xterm window
Shuffle Up	Takes the next window and moves it to the front
Shuffle Down	Takes the next window and moves it to the back
Refresh	Completely redraws the screen
Pack Icons	Moves all the icons on the window to the lower-left corner
Toggle Behavior	Switches between standard and customized window manager
Restart	Restarts the window manager
Quit	Leaves the window manager

We find New Window and Refresh to be relatively useful. Shuffling windows is a waste of time, because you can click the title bars of the windows you really want to see. Packing icons can be useful if you have lots of icons cluttering up your screen (which we rarely do). Toggle Behavior and Restart are useful only if you customize your window manager. Quit is handy if your system is set up so that you log out by leaving the window manager. Otherwise, it's useless, too.

The Parade of Motif Widgets

The Motif toolkit is a set of programming tools with prewritten bits of program that programmers can use to build their Motif applications. That wouldn't be very interesting except that the bits of program it includes are the ones that draw stuff on the screen. These so-called *widgets* include the usual things that windowing programs use, such as menus, pushbuttons, text boxes, and scroll bars. Motif widgets have become a *de facto* standard for X programs and have sprouted up in seemingly every application written for X Windows. Even those programs that use something other than Motif widgets very often make them look just like Motif programs, with the dull gray menus and buttons that UNIX users have gotten used to.

This section quickly describes the most common widgets. They're all designed to be easy to use, so even without reading the instructions, it's easy to guess how they work.

Menu widgets

Figure 4-8 shows the main window from the MotifBurger sample application that comes with Motif, with one of its pull-down menus selected. You make choices from a Motif menu in an obvious way: Click the place you want on the menu bar at the top of the application's window. If the menu has sub-entries (as most do), the next level menu drops down. Click the entry you want.

Figure 4-8:
An
application
menu.

You can also drive Motif applications from the keyboard. To choose a menu entry, hold down Alt (the left Alt key if you have two) and press the underlined letter in the menu entry. If there are submenus, press the up- and down-arrow keys to move to the entry you want, and then press Enter to select or Esc to ignore.

Occasionally, you see a couple of other minor variants of menus. *Tear-off* menus are similar to pull-down menus except that they have a dotted line across the top when you pull them down. If you click the dotted line and drag the menu to a convenient place, it stays there indefinitely so that you can use it whenever you want. We don't find this feature very useful because it clutters up the screen. (Motif's old arch rival, Open Look, had tear-off–like menus called *pushpins,* and Open Look proponents trumpeted them as a major advantage. Motif probably added them as much to shut up the competition as because anyone really wanted them.) Sometimes, *pop-up* menus also appear when you press the right mouse button, the way the root menu appears when you click outside any window. Pop-up menus work just like pull-down menus after they've popped up.

Figure 4-9 shows a window from the MotifBurger sample application. This window is pretty awfully designed because it's full of far too many different kinds of widgets. But it was intended as a demonstration of the various kinds of widgets, which it does just fine.

Let's look at the widget types, beginning from the left side of the figure.

Radio buttons

The Hamburgers Rare/Medium/Well Done box is called a *radio button* box because it sort of resembles the buttons on a car radio. You can click any one of the buttons to select it, but you can select only one radio button in a group.

Figure 4-9:
A bunch of
widgets.

You can recognize radio buttons because they're shaped like little diamonds.

You're supposed to be able to select radio buttons by holding down the Alt key and pressing the underlined letter, but in our experience, that doesn't always work. Use your mouse to be sure.

Toggle buttons

The list of hamburger condiments, from Ketchup to Mayonnaise, are *toggle buttons*. When you click one, it turns on if it was off, and turns off if it was on — sort of like a toggle switch. Unlike radio buttons, any or all of the toggle buttons in a group can be selected at a time.

You can recognize toggle buttons because they're little squares.

Scales or sliders

The Hamburger quantity thing is a *scale*. You can move it up or down with the mouse to control how many hamburgers to order. Although this scale looks pretty silly, in some cases, they're just what you want (the volume control on a sound application, for example).

Scales can be laid out either up and down or left and right. They work the same either way.

Option menus

The fries size control is an *option menu*. When you click it, the complete set of options appears, as shown in Figure 4-10. Move the cursor to the one you want and click. It shrinks back down and displays the selected option.

Text boxes

The little quantity box under fries is a *text box*. Click the cursor there, and then type the number of orders of fries you want. The usual text-editing characters, such as arrow keys and Backspace, work.

This text box is the smallest one we've ever seen. (Hey, it's just a sample application.) Most text boxes are large enough that the editing keys are useful. Many text windows also have scroll bars, which we discuss in the following section.

Figure 4-10:
How many
fries would
you like
with that?

Scrollable lists and scroll bars

The list of drinks starting with Apple Juice is a *scrollable list.* You can move the list up and down in its window by using the *scroll bar* to the right of the window. The little arrows move the list up and down a small, fixed amount. You can also drag the block between the arrows up and down to move the list directly.

After you've found the item you want, click it to select and highlight it. (We've selected Apple Juice here, but our favorite is Grape Juice, because it gives us the classic cool, purple mustache.)

Pushbuttons

The last controls here are *pushbuttons.* They come in two varieties: buttons with text and buttons with drawings. The two arrows for the drinks quantity are buttons with drawings. The Apply, Dismiss, and Reset buttons at the bottom of the window are buttons with text.

They all work in the same way. To select the button and do whatever the button does, click it.

Ta-Ta for Now

The last little detail is how to tell X Windows you're finished with it. The way you do that (we're getting tired of saying this) varies from one system to another. You have to stop the startup program, which is usually a terminal window named login or the window manager itself. If there is a window named login, go to the login window and type **exit** or **logout** to exit that shell, or kill it as explained in the preceding section.

If your startup program is the window manager, you must persuade the window manager to exit. You can't kill it the way you kill other programs, because the window manager doesn't have a particular window. In Motif, you move the cursor outside any window, press the first mouse button, and select the item labeled Quit from the menu that pops up. Motif pops up another box, incredulous that you claim that you want to leave a program as wonderful as itself, so you have to click OK to assure it that you are indeed such an ingrate.

Terminal Happenings

Even though X Windows enables you to run all of the coolest, gnarliest, newest, most graphicalest programs, guess what program people use the most? It's called xterm, and all it does is act like the kind of VT-100 dumb terminal that window systems are supposed to save us from. Such are the ways of progress.

The xterm program is one of the oldest programs that runs under X, and it has the greasy fingerprints of generations of programmers. As the README file in its source code notes, "This is undoubtedly the most ugly program in the distribution." So although xterm has more than 70 exciting options on the command line alone, we won't tell you about them.

Click, click

One place where xterm acts a little better than the dumb terminal it purports to emulate is in mouse handling. You can select text with the mouse and then paste the selected text into either the same or a different xterm window.

To select some text, move the mouse to the beginning of the text, press down the first (left) mouse button, and move the mouse to the end of the text. As you move the mouse, the selected text changes color. When you've selected it all, let go of the mouse button. Normally, xterm selects text character by character, but if you double-click rather than just press the mouse button, it'll select by word, and if you triple-click, it'll select by line. For users who don't believe in walking and chewing gum at the same time, there's an alternate way to select text: Move to the beginning of the selection, click the left button, and then move to the end of the selection and click the right button.

Either way, after you've selected the text, move the mouse to the window where you want to paste it and click the middle button. If, after you've selected the text, a program erases the window, you won't be able to see the selection any more, but it'll still be there and you can still paste it.

Most other programs that have text type-in areas use the same mouse conventions that xterm does, so you can select text from an xterm and paste it into other programs, and vice versa.

Coming in for a save

The other thing that makes xterm occasionally useful is that you can save a transcript of what goes on in the window into a file — a *log file*. To turn on logging, move the cursor into the xterm window, hold down the Ctrl key with your non-mouse hand, and then press and hold down the left mouse button to get a little menu like the one in Figure 4-11. Next, move the mouse down to Log to File, and let go of the mouse button. (This sequence isn't quite as hard as it sounds, fortunately.) A bunch of other options are on that menu, none of which we recommend other than the self-explanatory Redraw Window and Quit.

```
         Main Options
   Secure Keyboard
   Allow SendEvents
   Log to File
   Redraw Window
   Send STOP Signal
   Send CONT Signal
   Send INT Signal
   Send HUP Signal
   Send TERM Signal
   Send KILL Signal
   Quit
```

Figure 4-11:
A few xterm
menu
options.

After that, everything you type in that window, including all the backspaces and other correction characters to remind you of what a rotten typist you are, and everything that UNIX types back, is written to a file. What file? The answer varies, but usually, it's a file in your home directory called XtermLog.12345 where the last five digits are made up to be unique. Type **ls Xterm***, and you'll probably find it. When you're finished, do the same Ctrl and mouse dance and select Log to File again (it'll be checked to remind you that logging is on) to turn off the log.

Logging is an optional feature of xterm, and some systems have logging turned off permanently. In that case, if you try to turn on logging, the terminal will just beep.

Chapter 5
Files for Fun and Profit

• •

In This Chapter

▶ Listing information about files

▶ Showing who has permission to use files

▶ Duplicating a file

▶ Erasing a file

▶ Renaming a file

▶ Looking at what's in a file

▶ Printing a text file

▶ Giving a file to someone else

• •

A *file* is a bunch of information stored together, such as a letter to your mom or a database of customer invoices. Every file has a name. You will end up with tons of them.

This chapter explains how to work with files, including getting rid of the ones you no longer want.

Just as a reminder, you must log in before you can do any of the nifty things we talk about in this chapter (see Chapter 1). When you see the UNIX prompt (% or $), you are ready to rock and roll.

What Files Do You Have?

To see a list of your files (actually, a list of the files in the working directory, which Chapter 6 covers), type 1s and press Enter. (This is positively the last time we'll nag you to press Enter.)

This command stands for *list,* but could the lazy typists who wrote UNIX have used the other two letters? No-o-o. . . . This command lists all the files in your working directory. (Chapter 6 discusses directories and how to make lots of them.) The 1s command just shows the names of the files in alphabetical order, like this:

```
bin/        budget-96 budget-97 budget-98 daveg draft
jordan      Mail/     meg       news.junk zac
```

In some Linux systems, if the directory contains subdirectories, the subdirectory names appear in a different color if your screen handles colors, which is very handy. In BSD UNIX, subdirectory names also have a slash after them. (Chapter 6 talks about subdirectories, if you are wondering what we are talking about.)

Let's see the nitty-gritty details

For more information about your files, use the `-l` option *(long form listing)*, as follows:

```
ls -l
```

That's a small letter *el*, by the way, not a number *one*. This option tells `ls` to display tons of information about your files. Each line looks like this:

```
-rw-r—r—  1 johnl   users   250 Apr  6 09:57 junk3
```

Later in this chapter, in the section "Who can do what?" we explain all the information in this listing. For now, just notice that the right-hand part of the line shows you the size of the file (250 characters, in this example), the date and time the file was last modified, and the filename.

To switch or not to switch?

Lots of UNIX commands have *options.* (They are also called *switches,* because you switch the options on and off by typing or not typing them when you type the command. True geeks call them *flags.*) Options make commands both more versatile and more confusing. Probably the most widely used option is the `-l` option for the `ls` command, which tells `ls` to display lots of information about each file. When you type a command with one or more options, keep these rules handy:

✔ Leave a space after the command name (the command `ls`, for example) and before the option (the `-l` part).

✔ Type a hyphen as the first character of the option (`-l`, for example).

✔ Type a space after the option if you want to type more information on the command line after the option.

✔ If you want to include more than one option, type another space, another hyphen, and the next option. You can usually string multiple options together after one hyphen; for example, `-al` means you want option `a` and option `l`.

Making a long listing stop and start when you're ready

If you have a lot of files, the ls listing may fly right off the top of your screen. If you have this problem, type the following line:

```
ls | more
```

The vertical bar is called a *pipe.* (We talk more about the pipe in Chapter 7.) The | more option after the basic ls command tells UNIX to stop listing information to the screen just before the first file disappears from view. Press the spacebar to see the next screen of filenames.

Let's see 'em all

You may have more files in your directory than you think. UNIX enables you to make things called *hidden files,* which are just like regular files except that they don't appear in normal ls listings. It's easy to make a hidden file — just start its filename with a period.

You can see your hidden files by typing the following:

```
ls -a
```

To see all the information about your hidden files, type the following:

```
ls -al
```

This command combines the -a and -l options together so that you see the long version of the complete listing of files. You could get the same thing by typing:

```
ls -a -l
```

but that would require typing an extra character and an extra space, an anathema to lazy UNIX typists.

Roger, I Copy

You can make an exact duplicate of a file. To do this, you must know the name of the file you want to copy, and you must create a new name to give to the copy. If a file contains your January budget (called budget.jan, for example) and you want to make a copy of it to use for the February budget (to be called budget.feb, for example), type this line:

```
cp budget.jan budget.feb
```

The lazy typists strike again. Be sure to leave spaces after the cp command and between the existing and new filenames. This command doesn't change the existing file (budget.jan); it just creates a new file with a new name, but with the same contents.

A good way to lose some work

What if a file named budget.feb *already* exists? Tough cookies! UNIX blows it away and replaces it with a copy of budget.jan. It truly is an excellent idea to use the ls command first to make sure that you don't already have a file with the new name you have chosen.

In Linux and UNIX System V Release 4, you can use the -i switch to ask cp to inform you whether a file with the new name already exists. If it does, the -i switch asks you whether to proceed. If you have this version of UNIX, type cp -i rather than just cp to use this nifty little feature.

If all goes well and cp works correctly, it doesn't give you any message. Blessed silence on the part of UNIX usually means that all is well. You should use the ls command to check that the new file really does exist, just in case.

What's in a name?

When you create a file, you give it a name. UNIX has rules about what makes a good filename:

✔ Filenames can be pretty long; they're not limited to eight characters and a three-character extension, like some operating systems we could name. On older versions of UNIX, the limit is 14 characters for a filename; newer versions have a huge limit — in the hundreds of characters — so you can call a file
Some_notes_I_plan_to_get_around_to_typing_up_eventually_
if_I_live_that_long.

✔ Don't use weird characters that mean something special to UNIX or some shell you might encounter. Stay away from the following characters when you name files:

```
<   >   '    "     *
{   }   ^    !     \
[   ]   #    |     &
(   )   $    ?     ~
```

Stick mainly to letters and numbers.

✔ Don't put spaces in a filename. Although some programs let you put them in, spaces cause nothing but trouble, because other programs simply cannot believe that a filename might contain a space. Don't borrow trouble. Most UNIX people use periods to string together words to make filenames, such as budget.jan.98 or pumpkin.soup. Underscores work, too.

✔ UNIX considers uppercase and lowercase letters to be completely different. Budget, budget, BUDGET, and BuDgEt are all different filenames.

Nuking Files Back to the Stone Age

You can also get rid of files by using the command that the lazy typists call rm. To erase (delete, remove — it's all the same thing) a file, type the following:

```
rm budget.feb
```

If all goes well, UNIX reports nothing, and you see another prompt. Use ls to see whether the rm command worked and the file is gone.

Watch out! Under most circumstances, there is *no way* to get a file back after you delete it.

To be safe, you can use the -i option to ask rm to ask you to confirm deletion of the file. This is a particularly good idea if you use wildcards to delete a group of files at once. (See Chapter 7 for more on wildcards.) For example, if you type

```
rm -i last-years-budget
```

UNIX asks the following:

```
rm: remove 'last-years-budget'
```

Press Y to delete the file or N to leave it alone.

Big, big trouble

If you delete something really, really important and you will be called on to perform ritual seppuku if you can't get it back, don't give up hope. Your local UNIX guru should make things called *backups* on some regular basis. Backups contain copies of some or all the files on the UNIX system. Your files may be among those on the backup. Go to the guru on bended knee and ask whether the file can be restored. If the file wasn't backed up recently, you may get an older version of it, but, hey — it's better than the alternative.

Even before you get yourself into this kind of pickle, you may want to ask your UNIX expert to confirm that regular backups are made. Make sure that your important files are included in the backups. If no one is making regular backups, panic! This is not a safe situation. You'd better talk to your system administrator about getting a tape backup system.

Good housekeeping

You should get rid of files you no longer use, for several reasons:

- ✔ It becomes confusing when you have all kinds of files lying around, and it's difficult to remember which ones are important.
- ✔ The useless files take up disk space. Whoever is in charge of your UNIX system probably will bother you regularly to "take out the garbage" — that is, to get rid of unnecessary files and free up some disk space.

On the other hand, making extra copies of files can be a good idea. If you have been working on a report for three weeks, it isn't a bad idea to make an extra copy every day or so. That way, if you make some revisions that, in hindsight, were stupid, you can always go back to a previous revision.

What's in a Name (Reprise)

Having given a file a name, you may want to change it later. Maybe you spelled it wrong in the first place. In any case, you can rename a file by using the mv (lazy typist-ese for *move*) command.

Suppose that you made a file called bugdet.march. Oops, dratted fingers. . . . Type the following line to correct the error in the filename:

```
mv bugdet.march budget.march
```

After mv, you type the current name of the file and then the name you want to change it to. Note that it can be harder to retype the same typo than to type the name correctly!

Because you can't have two files with the same name in the same directory, if a file already has the name you want to use, mv thoughtfully blows away the existing file (probably not what you want to do). Type carefully. Linux and SVR4 users can use mv -i (like cp -i) to prevent inadvertent file clobbering.

Want to hide a file so that it doesn't appear in your directory listing? Use a period (.) as the first letter of the filename. To see all of your files, including hidden files, type

```
ls -al
```

Looking at the Guts of a File

We have been slicing and dicing files for a while now, but you still haven't seen what's inside one. There are two basic types of files:

- ✔ Files that contain text that UNIX can display nicely on-screen
- ✔ Files that contain special codes that look like monkeys have been at the keyboard when you display the files on-screen

The first type of files are called *text files.* The second type comprises spreadsheet files, database files, program files, and just about everything else. Text editors make text files, as do a few other programs.

To display a text file, type the following line:

```
cat eggplant.recipe
```

If you want to see the guts of a file that isn't named eggplant.recipe, substitute your file's name. The cat stands for *catalog,* or maybe *catenate* — who knows? We're surprised that the lazy typists didn't call it something like q. If you try to use cat with a file that doesn't contain text, your screen looks like a truck ran over it — but you won't hurt anything. Sometimes the garbage in the file can put your terminal in a strange mode in which characters you type don't appear or appear as strange Greek squiggles. See Chapter 22 to learn how to "un-strange" your terminal.

If the file is long, the listing goes whizzing by. (You find out how to look at the file one screen at a time in Chapter 7.) To see just the first few lines of the file, you can type the following line:

```
head eggplant.recipe
```

Most versions of the `head` command display the first ten lines.

You can ask UNIX to guess at what's in a file by using the `file` command. If you type

```
file filename
```

(replacing *filename* with the name of the file you are wondering about), UNIX takes a guess at what's in the file by looking at it. It says something like this:

```
letter.to.jordan:    ascii text
```

or this

```
unix4d:    directory
```

Is This a Printout I See before Me?

If a file looks okay on-screen when you use the `cat` command, try printing it. If you use UNIX System V, type the following line to print your famous eggplant dish:

```
lp eggplant.recipe
```

If you use BSD UNIX or Linux, type the following:

```
lpr eggplant.recipe
```

Assuming that you have a printer that is hooked up, is turned on, and has paper, and that your user name is set up to use it, the `eggplant.recipe` file prints. If it doesn't, see Chapter 9 to straighten things out. If your computer is blessed with a network, the printed copy may come out down the hall or on another floor. In one inexplicable case, when users in New York printed any file, the copies ended up on a printer somewhere in Japan. If your printer isn't attached directly to your computer, you probably have to ask for advice about where to pick up the printout. If you can print files on more than one printer, you use the `-d` or `-P` option with the printer name to tell UNIX which printer you want to use (see Chapter 9).

Who Goes There?

Unlike some operating systems we could name (such as . . . oh, Microsoft Windows, f'rinstance), UNIX was designed from the beginning to be used by more than one person. Like all multiuser systems, UNIX keeps track of who owns what file and who can do what with each file. *Permissions* attached to each file and directory determine who can use them.

Permissions come in three types:

▶ **Read permission** enables you to look at a file or directory. You can use `cat` or a text editor to see what's in a file that has read permission. You also can copy this type of file. Read permission for a directory enables you to list the directory's contents.

▶ **Write permission** enables you to make changes to a file. Even if you can write (change) a file, you can't necessarily delete it or rename it; for those actions, you must be able to write in the directory in which the file resides. If you have write permission in a directory, you can create new files in the directory and delete files from it.

▶ **Execute permission** enables you to run the program contained in the file. The program can be a real program or a shell script. If the file doesn't contain a program, execute permission doesn't do you much good and can provoke the shell to complain bitterly as it tries (from its rather dim point of view) to make sense of your file. For a directory, execute permission enables you to open files in the directory and use `cd` to get to the directory to make it your working directory.

Rock groups, pop groups, and UNIX groups

Every UNIX user is a member of a group. When the system administrator created your user name, she or he assigned you to a group. To see which group you are in, type this line:

```
id
```

You see something like the following:

```
uid=113(margy) gid=102(guest) groups=102(guest),101(book),
         103(cheese)
```

Groups usually indicate the kind of work you do. UNIX uses groups to give a bunch of people the same permissions to use a set of files. All the people who work on a particular project are usually in the same group so that they can look at and perhaps change each other's files.

If you are part of the accounting department, for example (it's a dirty job, but someone has to do it), you and the other accounting staff members might need read, write, and execute permission for basically the same files. People in other departments should not have the same access to accounting programs and data. The system administrator probably made a group called something like `acctg` and put all you accounting boys and girls in it.

In Linux and BSD, you can be in several groups at a time, which is handy if you're working on several projects. To find out what groups you are in, type groups.

That's mine!

Every file and directory has an owner and a group owner. The owner is usually the person who made the file or directory, although the owner can sometimes change the ownership of the file to someone else. The group owner is usually the group to which the owner belongs, although the owner can change a file's group owner to another group.

If you use Linux or System V, you can change who owns a file with the chown command (described later in this chapter).

Who can do what?

To see who can do what to a file, use the ls command with the -l option. Type this line:

```
ls -l myfile
```

You see something like the following:

```
-rw-r—r—   1 margy    staff   335 Jan 22 13:23 myfile
```

If you don't specify a filename (in this case, myfile), UNIX lists all the files in the directory, which is often more useful. For every file, this listing shows all the following information:

✔ Whether it is a file, symbolic link, or directory. The first character in the line is a hyphen (-) if it is a file, an *l* if it is a symbolic link, and a *d* if it is a directory.

✔ Whether the owner can read, write, or execute it (as shown by the next three characters, 2 through 4, on the line). The first character is an *r* if the owner has read permission or a hyphen (-) if not. The second character is a *w* if the owner has write permission or a hyphen (-) if not. The third character is an *x* (or sometimes an *s*) if the owner has execute permission or a hyphen (-) if not.

✔ Whether the members of the group owner can read, write, or execute the file or directory (as indicated by the next three characters, 5 through 7). An *r, w,* or *x* appears if that permission is granted; a hyphen (-) appears if that permission is not granted.

✔ Whether everyone else can read, write, or execute the file or directory (as indicated by the next three characters, 8 through 10). An *r, w,* or *x* appears if that permission is granted; a hyphen (-) appears if that permission is not granted.

✔ The link count — that is, how many links (names) this file has. For directories, this number is the number of subdirectories the directory contains plus 2 (don't ask).

✔ The owner of the file or directory.

✔ The group to which the file or directory belongs (group owner).

✔ The size of the file in bytes (characters).

✔ The date and time the file was last modified.

✔ The filename — at last!

Permissions by number

It is not too difficult to figure out which permissions a file has by looking at the collection of *r*s, *w*s, and *x*s in the file listing. Sometimes permissions are written another way, however: with numbers. Only UNIX programmers could have thought of this. (This is an example of lazy typists at their finest.) Numbered permissions are sometimes called *absolute permissions* (perhaps because they are absolutely impossible to remember).

When permissions are expressed as a number, it is a three-digit number. The first digit is the owner's permissions, the second digit is the group's permissions, and the third digit is everyone else's permissions. Every digit is a number from 0 to 7. Table 5-1 lists what the digits mean.

Table 5-1	Absolute Permissions Decoded
Digit	*Permissions*
0	None
1	Execute only
2	Write only
3	Write and execute
4	Read only
5	Read and execute
6	Read and write
7	Read, write, and execute

Why those numbers?

You may well ask why numbers 0 to 7 were assigned to permissions. They weren't assigned at random. For those of you who remember New Math from fourth grade, all this makes sense if you think in binary (base 2).

Think of every permission digit as a 3-digit binary number, like 010 (that's binary for 2). The first digit is 1 if you have read permission, or 0 if you don't. The second digit is 1 if you have write permission, or 0 if you don't. The third digit is 1 if you have read permission, or 0 if you don't.

So, the permission digit 6, which is 110 in binary, means that you can read and write, but not execute. If this still doesn't make sense, find a fourth-grader to work it out for you.

If Mom says no, go ask Dad

If you own a file or directory, you can change its permissions. You use the chmod (for *change mode*) command to do it. You tell chmod the name of the file or directory to change and the new permissions you want the file to have for yourself (the owner), your group, and everyone else. You can either type the numerical absolute permissions (such as **440**) or use letters.

To use letters to type the new permissions, you use a cryptic collection of letters and symbols that consists of the following:

- Whose permissions you are changing: u for user (the file's owner), g for the group, o for other (everyone else), or a for all three.

- If the permission should be + (on, yes, OK) or - (off, no, don't let them).

- The type of permission you're dealing with: r for read, w for write, and x for execute.

Type the following line, for example, to allow everyone to read a file called announcements:

```
chmod a+r announcements
```

This line says that the user/owner, group, and everyone else can read the file. To not let anyone except the user/owner change the file, type this line:

```
chmod go-w announcements
```

You can also use numeric (absolute) permissions with chmod. To let the user/owner and associated group read or change the file, type the following:

```
chmod 660 announcements
```

This sets the owner permission to 6 (read and write), the group permission to 6, too, and everyone else's permission to 0 (can't do anything).

You can change the permissions for a directory in exactly the same way you do for a file. Keep in mind that *read, write,* and *execute* mean somewhat different things for a directory.

Finding a new owner

When someone gives you a file, he or she usually copies it to your home directory. As far as UNIX is concerned, the person who copied the file is still the file's owner. In Linux and System V, you can change the ownership of a file you own by using the chown command.

You tell chown the new owner for the file and the filename or filenames whose ownership you are changing. For example:

```
chown john chapter6
```

This command changes the ownership of the file named chapter6 to john. Keep in mind that only you can give away files you own; if you put a file in someone else's directory, it's polite to chown the file to that user.

Another way to change the owner of a file is to make a copy of the file. Suppose that Fred puts a file in your home directory and he still owns it. You can't use chown to change the ownership, because only the owner can do that. (We have a chicken-before-the-egg problem here.) You *can* get owner-ship of a file if you copy the file. When you copy a file, you own the new copy. Then delete the original.

File seeks new group; can sing, dance, and do tricks

If you own a file or directory, you can change the group that can access it. The chgrp command enables you to change the name of the group associated with the file. Take the following command, for example:

```
chgrp acctg billing.list
```

This command changes the group associated with the file billing.list to the group called acctg.

Chapter 6

Directories for Fun and Profit

• •

In This Chapter

▶ Defining a directory

▶ Getting to the right directory

▶ Defining a home directory

▶ Making a new directory

▶ Erasing a directory

▶ Renaming a directory

▶ Moving a file from one directory to another

▶ Organizing your files

▶ A map of UNIX

• •

*F*iles are great — they're where you store all your important information, as well as where UNIX itself and all your programs are stored. In fact, UNIX systems have tens of thousands of files, even before you create a single one. Imagine typing your ls command and getting a list of 10,000 filenames? Not pretty (or fast).

To avoid this situation, UNIX has things called *directories,* which enable you to divide your files into groups. This chapter explains how to organize your UNIX files into directories and how to find things after you have done so.

Good News for Windows and DOS Users

We have good news about UNIX for you experienced Windows and DOS users. UNIX works almost exactly the same as Windows and DOS do when it comes to directories and files. Actually, it's the other way around — a guy named Mark added directories to DOS back in 1982, and ripped off . . . er, emulated the way UNIX did things — with a few confusing changes, of course.

Briefly, Windows and DOS users should know the following things about UNIX directories:

- ✔ All those backslashes (\ ) you learned to type in Windows and DOS turn into regular slashes (/) in UNIX. No one knows why Mark decided that DOS slashes should lean backward. We're sure he had a very good reason, of course — maybe the / key was broken on his keyboard.

- ✔ The UNIX cd (change directory) command works (more or less) like the DOS CD command; remember not to capitalize it in UNIX.

- ✔ The UNIX command for making a directory is mkdir rather than the DOS MD command. To remove a directory in UNIX, you use the rmdir command rather than the DOS RD command. (Where were the lazy typists when we needed them?) These two commands also work (more or less) like the DOS versions. Don't capitalize them, either.

- ✔ As always, UNIX believes that uppercase and lowercase letters have nothing to do with each other. They are completely different, so be sure to use the correct capitalization when you type directory names and filenames.

- ✔ If you really like DOS commands and want to make UNIX understand them, you can make shell scripts (the UNIX equivalent of DOS batch files) that enable you to type DIR or COPY while you are using UNIX. (Chapter 12 tells you how to make shell scripts.) Or if you absolutely fall in love with UNIX commands — and who doesn't! — you can make DOS batch files on your PC so that you can type ls and cp while you are using the PC.

If you understand directories and paths intuitively from your vast experience with PCs, skip forward to the sidebar "Getting the big picture."

What Is a Directory?

A *directory,* for the rest of you people, is a group of files, or a work area. (Windows 95 and Macintosh users may recognize this as a *folder.*) You give a directory a name, such as Budget or Letters or Games or Harold. You can put in a directory as many files as you want. Directories divide your disks into manageable chunks.

The good thing about directories (also sometimes called *subdirectories,* for no good reason) is that you can use them to keep together groups of related files. If you make a directory for all your budget files, those are the only files you see while you are working in that directory. Directories make it easy to concentrate on what you are doing so that you're not distracted by the zillions of other files on the disk.

You can make directories, move files into them, rename directories, and get rid of them. This chapter describes the commands that perform each of these stunts.

Divide and Conquer

Interestingly, a directory can contain other directories. You might have a directory called Budget, for example, for your departmental budget. The Budget directory might contain several other directories (also called subdirectories) such as Year1998, Year1999, and Estimates. If a directory contains so many files that you can't find things, you should create some subdirectories to divide things up.

Files and directories are stored on disks. Every disk has a main directory that contains everything on the disk. This directory is called the *root directory*. The designers of UNIX were thinking of trees here, not turnips. They imagined an upside-down tree with the root at the top and the branches reaching downward, like the picture in Figure 6-1. This arrangement of directories is called a *tree-structured directory*.

Figure 6-1: A tree-structured directory.

Strangely, you don't type root when you are talking about the root directory. Rather, you type /. Just like that: A single slash means "root" in UNIX-ese.

Paths to power

Unfortunately, UNIX never shows you the directory structure as a nice picture, like Figure 6-1. That would be too easy. Rather, to tell UNIX which file you want to use, you type its pathname. The *pathname* is the step-by-step map UNIX follows to get to the file, starting at the root. The pathname for the file named `freds.99.estimate` in Figure 6-1, for example, contains these steps:

`/`	The root, where you start.
`Budget`	The name of the first directory you move to on your way to the file.
`/`	Confusingly, this slash doesn't refer to another root; it's just the character used to separate one name from the next in the pathname.
`Year1999`	The next directory on your way to the file.
`/`	Another separator character.
`freds.99.estimate`	The filename you want.

When you type this pathname, you string it all together, with no spaces, as follows:

```
/Budget/Year1999/freds.99.estimate
```

Luckily, you don't have to type big, long pathnames like this one very often; it's devilishly hard to get all that right on the first try!

Family matters

You can also think of the tree structure of directories as a family tree. In this way of thinking, the `Year1999` directory is a *child* of the `Budget` directory, and the `Budget` directory is the *parent* of the `Year1999` directory. You will see these terms sometimes if you read more about UNIX.

Names for directories

Choose names for directories in the same way that you choose names for files: Avoid funky characters and spaces, don't make the name so long that you will never type it correctly, and so on. Some people capitalize the first letter of directory names so that they can tell what's a directory and what's a file. When you use `ls` to list the contents of a directory, the command lists both filenames and the names of subdirectories. When you use capitalization to distinguish between directory names and filenames, you can quickly tell which are which.

Getting the big picture

If you have a UNIX workstation that's all your own, most or all the files on its hard disk are yours. If you have a terminal and share a UNIX computer with others, the computer's hard disk has files that belong to all the users. As you can imagine, we are talking about oodles of files. To keep the files — and the users! — organized, there are lots of different directories.

There are lots of directories for the UNIX program files themselves, program files for other programs, and other stuff you definitely are not interested in. The files that belong to users (such as yourself) usually are stored in one area. A directory called /usr (or sometimes /home) contains one subdirectory for every user. If your user name is zacyoung, for example, the /usr directory contains a subdirectory called zacyoung, which contains your files.

There's No Place Like Home

Every user has a home directory (sweet, isn't it?) in which you store your personal stuff, mail, and so on. When you log in, UNIX starts you working in your home directory, where you work until you move somewhere else. Your home directory is your subdirectory in the /usr (or /home) directory, so Zac Young's home directory is /usr/zacyoung. (Zac is only two years old, but we're sure that he'll need a home directory shortly.)

Because most UNIX systems involve lots of people sharing disk space and files, UNIX has a security system to prevent people from reading each other's private mail or blowing away each other's work (accidentally, of course). Chapter 5 talks about the security system. In your home directory, you usually have the right to create, edit, and delete all the files and subdirectories. You can't do this in someone else's home directory unless the directory's owner gives you permission.

I've been working in the directory

Whenever you use UNIX, the directory you are currently working in is the *working* directory. Some people call it the *current* directory, which also makes sense.

When you first log in, your home directory is your working directory. Although you start in your home directory, you can move around. If you move to the /Budget directory, for example, the /Budget directory becomes the working directory. (Your home directory is still your home directory — it never moves.)

If you forget where you are in the directory structure, you can ask UNIX. Type the following to ask UNIX where you are:

```
pwd
```

This line is short for *print working directory*. UNIX doesn't print the information on paper; it just displays it on your screen. You see something like the following:

```
/Budget/Year1999
```

When you use the ls command (or most other UNIX commands), UNIX assumes that you want to work with just the files in the working directory. The ls command lists just the files in the working directory unless you tell it to look somewhere else.

To move to another directory to do some work (if you are tired of working on the budget and want to get back to that recipe for pumpkin soup, for example), you can change directories. To move from anywhere in the /Budget directory to the /Recipes directory, type the following line:

```
cd /Recipes
```

Remember that cd is the *change directory* command. After the cd (and a space), you type the directory you want to go to. You can tell UNIX exactly which directory you want in two ways:

- ✔ Type a *full pathname,* or *absolute pathname* (the pathname starting at the root, as you did earlier). In the /Recipes example, the slash at the beginning of the pathname indicates that the pathname starts at the root.
- ✔ Type a *relative pathname* (the pathname starting from where you are now).

This is confusing, we know, but UNIX has to know exactly which directory you want before it makes the move. Because there can be more than one directory called Recipes on the disk, UNIX has to know which one you want.

When you type a full pathname starting at the root directory, the pathname starts with a /. When you type a relative pathname starting at the current working directory, the pathname doesn't start with a /. That's how UNIX (and you) can tell which kind of path it is.

If you are in the /Budget directory (on the /Budget branch of the directory tree) and want to go to the Year1999 subdirectory (a branchlet off the main /Budget branch), for example, just type cd Year1999. To go to a different branch or to move upward toward the root, you must use the slashes. To move from the /Budget/Year1999 branchlet back to the main /Budget branch, type cd /Budget. To move from the /Budget branch to the /Recipes branch, for example, type cd /Recipes.

If you try to move to a directory that doesn't exist, or if you incorrectly type the directory name or pathname, UNIX says:

```
Dudegt: No such file or directory
```

(or whatever directory name you typed).

I want to go home!

If you move to another directory (/Oz, for example) and want to get back to your home directory (/Kansas, that is), you can do so as easily as clicking the heels of your ruby slippers together three times. (Or were they glass slippers?) Just type the following line:

```
cd
```

When you don't tell UNIX where you want to go, it assumes that you want to go home.

Putting Your Ducks in a Row

As with everything else in life (if we may be so bold as to suggest it), it pays to be organized when you are naming files and putting them in directories. If you don't have at least a little organization, you will never find anything. Think about which types of files you will make and use. (Word processing files? Spreadsheet files?) Then make a directory for every type of file or for every project you are working on. This section shows you how.

Making directories

Before you make a directory, be sure that you make it in the right place. Remember that you type the following line to display your working directory (that is, the current directory):

```
pwd
```

The most likely place to make a subdirectory is in your home directory. If you're not there already, type the following line to go back home:

```
cd
```

When you create a directory, you give it a name. To create a directory called Temp to hold temporary files, type the following line:

```
mkdir Temp
```

Most people have a directory called Temp to hold files temporarily. These files can be the ones you need to keep just long enough to print, to copy to a floppy disk or tape, or whatever. Anyway, you have one now, too. To confirm that the Temp directory is there, type this line:

```
ls
```

You can even go in there and look around by typing the following (and pressing Enter after typing the first line):

```
cd Temp
ls
```

When you create a directory, it starts out empty (it contains no files).

Most people have directories with names something like the following:

Mail   For electronic mail (see Chapter 17).

Docs   For miscellaneous documents, memos, and letters.

Temp   For files you don't plan to keep. Use Temp to store files you plan to throw away soon. If you put them in some other directory and don't erase them when you finish with them, you may forget what they are and be reluctant to delete them later. Directories commonly fill up with junk in this way. Make it a rule that any files left in the Temp directory are considered deletable.

bin   For programs that you use but that aren't stored in a central place. Your system administrator may have already made you your own bin directory. (See Chapter 12 for information about the bin directory and making your own programs.)

You can also make one or more directories to contain actual work.

Dot and dot dot

There are two funny pseudo-directory names you can use — especially with the cd and ls commands. One is . (a single dot), which stands for the current directory. You type the following line, for example, to tell UNIX to list the files in the current directory:

```
ls .
```

This is pretty pointless, of course, because typing the following line does exactly the same thing:

```
ls
```

Okay, forget about . (the single dot). But .. (the double dot, or dot dot) can be useful. It stands for the parent directory of the current working directory. The *parent* directory is the one of which the working directory is a subdirectory. It is one level up the tree from where you are now. If you are in the directory /usr/home/zacyoung/Budget, for example, the .. (dot dot, or parent) directory is /usr/home/zacyoung.

Suppose that you type the following:

```
ls ..
```

You see a list of the files in the parent directory of where you are now. This can save you some serious typing (and the associated errors).

Neat operations you can perform on directories

After you have some directories, you may want to change their names or get rid of them. You also may want to move a file from one directory to another. Let's try that first.

Transplanting files

Chapter 5 describes the use of the mv command to rename a file. You can use the same command to move files from one directory to another. To get the mv command to move files rather than just rename them, you tell the mv command two things:

    ✔ The name of the file you want to move.

    ✔ The name of the path where you want to put it.

If you want, you can rename the file at the same time you move it, but let's keep things (comparatively) simple. Suppose that you put the file `allens.99.estimates` into the `/Budget/Year1998` directory rather than in `/Budget/Year1999`. The easiest way to move it is to go first to the directory in which it is located. In this example, you type the following line:

```
cd /Budget/Year1998
```

Use `ls` to make sure that the file is in the current directory. After you are sure that the file is there, you can move it to the directory you want by typing the following line:

```
mv allens.99.estimates /Budget/Year1999
```

Be sure to type one space after `mv` and one space between the name of the file and the place you want to move it to. If you use `ls` again, you discover that the file is no longer in the working directory (`Year1998`). You should change to the directory to which you moved the file and use `ls` to make sure that the file is there. Make one typing mistake in a `mv` command, and you can move a valuable file to some unexpected place.

Amputating unnecessary directories

You can use the `rmdir` command to remove a directory, but what about the files in the directory? Are they left hanging in the air with the ground blown out from under them? Nope; you must either get rid of the files in the directory (delete them) or move them elsewhere before you can hack away at the directory.

To erase a directory, do the following:

    1. Use the `rm` command to delete any files you don't want to keep.

    (See Chapter 5 for the gory details of using the `rm` command.)

    2. If you want to keep any of the files, move them to somewhere else by using the `mv` command (as explained in the preceding section).

    3. Move to some other directory when the directory you want to delete is empty.

    UNIX doesn't let you delete the current working directory. The easiest thing to do is to move to the working directory's parent directory, as follows:

```
cd ..
```

4. Remove the directory by typing the following:

```
rmdir OldStuff
```

Replace OldStuff with the name of the directory you want to ax.

5. Use ls **to confirm that the directory is gone.**

You can delete a directory and all the files in it, or even a directory and all the subdirectories and files in them, but this is pretty dangerous stuff. You usually are better off sifting through the files and deleting or moving them in smaller groups. If you're interested in a *really* dangerous command, which we shouldn't even be telling you about, you can type rm -r to remove a directory and all its files and subdirectories in one fell swoop.

Renaming a directory

If you have used DOS, you will be thrilled to learn that in UNIX, you can rename a directory after you create it. (DOS doesn't let you do this, at least not in early versions.) Again, the mv command comes to the rescue.

To rename a directory, you tell mv the current directory name and the new directory name. Go to the parent directory of the directory you want to rename and then use the mv command. To rename the /Budget directory /Finance, for example, go to the / directory (type cd /) and then type this line:

```
mv Budget Finance
```

Remember to make sure first that a directory with that name isn't already there. If it is, UNIX moves the first-named directory to become a subdirectory of the existing directory. In other words, if a /Finance directory is already there, /Budget moves to become /Finance/Budget. Could be handy, if that's what you have in mind. Then again, it could drive you out of your mind if that's not what you expected.

A Map of UNIX

Most UNIX systems have thousands, or even tens of thousands, of files. They are stored in hundreds of directories. Luckily, you don't care about most of these directories, because they contain nothing but the files that make up the murky technical underbelly of UNIX.

You may, however, need to find something in some directory other than your own safe, well-lit home directory. Table 6-1 is a guide to some directories that you are likely to find on your UNIX system. (Not every UNIX system has all these directories, but most do.)

Table 6-1   Popular UNIX Directories and What They Contain

Directory Name	What It Contains
/bin	Standard system commands.
/usr/bin	More standard system commands.
/usr/ucb/bin	Even more standard system commands (the ones written at Berkeley).
/usr/local/bin	Nonstandard, locally installed system commands.
/dev	Contains connections to devices, such as tape drivers, rather than real files. UNIX uses a terribly clever trick for referring to hardware devices as if they were files.
/etc	Miscellaneous system files. Not real interesting to nonweenies.
/home	Contains a home directory for each user. (If you don't see /home, try /usr.)
/lib	Program libraries and the like. (See comment about /etc.)
/usr/lib	More program libraries and the like. (Ditto.)
/usr/news	Usenet news articles, if they happen to be stored on your system. (Even if you have the news programs discussed in Chapter 19, the articles may be on another computer.)
/tmp	Small temporary files.
/usr/tmp	Larger temporary files.
/usr/src	On systems that come with source code, the source code to the system. (Fascinating to programmers; not so fascinating otherwise.)
/var/src	Another place where source code can be found.
/usr/man and /usr/catman	Text of online manual pages.

Chapter 7
Cute UNIX Tricks

• •

• •

*N*ow you know how to work with files and how to type some commands to UNIX. (You type them to the shell, as you know, but let's not get bogged down in that here.) UNIX has a clever way to increase the power of its commands: *redirection*. This chapter shows you how to use redirection and how to use wildcards to work with groups of files.

This Output Is Going to Havana: Redirection

When you use a UNIX command like ls, the result (or *output*) of the command is displayed on-screen. The standard place, in fact, for the output of most UNIX commands is the screen. There is even a name for this: *standard output.* As you can imagine, there is also *standard input,* usually the keyboard. You type a command; if it needs more input, you type that, too. The result is output displayed on-screen — all very natural.

You can pervert this natural order by *redirecting* the input or output of a program. A better word is *hijacking.* You say to UNIX, "Don't display this output on-screen — instead, put it somewhere else." Or, "The input for this program is not coming from the keyboard this time — look for it somewhere else."

The "somewhere else" can be any of these sources:

- ✔ **A file:** You can store the output of ls (your directory listing) in a file, for example.
- ✔ **The printer:** Useful only for output. Getting input from a printer is a losing battle.
- ✔ **Another program:** This gets really interesting, when you take the output of one program and feed it to another program!

Bunches of UNIX programs are designed primarily to use input from a source other than the keyboard and to output stuff to someplace other than the screen. These kinds of programs are called *filters*. Readers old enough to remember what cigarettes are may recall that the really advanced ones had a filter between the cigarette and your mouth to make the smoke smoother, mellower, and more sophisticated. UNIX filters work in much the same way, except that they usually aren't made of asbestos.

The only exception to this redirection business is with programs, such as text editors and spreadsheets, that take over the entire screen. Although you can redirect their output to the printer, for example, you won't like the results (nor will your coworkers, as they wait for a pile of your garbage pages to come out of the printer). Full-screen programs write all sorts of special glop (they give instructions) to the screen to control where stuff is displayed, what color to use, and so forth. These instructions don't work on the printer because printers use their own, different kind of glop. The short form of this tip is that *redirection and editors don't mix.*

Grabbing output

So how do you use this neat redirection stuff, you ask? Naturally, UNIX does it with funny characters. The two characters ‹ and › are used for redirecting input and output to and from files and to the printer. You use another character (|) to redirect the output of one program to the input of another program.

To redirect (or *snag,* in technical parlance) the output of a command, use ›. Think of this symbol as a tiny funnel *into which* the output is pouring. (Hey, we use any gimmick we can to remember which funny character is which.) To make a file called list.of.files that contains your directory listing, for example, type the following line:

```
ls > list.of.files
```

UNIX creates a new file, called list.of.files in this case, and puts the output of the ls command into it.

If `list.of.files` already exists, UNIX blows away the old version of the file. If you don't want to erase the existing file, you can tell UNIX to add this new information to the end of it (*append* the new information to the existing information). To do this, type the following line:

```
ls >> list.of.files
```

The double `>>` symbol makes the command append the output of `ls` to the `list.of.files` file, if it already exists. If `list.of.files` doesn't exist already, `ls` creates it.

Some (but not all, of course) versions of the C shell check to see whether the file already exists and refuse to let you wreck an existing file with redirection. If your C shell works like this, to overwrite the file, use `rm` to get rid of the old version. The command that tells the C shell not to clobber an existing file when creating a new file from redirection is `set noclobber`. To turn this protection off, you can use the `unset noclobber` command.

Redirecting input

Redirecting input is useful less often than redirecting output, and we can't think of a single, simple example in which you would want to use it. Suffice it to say that you redirect input just like you redirect output, but you use the `<` character rather than the `>` character.

Gurgle, Gurgle: Running Data through Pipes

It can be really useful to redirect the output of one program so that it becomes the input of another program. This process is the electronic equivalent of whisper-down-the-lane, with each program doing something to the information being whispered.

To play whisper-down-the-lane with UNIX, you use a *pipe*. The symbol for a pipe is a vertical bar (`|`). Search your keyboard for this character. It's often on the same key with `\` (the backslash). Sometimes the key shows the vertical bar with a gap in the middle, but the gap doesn't matter. If you type two commands separated by a `|`, you tell UNIX to use the output of the first command as input for the second command.

Gimme just a little at a time

When you have many files in a directory, the output of the `ls` command can go whizzing by too fast to read, which makes it impossible to see the files at the beginning of the list before they disappear off the top of the screen. A UNIX program called `more` solves this problem. The `more` program displays on the screen the input you give it, but it pauses as soon as it fills the screen and waits for you to press a key to continue. To display your list of files one screenful at a time, type this line:

```
ls | more
```

This line tells the `ls` command to send the file listing to the `more` command. The `more` command then displays the listing. You can think of the information from the `ls` command gurgling down through the little pipe to the `more` command. (We think of it this way.)

The `cat` and the fiddle . . . er, file

As explained in Chapter 5, you can use the `cat` command to display the contents of a text file. If the text file is too long to fit on-screen, however, the beginning of the file disappears too fast to see. You can display a long file on-screen one screenful at a time in these two ways:

 ✔ Redirect the output of the `cat` command to `more` by typing the following line (assuming that the file is called `really.long.file`):

```
cat really.long.file | more
```

 ✔ Just use the `more` command by typing this line:

```
more really.long.file
```

If you use the `more` command without a pipe (without the `|`), `more` takes the file you suggest and displays it on-screen a page at a time.

Sorting, sort of

A program called `sort` sorts a file line-by-line in alphabetical order. It alphabetizes all the lines according to the first letter in each line. Each line in the file is unaffected; just the *order* of the lines changes.

Suppose that you have a file called `honors.students`, which looks like this:

```
Meg Young
Shelly Horwitz
Neil Guertin
Stuart Guertin
Sarah Saxon
Zac Young
Gillian Guertin
Tucker Myrhe
Andrew Guertin
Megan Riley
Chloe Myrhe
```

To sort it line by line into alphabetical order, type the following:

```
sort honors.students
```

The result looks like this:

```
Andrew Guertin
Chloe Myrhe
Gillian Guertin
Meg Young
Megan Riley
Neil Guertin
Sarah Saxon
Shelly Horwitz
Stuart Guertin
Tucker Myrhe
Zac Young
```

However, the list appears on the screen and nowhere else. If you want to save the sorted list, type the following:

```
sort honors.students > students.sorted
```

You can also sort the output of a command, as follows:

```
ls | sort
```

Because `ls` displays filenames in alphabetical order anyway, of course, this last example doesn't do you much good. But if you want the filenames in *reverse* alphabetical order (we're stretching for an example here), you can use the `-r` option with the `sort` command, like the following:

```
ls | sort -r
```

If you are sorting numbers, be sure to tell UNIX. Otherwise, UNIX sorts the numbers alphabetically (the sort of imbecilic and useless trick only a computer would do). To sort numbers, use the -n option, as follows:

```
sort -n order.numbers
```

For example, suppose that your file of honors students contained total test scores, like the following:

```
10000  Meg Young
8000   Shelly Horwitz
7000   Neil Guertin
5000   Stuart Guertin
9000   Sarah Saxon
5000   Zac Young
8000   Gillian Guertin
7000   Tucker Myrhe
11000  Andrew Guertin
6000   Megan Riley
7000   Chloe Myrhe
```

When you alphabetize things as letters, not as numbers, a "1" comes before an "8" no matter what, even if it's the first letter of "10". When you alphabetize things as numbers, "10" comes after "8", not before it. If you sort this file as letters, with this command:

```
sort honors.students
```

you get this:

```
10000  Meg Young
11000  Andrew Guertin
5000   Stuart Guertin
5000   Zac Young
6000   Megan Riley
7000   Chloe Myrhe
7000   Neil Guertin
7000   Tucker Myrhe
8000   Gillian Guertin
8000   Shelly Horwitz
9000   Sarah Saxon
```

This does not show the bonus amounts in any useful order. If you sort the file as numbers, with this command:

```
sort -n honors.students
```

you get this more useful listing:

```
5000    Stuart Guertin
5000    Zac Young
6000    Megan Riley
7000    Chloe Myrhe
7000    Neil Guertin
7000    Tucker Myrhe
8000    Gillian Guertin
8000    Shelly Horwitz
9000    Sarah Saxon
10000   Meg Young
11000   Andrew Guertin
```

If the file contains letters, not numbers, the -n option has no effect.

Can we get that on paper?

Being able to print the output of a command is terrifically useful when you want to send to a printer something that normally appears on-screen. To print a listing of your files, for example, type this line:

```
ls | lp
```

Users of Linux and BSD UNIX have to use the lpr command rather than lp. (Chapter 9 explains other stuff about printing.)

You can use more than one pipe if you want to be really advanced. To print a listing of your files in reverse order, for example, you can use this convoluted command:

```
ls | sort -r | lp
```

Wild and Crazy Wildcards

When you type a command, you may want to include the names of a bunch of files on the command line. UNIX makes the typing of multiple filenames somewhat easier (as though we should be grateful) by providing wildcards. *Wildcards* are special characters (still more of them to remember!) that have a special meaning in filenames. There are two wildcards:

?	means "any single letter"
*	means "anything at all"

Pick a letter, any letter

You can use one or more ? wildcards in a filename. Each ? stands for exactly one character — no more, no less. To list all your files that have two-letter names, for example, you can type this line:

```
ls ??
```

The command `ls budget??` lists all filenames that start with *budget* and have two — and only two — characters after *budget,* like `budget98` and `budget99`; the combination doesn't match `budget1` or `budget.draft` or `Budget98` (because of the uppercase B, remember).

Stars (***) in your eyes

The * wildcard stands for any number of characters. To list all your files that have names starting with a *c,* for example, type the following:

```
ls c*
```

This specification matches files named `customer.letter`, `c3`, and just plain `c`. The specification `budget.*` matches `budget.1999` and `budget.draft`, but not `draft.budget`. The name `*.draft` matches `budget.draft` and `window.draft`, but not `draft.horse` or plain `draft`. By itself, the filename `*` matches everything. (Watch out when you let the asterisk go solo!)

Are kings or deuces wild?

Unlike some other kinds of operating systems (we won't name any, but one system's initials are *DOS*), UNIX handles the ? and * wildcards in the same way for every command. You don't have to memorize which commands can handle wildcards and which ones cannot. In UNIX, they all can handle wildcards.

Wildcards commonly are used with the `ls`, `cp`, `rm`, and `mv` commands. For example, to copy all the files from the current directory to the `temp` directory, you can type:

```
cp * temp
```

WARNING!

Look before you delete!

The combination of wildcards and the rm command is deadly. Use wildcards with care when you delete files. You should look first at the list of files you are deleting to make sure that it is what you had in mind. *Before* you type the following command, for example, to delete a bunch of files:

        rm *.97

type the following line and look at the resulting list of files:

        ls *.97

There might be something worth keeping that you forgot about in that list of .97 files.

The most deadly typo of all is this one (***do not type this line!***):

        rm * .97

There's a space between the * wildcard and the .97. Although you may have thought that you were deleting all files ending with .97, UNIX thinks that you have typed two filenames to delete:

* This "filename" deletes all the files in the directory.

.97 This filename deletes a file named .97. (Yes, filenames can start with a period.) Of course, by the time UNIX tries to delete this (nonexistent) file, it has already deleted all the files in the directory!

You end up with an empty directory and lots of missing files. Watch out when you use rm and * together!

Wildcards for DOS users

Although UNIX wildcards look just like DOS wildcards and they work in almost the same way, they have a few differences:

- ✔ Because UNIX filenames don't have the three-letter extensions that DOS filenames use, don't use *.* to match all files in a directory. That will only match files that actually have a dot in their names. A simple * will do the trick.

- ✔ In DOS, you cannot put letters after the * wildcard — DOS ignores the letters following the asterisk. In DOS, *d*mb* is the same as *d**, for example. It's dumb, we know. The good news is that UNIX is not so dumb. In UNIX, d*mb works just the way you want it to.

UNIX Is History!

We make fun of the C shell a lot (and rightly so), but when Bill wrote it, he added a lovely feature called *history*. BASH does history, too, even more nicely than the C shell. And the Korn shell has a way to do history that is clunky but serviceable.

History enables you to issue UNIX commands again without having to retype them, a big plus in our book. Bourne shell users might as well skip the rest of this chapter, because it will just make you jealous (or it'll make you bite the bullet and switch to the BASH shell, by typing bash).

Here's how history works. The shell stores a list of the commands that you've given, in a *history list*. Then you can use the list to repeat commands exactly as you typed them the first time or to edit previously used commands so that you can give a similar command.

The C shell throughout history

In the C shell, you can type ! ! and press Enter to repeat the last command you typed. The shell displays the command and then executes it.

You can also rerun the last command line that begins with a particular bunch of letters. If you type

```
!find
```

the C shell repeats the last command line that began with the text *find*. You don't have to type an entire command. If you type

```
!fi
```

it looks for the last command you typed that started with *fi*, which might be a find command or file command.

To see the history list, type history. You see a list like the following:

```
1  20:26   ls
2  20:26   ls -l
3  20:26   ls -al
4  20:26   history
5  20:26   cat junk3
6  20:26   cat .term
7  20:26   history
8  20:27   history
```

There are the commands you have just typed, in the order that you typed them. The list is numbered, so that you can refer to the commands by number. After the number comes the time that you typed the command (if you care), followed by the command you typed.

If you want to repeat a command, you can type a ! followed by the number of the command. For example, if you type

```
!3
```

the C shell repeats command number 3 on the list (in this case, `ls -al`).

You can also repeat a command with a modification. Suppose that you just typed this command:

```
find . -name budget.98 -print
```

Now you want to give the same `find` command, but this time you're looking for a file named `budget.99`. Instead of tediously, arduously retyping the line, character by character and keystroke by keystroke, worrying anxiously about a possible typo with every key you press, you can tell the C shell to repeat the last command, substituting *99* for *98*. The command is:

```
^98^99
```

You type a caret (^), the old text, another caret, and the text to substitute. Voilà! The C shell displays the new command and then executes it.

BASH throughout history

BASH can do all the cool history tricks that the C shell can, with some additional acrobatics. When BASH displays your history list, it usually stores the last 500 commands you typed, so the list can be huge. To see it a page at a time, type the following command:

```
history | more
```

To see the last nine commands on the history list, type:

```
history 9
```

Here comes the neat part — you can use the arrow keys to flip back through your commands. When you press the up arrow (or Ctrl+P, for *previous*), BASH shows you the previous command from the history list. You can press Enter to execute the command. You can keep pressing the up arrow (or Ctrl+P) until you get to the command you want. If you go past it, you can move back down your history list by pressing the down arrow (or Ctrl+N, for *next*).

Instant script — just add water

For those of you who know what a shell script is, you can use the `history` command to create an instant script.

Here's how to use the `history` command to create a script. Give the commands that you want to include in the script, in the order in which you want them to occur. Then type `history` to display the list of commands. Note how many of the previous commands you want to include in the scripts; for this example, perhaps it's the last eight commands. Type a command like the following (for the C shell):

```
history -h 8 >myscript
```

If you use BASH, type this:

```
history 8 > myscript
```

In the Korn shell, type:

```
fc -l 8 > myscript
```

This command lists the last eight commands and stores the list in a file called `myscript`. It's good idea to ask for more commands from your history list than you think you need, because you can always delete them from your script. You need to use a text editor to clean up the script anyway, deleting the command numbers and times.

This feature is downright useful and typo-saving! Of course, DOS 6.2 has it, too, but who's counting?

After you have displayed a command from your history list on the command line, you can edit it before you press Enter to execute it. Use the left and right arrow keys (or Ctrl+B and Ctrl+F, for *backward* and *forward*) to move the cursor. When you type characters, BASH inserts them on the command line where the cursor is.

The folks at the Free Software Foundation who wrote BASH are big emacs fans (as are we), because you can use most emacs editing commands to edit the command on the command line. For example, Ctrl+A moves your cursor to the beginning of the line, Ctrl+E moves it to the end of the line, Esc-F moves it forward by a word, and so forth. For users who, for some reason, prefer `vi` to emacs, if you press Esc Enter, it changes to a `vi`-like editor, where you search for history commands with Ctrl+R and Ctrl+S.

But enough about BASH and history. You get the general idea!

The Korn shell throughout history

We don't use the Korn shell much, because we've become rather fond of BASH, but the Korn shell can do history, too. The `history` command lists your history list, as does the more cryptic `fc -l` command. To repeat the last command, just type `r` and press Enter. That's it — just `r`. To repeat the last `cat` command, type the following:

```
r cat
```

To repeat the last command, but replace *98* with *99*, type

```
r 98=99
```

The Korn shell enables you to edit your previous commands in all kinds of fancy ways, but it's confusing to do, so we suggest you switch to the BASH shell if you long to edit and reissue commands.

Do I Have To Type the Same Things Every Time I Log In?

Most users find that, every time they log in, they type the same commands to set up the computer the way they like it. You may typically change to your favorite directory, for example, and then change the terminal settings (see the next section), check your mail, or do any of a dozen other things.

The Bourne, Korn, and BASH shells look for a file called `.profile` in your home directory when you log in. If the `.profile` file exists, UNIX executes the commands in that file. The C shell has two corresponding files: `.login` (which it runs when you log in) and `.cshrc` (which it runs every time you start a new C shell, either at login time or when you type `csh`).

Your system administrator probably gave you a standard `.profile` or `.login` file when your account first was set up. It is *definitely* not a good idea to mess with stuff that's already there. You might end up unable to log in and then have to crawl to your system administrator and beg for help. So, don't say we didn't warn you.

The standard `.profile`, `.login`, and `.cshrc` files vary considerably (why do we even finish this sentence — you know what we're going to say) from one system to another, depending on the tastes of the system administrator. These files usually perform the following tasks:

✔ Sets up the search path the shell uses to look for commands

✔ Arranges to notify you when you have new mail

✔ (Sometimes) changes the shell prompt from the usual $ or % to something more informative

If you always type the same commands when you log in, it is fairly safe to add new commands at the end of .profile or .login. If you do most of your work in the directory bigproject, for example, you might add the following three lines to the end of the file your shell uses to start up your UNIX session (.profile or .cshrc):

```
# change to bigproject, added 3/98
cd bigproject
echo Now in directory bigproject.
```

The first line is a comment the computer ignores but is useful for humans trying to figure out who changed what. Any line that starts with a pound sign (#) is a comment. The second line is a regular cd command. The third line is an echo command that displays a note on-screen to remind you of the directory you're in.

If you use the C shell, a frequently useful command to put in .login is this one:

```
set ignoreeof
```

Normally, if you press Ctrl+D in the shell, the shell assumes that you're finished for the day and logs you out — in keeping with the traditional UNIX "you asked for it, you got it" philosophy. Many people think that you should be more explicit about your intention to log out and use ignoreeof to tell the shell to ignore a Ctrl+D (refer to the following section to see what eof has to do with Ctrl+D) and log out only when you type exit or logout.

Terminal Options

About 14 zillion different settings are associated with each terminal or pseudo-terminal attached to a UNIX system, any of which you can change with the stty command. More than 13 zillion of the 14 zillion shouldn't be messed with, or your terminal will vanish in a puff of smoke (as far as UNIX is concerned) and you will have to log in all over again or even get your system administrator to undo the damage. You can, however, safely change a few things.

All the special characters that control the terminal, such as Backspace and Ctrl+Z, are changeable. People often find that they prefer characters other than the defaults, for any of several reasons: They became accustomed to something else on another system, the placement of the keys on the keyboard makes some choices more natural than others, or their terminal emulator is dumb about switching Backspace and Delete. The special characters that control the keyboard are listed and described in Table 7-1.

Table 7-1		Terminal-Control Characters
Name	*Typical Character*	*Meaning*
erase	Ctrl+H	Erases (backspaces over) the preceding character
kill	Ctrl+U	Discards the line typed so far
eof	Ctrl+D	Marks the end of input to a program
swtch	Ctrl+Z	Pauses the current program (see Chapter 16)
intr	Ctrl+C	Interrupts or kills whichever program is running
quit	Ctrl+\	Kills the program and writes a core file

To tell stty to change any of these control characters, you give it the name of the special character to change and the character you want to use. If, as is common, you want to use a control character, you can type a caret (^ — the thing above the 6 on the key in the row of keys across the top of the keyboard) followed by the plain character, both enclosed in quotation marks. As a special case, ^? represents the Del or Delete key. The Tab key is represented as ^I. The Backspace key is usually ^H. To make the Delete key the erase character and Ctrl+X the kill character, for example, type this line:

```
stty erase '^?' kill '^X'
```

If you're feeling perverse, you can set the various control characters to whatever you want. You can make the erase character q and the intr character 3, although doing so makes it difficult to get any work done, because you couldn't use *q* or *3* in anything you type.

The other thing you can change is the *terminal output stop mode,* which controls whether background jobs can display messages on your terminal. (Chapter 13 explains what this means.) To allow output from background jobs to display on your terminal, turn off output stop mode by typing the following:

```
stty -tostop
```

To prevent output from background jobs or, more exactly, to make background jobs stop and wait when they want to display something, turn on output stop mode by typing this line:

```
stty tostop
```

All these `stty` commands usually go in the `.login` or `.profile` file so that the terminal is set up the way you want every time you log in.

Chapter 8
Where's That File?

Doncha love to set up lots of different directories so that you can organize your files by topic, program, date, or whatever suits you? We do. But, after you have files in all those directories, however, it is also easy to lose them. Is that budget memo in your Budget directory, your Memos directory, your ToDo directory, Fred's Budget.Stuff directory, or somewhere else?

Two programs can help you find files: find and grep. Alternatively, you can use the ln command to create links to your files so that a file can appear in several directories at a time, and you have that many more opportunities to find it.

Beating the Bushes

UNIX systems have lots of files. Lots and lots. Tens of thousands, to be more specific. So where's the memo you wrote last week?

Peering into every directory

The first approach to finding a lost file is to use the brute-force method. Starting in your home directory, use `ls` to search through each of your directories. In every directory, type the following line:

```
ls important.file
```

Replace *important.file* with the name of the file you are looking for. If the file is in the current directory, `ls` lists it. If the file isn't there, `ls` complains that it can't find it. This approach can take a while if you have a lot of directories. An additional drawback is that you won't find the missing file if it has wandered off to someone else's directory.

If you know — or think you know — that your file is nearby, you can use * (asterisk) wildcards in directory names. (Wildcards are covered in Chapter 7. They enable you to work with lots of files or directories at once.) To find *important.file* in any of the subdirectories in the working directory, type the following:

```
ls */important.file
```

This technique doesn't work if you have directories within directories: It looks only one level down.

When you care enough to know the filename

With luck, you know the name of the file you have lost. If so, you can use the `find` program to find it. When you use `find`, you tell it the name of the file and the place to start looking. The `find` program looks in the directory you indicate, and in all that directory's subdirectories.

Links to shadow files

You may run into a situation in which a file seems to be in several directories at one time (*Twilight Zone* music here, please). Windows, DOS, and Mac users know that this is patently absurd. Surprise! In UNIX, you *can* have a file in several places at the same time. It can even have several different names. It can be mighty useful, in fact, for a file to be in, for example, the home directories of several people at one time so that they all can easily share it.

To achieve this magical feat, you use *links*. We discuss links in the section "A File by Any Other Name," later in this chapter. In the meantime, don't panic if you see a file lurking around in one place when you're sure that it belongs somewhere else.

Suppose that you are working in your home directory. You think that a file called tiramisu is in there somewhere. Type this line:

```
find . -name tiramisu -print
```

That is, you type these elements:

- ✔ find (just like you see it here).
- ✔ A space.
- ✔ The directory in which you want the program to begin looking. If it is the working directory, you can type just a period (which means "right here").
- ✔ Another space.
- ✔ -name to mean that you will specify a filename.
- ✔ Another space.
- ✔ The name of the file you want to find (**tiramisu**, in this case).
- ✔ Yet another space.
- ✔ -print to tell UNIX to print (on-screen) the full name, including the directory name, to let you know where UNIX finds the file. If you omit this step, and find finds the file, it doesn't tell you. (We know that this is pretty stupid, but computers are like that.) If you use UNIX SVR4 or Solaris, you will notice that they fixed up the find command so that it warns you rather than run the command pointlessly.

The find program uses a *brute-force* approach to locate your file. It checks every file in all your directories. This can take a while. When find finds the file, it prints the name and keeps going. If the program finds more than one file with that name, find finds them and reports them all. After find has printed a found file, you usually will want to stop the program (unless you think that there is more than one match). You stop find by pressing Ctrl+C or Delete.

If the find command doesn't work and you think that the file might be in some other user's directory, type the same find command and replace the . (dot) with a / (slash). This version tells find to start looking in the root directory and to search every directory on the disk. As you can imagine, this process can take some time, so try other things first.

When you know where to search

Rather than use a period to tell find to begin looking in the current working directory, you can use a path name. You can type this line, for example:

```
find /usr/margy -name tiramisu -print
```

This command searches Margy's home directory and all its subdirectories. (Her home directory name may be something different; see Chapter 6.) To search the entire disk, use the slash (/) to represent the root of the directory tree:

```
find / -name tiramisu -print
```

If your disk is large and full of files, a search from the root directory down can take a long time — as long as half an hour on a very large and busy system.

You can even type several directories. To search both Margy's and John's home directories for files named white.choc.mousse, for example, type this line:

```
find /usr/margy /usr/john1 -name white.choc.mousse -print
```

If you use the BASH or C shell, rather than type the home directory name, you can type a tilde (~) and the user name; the shell puts in the correct directory name for you:

```
find ~margy ~john1 -name white.choc.mousse -print
```

Well, I know part of the filename

You can use wildcard characters in the filename if you know only part of the filename. (Remember the * and ? characters that act as "jokers" in filenames?) Use ? to stand for any single character; use * to stand for any bunch of characters. There is a trick to this, however: If you use * or ? in the filename, you have to put quotation marks around the filename to keep the shell from thinking that you want it to find matching names in only the current directory.

You can search the entire disk for files that start with budget, for example, by typing this line:

```
find / -name "budget*" -print
```

If you leave out the quotation marks, the search may look like it worked, but find probably hasn't done the job correctly.

Directory assistance

You can look for lost directories in addition to lost files. Give the find command the option -type d, as follows:

```
find / -name "Budget*" -type d -print
```

This command searches the entire disk for directories that begin with
`Budget`.

Remote searches

If your system uses NFS (Network File System; see Chapter 21), some or
all of the directories and files on your machine may really be on other
computers. The `find` command doesn't care where files are and cheerfully
searches its way into any directory it can get to. Getting to files over a
network is about half as fast as getting to files stored locally, so telling `find`
to look through a lot of files stored on a network can take a long time.
Consider having a long lunch while it does its thing.

Suppose that you're looking for Dave's famous stuffed squid recipe. The
obvious way to look for it is with the following line:

```
find ~dave -name stuffed-squid -print
```

If you know that Dave's files are stored on machine `xuxa`, however, the
following command can be much faster:

```
rsh xuxa "find ~dave -name stuffed-squid -print"
```

See Chapter 21 for details about the `rsh` command.

When you find them

After you find the file or files you were looking for, you can do more than
just look at their names. If you want, you can tell the `find` command to do
something with every file it finds.

Rather than end the `find` command with the `-print` option, you can use
the `-exec` option. It tells `find` to execute a UNIX shell command every time
it finds a file. Take the following command, for example:

```
find . -name "report*" -exec lpr {} ";"
```

This command tells the `find` command to look for files with names beginning with `report`. Every time it finds such a file, it runs the `lpr` program
and substitutes the name of the file for the {}. (You type two curly braces,
which was some nerd's idea of a convenient place holder.) The semicolon

indicates the end of the UNIX shell command. (You have to put quotation marks around the semicolon, or the shell hijacks it and thinks that you want to begin a new shell command. If that didn't make sense, take our word for it and remember to put quotation marks around the semicolon when you use find.) Every time find finds a filename beginning with report, this command prints the file it found.

You can use almost any UNIX command with the -exec option, so, after you have found your files, you can print, move, erase, or copy them as a group. A slight variation is to use -ok rather than -exec. The -ok option does the same thing except that, before it executes each command, find prints the command it's about to run, followed by a question mark, and waits for you to agree that that would be a good thing to do. Press Y if you want to do it, and press N if you want it to skip that particular command.

By using find and -exec rm, you can delete many unwanted files in a hurry. If you make the smallest mistake, however, you can delete many important and useful files equally as quickly. We don't recommend that you use find and rm together. If you insist, however, please use -ok to limit the damage.

It's bigger than a breadbox . . .

"Hmm . . . I don't remember what the file is called, but I'm looking for a letter I wrote to Tonia, so it should contain her mailing address in the heading . . . that's 1471 Arcadia . . . How do I find it. . . .?"

This is a situation for grep — a great program with a terrible name. It stands for, if you can believe it, *g*lobal *r*egular *e*xpression and *p*rint, or some such thing. The grep command looks inside files and searches for a series of characters. Every time it finds a line that contains the specified characters, it displays the line on-screen. If it is looking in more than one file, grep also tells you the name of the file in which the characters occur. You control which files it looks in and which characters it looks for.

There are three grep programs: grep, egrep, and fgrep. They are very similar, so we just talk about grep. (Fgrep is faster but more limited, and egrep is more powerful and more confusing.)

To look in all the files in the working directory (but not in its subdirectories) for the characters 1471 Arcadia, type this line:

```
grep "1471 Arcadia" *
```

That is, type the following elements:

- ✔ grep (just as you see it here).
- ✔ A space.
- ✔ The series of characters to look for (also called the *search string*). If it consists of several words, enclose it in quotation marks so that grep doesn't get confused.
- ✔ A space.
- ✔ The names of the files to look in. If you type * here, grep looks in all the files in the current directory.

The grep program responds with a list of the lines in which it found the search string, as follows:

```
ts.doc: 1471 Arcadia Lane
tonia.letter: 1471 Arcadia La.
```

The program lists the name of the file and then the entire line in which it found the search string.

You can do lots of things with grep other than look for files. In fact, we could write entire (small) books about using grep. For our purposes, however, here are some useful options when you use grep to look for files.

If you want just to see the filenames and you don't want grep to show you the lines it found, use the -l (for *list*) option. (That's a small letter *l*, not a number one.) Suppose that you type this line:

```
grep -l "1471 Arcadia" *
```

The grep program responds with just a list of filenames, as shown here:

```
ts.doc
```

```
tonia.letter
```

It might be a good idea to tell grep not to worry about uppercase and lowercase letters. If you use the -i (for *ignore* case) option, grep doesn't distinguish between uppercase and lowercase letters, as in the following example:

```
grep -i DOS *
```

With this command, `grep`, which is extremely literal-minded, finds both references to DOS and some "false hits":

```
fruit.study: salads; in Brazil, avocados are used in
desserts.

chapter.26: DOS vs. UNIX

chapter.30: Dos and Don'{À
```

Finally, if you don't know the exact characters that occur in the file, you can use `grep`'s flexible and highly powerful (that is, cryptic and totally confusing) expression-recognition capabilities, known in nerd-speak as *regular expressions*. The `grep` program has its own set of wildcard characters, sort of but not very much like the ones the shell uses to enable you to specify all kinds of amazing search strings. If you are a programmer, this can be very useful, because you frequently need to find occurrences of rather strange-looking stuff.

The reason we mention this is that `grep`'s wildcard characters include most punctuation characters, namely:

```
.  *  [  ]  ^  $
```

So, if you include any of these characters in a search string, `grep` doesn't do what you expect. To type any of these characters in a search string, precede them with a backslash (\). To search for files containing *C.I.A.*, for example, type this line:

```
grep "C\.I\.A\." *
```

Actually, the period (.) is `grep`'s wildcard character, like the question mark (?) in the shell. In this example, if you hadn't preceded the periods with backslashes, `grep` would have matched not only *C.I.A.* but also *CHIFAS* (a Peruvian dialect word meaning *Chinese restaurants,* in case you were wondering) and lots of other things. But don't press your luck — use the backslashes with punctuation marks to be safe.

Searching is slow!

Because the `grep` and `find` commands can take a couple of minutes to do their work, you may want to run them in the background (see Chapter 13). To do this, redirect their output to a file so that you can review the results of the search at your leisure. End the command with an ampersand (&), which tells UNIX to run the command in the background. For example, you can type these two commands, pressing Enter after each one:

```
find / -name "budget*" -print > budget.files &
grep "chocolate mousse" * > mousse.recipe.files &
```

TIP

Quick 'n' dirty database

You can use `grep` to treat a text file like a quick and dirty database. By using a text editor, for example, you can make a file called `411` that contains the names and phone numbers of your friends and associates, with one entry per line, as follows:

```
Jordan Young, 555-4673
Meg Young, 555-5485
Zac Young, 554-8649
```

To look up someone's phone number, you just type this line:

```
grep Meg 411
```

The `grep` program displays the line or lines of the file containing the name or names you asked for.

The `grep` program is widely used by UNIX enthusiasts for searching all kinds of files for all kinds of information. As long as each item fits on one line, you can keep all sorts of data in this kind of cheap database file. One of our favorite files is called *restaurants,* which has lines that look like this:

```
Chef Chung's Cheap 555-3864
```

So, if you're in the mood for something cheap, you can say

```
grep -i cheap restaurants
```

When the jobs end, you can type the following commands to see what they found:

```
cat budget.files
cat mousse.recipe.files
```

A File by Any Other Name

Sometimes, it's nice for a file to be in more than one place (that budget file we keep mentioning, for example). If you were working on it with someone else, it would be nice if it could be in both your home directory and your coworker's home directory so that neither of you would have to use the cd command to get to it.

A nice feature of UNIX (and you thought there weren't any!) is that this is possible — even easy. A single file can have more than one name, and the names can be in different directories.

Take, for example, two authors working on a book together (a totally hypothetical example). The chapters of the book are in John's directory: /usr/johnl/book. But what about Margy? It's annoying to have to type the following line every time work on the book begins:

```
cd /usr/johnl/book
```

Instead, it would be nice if the files could also be in /usr/margy/book.

How can you be in two places at once when you're not anywhere at all?

The way to do this is with the ln (for *link*) command. You tell ln two things:

- The current name of the file or files you want to create links to
- The new name

Let's start with just one file. Margy wants to make a link to the file named chapterlog (it contains the list of chapters). The file is in /usr/johnl/book. In her book directory, Margy types this line:

```
ln /usr/johnl/book/chapterlog booklog
```

UNIX says absolutely nothing; it just displays another prompt. (No news is good news.) But it just created a *link,* or new name, to the existing chapterlog file. The file now appears also in /usr/margy/book as booklog. You've got only one file (UNIX doesn't make a copy of the file or anything tacky like that) with two names.

How to play the links

After you create a link by using ln, the file has two names in two directories. The names are equally valid. It isn't as though /usr/johnl/book/chapterlog is the "real" name and /usr/margy/book/booklog is an alias. UNIX considers both names to be equally important links to the file.

How to delete links

To delete a link, you use the same rm command you use to delete a file. In fact, rm always just deletes a link. It just so happens that, when there are no links to a file, the file dries up and blows away. So, when you rm a file that has just one name (link), the file is deleted. When you rm a file that has more than one name (link), the command deletes the specified link (name), but the file remains unchanged, along with any other links it may have had.

How to rename a link

You can use the old mv command to rename a link, too. If Margy decides that it would be less confusing for the book-status file to have the same name in both places (as it stands now, it's chapterlog to John and booklog to Margy), she can type this line:

```
mv booklog chapterlog
```

You can even use the mv command to move the file to another directory.

How to link a bunch of files

You can also use ln to link a bunch of files at the same time. In this case, you tell ln two things:

✔ The bunch of files you want to link, probably using a wildcard character such as chapter*. You also can type a series of filenames or a combination of names and patterns. (UNIX may be obscure, but it's flexible.)

✔ The name of the directory in which you want to put all the new links.

The ln command uses the same names the files currently have when it makes the new links. It just puts them in a different directory.

The chapterlog business in the preceding example works so well that Margy decides to link to all the files in /usr/john1/book. To make links in /usr/margy/book, she types this line:

```
ln /usr/john1/book/* /usr/margy/book
```

This command tells UNIX to create links for all the files in /usr/john1/book and to put the new links in /usr/margy/book. Now every file that exists in /usr/john1/book also exists in /usr/margy/book. Margy uses the ls command to look at a file listing for her new book directory. It contains all the book files. This arrangement makes working on the files much more convenient.

Linking once and linking twice

The `ln` command links all the files that exist at the time the command was given. If you add new files to either `/usr/margy/book` or `/usr/john1/book`, the new files are not automatically linked to the other directory. To fix this situation, you can type the same `ln` command every few days (or whatever frequency makes sense). The command tells you that lots of files are already identical in the two directories and makes links for the new files.

If you have linked to someone else's files, you may have permission to read those files but not to change or write to them. When you ask `ln` to make the new links, if it tries to replace a file you couldn't write to, it says something like this:

    ln: chapter13: 644 mode?

See Chapter 25 for the exact meaning of this uniquely obscure message. Press Y if you want to replace the file, which you probably do in this case. Press N if you don't want to replace the file.

How to link across the great computer divide

All this talk about links assumes that the files you are linking to are on the same file system (that's UNIX-speak for *disk* or *disk partition*). If your computer has several hard disks, or if you are on a network and use files on other computers (through NFS or some other system, as explained in Chapter 21), some of the files you work with may be on different file systems.

Here's the bad news: The `ln` command can't create links to files on other file systems. Bummer. But there's good news for some readers: Linux, BSD, and SVR4 systems (that is, any System V and older AT&T-ish systems) have things called *soft links,* or *symbolic links* (*symlinks,* for short), that are almost as good.

Soft links enable you to use two or more different names for the same file. Unlike regular links (or *hard links*), however, soft links are just imitation links. UNIX doesn't consider them to be the file's real name.

Making soft links (for users of Linux, UNIX BSD, and SVR4 only)

To make a soft link, add the `-s` option to the `ln` command.

Suppose that you want a link in your home directory to the `recipe.list` file in `/usr/gita`. In your home directory, you type this line:

```
ln /usr/gita/recipe.list gitas.recipes
```

Rather than respond with serene silence, UNIX responds with this line:

```
ln: different file system
```

Drat! Gita's home directory is on a different file system from yours—perhaps even on a different computer. So you make a soft link by sticking an `-s` into the command:

```
ln -s /usr/gita/recipe.list gitas.recipes
```

As usual, no news is good news; `ln` says nothing if it worked. Now there appears to be a file in your home directory called `gitas.recipes` — all through the magic of soft links. You still have only one file, but there's an extra link to it.

Using soft links (for users of Linux, UNIX BSD, and SVR4 only)

You can look at, copy, print, and rename a soft-linked file as usual. If you have the proper permissions, you can edit it. If Gita deletes her file, though, the file vanishes. Your soft link now links to an empty hole rather than to a file, and you get an error message if you try to use the file. UNIX knows that the soft link isn't the file's "real" name. When you see a soft link in a long `ls` listing, UNIX gives the name of the soft link and also the name of the file it refers to.

If you try to use a file and UNIX says it isn't there, check to see whether it's a dangling soft link (a link to a nonexistent file). Type `ls -l` to see whether the file is a soft link. If it is, use another `ls -l` on the real filename to make sure that the file really exists.

To get rid of a dangling soft link, use the `rm` command to delete it.

Chapter 9

Printing (The Gutenberg Thing)

● ●

In This Chapter

▶ How to send stuff to the printer

▶ How to find the printer

▶ Stupid printing tricks

● ●

Printing Stuff

Unless you happen to work in the paperless office of the future (reputed to be down the hall from the paperless bathroom of the future), from time to time you will want to print stuff. The good news is that it's usually easy to do so. The bad news is that nothing is as easy as it should be.

The major extra complication is that the way to print things is different on UNIX BSD and System V systems. (Remember which one you have? Refer to Chapter 2 if you don't. You may have written it on the Cheat Sheet in the front of the book.) We start by explaining how you print something already in a file; then we go on to the fancy stuff.

There's a daemon in System V

If you use UNIX System V, the way you print stuff is, in theory, simplicity itself: You use the `lp` command. If you have a file called `myletter`, for example, you print it by typing this line:

```
lp myletter
```

UNIX responds with this important information:

```
request id is dj-2613 (1 file)
```

Usually, this is all you need to do. UNIX responds to your request to print by telling you the request ID of the print job, which you probably don't care about. Sometimes you will want to pretty up the way the printout looks by leaving wider margins; we talk about that later in this chapter.

The lp command doesn't print the file. That would be much too simple. What it does is leave a note for another program buried deep inside UNIX, and this buried program prints your file. The theory behind this arrangement is that a bunch of people may want to use the printer, and it would be a pain if you had to wait for the printer to be free. So lp puts your file on a list; the other program (called a *daemon*, pronounced "demon") runs down the list and does the printing so that you don't have to wait. The *request ID* is the name lp gives to the note it leaves for the daemon. You can ignore it unless you change your mind and decide that you don't want to print that file after all.

More daemons in BSD and Linux

If you use Linux or BSD UNIX, printing is just as easy as printing with System V, except that you use the command lpr rather than lp. If you have a file called myletter, for example, you print it by typing this line:

```
lpr myletter
```

Some systems, notably SVR4 and Solaris, have both the lp and the lpr commands. If you have these versions of UNIX, either command should work equally well. Note that the lpr command doesn't report a request ID.

Finding Your Printout

As far as UNIX is concerned, its only job is to send your file to the printer. Now the real work begins: *finding* your printout.

If your UNIX system is attached to a network, chances are that your printer is attached to some other computer rather than to yours. This means that you may have to go looking for it to find your printouts.

You may have to ask people in nearby cubicles or stand very still in the center of the office and listen for the sound of printing (a gentle whir and click from most laser printers). If all else fails, ask your system administrator. There may be more than one printer your UNIX system can use, so your system administrator may be the only person who can tell you which printer your printout is on.

Aha! There's the printer! If you're lucky, no one else has printed anything recently, so the paper on top of the printer is all yours. It is more likely that lots of people have printed stuff and a pile of paper is on top of the printer — only some of which is yours.

Every printout should have in front of it a sheet that identifies the file printed, with the user name, time, and other odds and ends that seemed relevant to the person who configured the printer. It's considered tacky to root through the stack, pick out your own pages, and leave the rest in a heap. Instead, separate the printouts and leave them on the table or in printout racks (if there are any) with the user names visible. With luck, others will do the same for you. If you can't find your printout on the printer, maybe someone else has already separated and stacked the printouts. Or maybe other users have decided that your printout looked more interesting than theirs and took it off the printer to read it.

Printers, printers, everywhere

A reasonably large installation probably has several printers. When you use the lp or lpr command, UNIX picks one printer as the default. If you use lp, you use the -d option (that's a lowercase *d* — remember that UNIX cares about these things) to identify the printer. To print your file on a printer called draft, for example, you type this line:

```
lp -ddraft myletter
```

If you use lpr, the analogous option is -P (that's an uppercase *P*), so the command you type is as follows:

```
lpr -Pdraft myletter
```

In either case, don't type a space between the -d or -P and the printer name.

Calling all printers

The list of available printers depends on the whims of the system administrator. Dot-matrix impact printers use a ribbon, like a typewriter. Inkjet printers spray letter patterns on the page. Laser printers work like photocopiers, except the copier's glass and camera are replaced by a computer-controlled light.

It's generally not too difficult to get a list of printers known to the system. If you use the lp command to print, type the following line to get a list of available printers:

```
lpstat -a all
```

Woodsman, spare that file!

When you tell UNIX to print a file, the file doesn't print immediately. UNIX makes a note to print the file and remembers its filename.

What if you delete the file before UNIX has a chance to print it? If you print with `lp`, you get a nasty message, because UNIX can't find the file. If you print with `lpr`, the file is printed normally, because UNIX makes a copy of the material to print.

To force `lp` to copy the file, use the `<` command-line operator. To send a copy of the file `myfile` to the printer, for example, type this line:

```
lp < myfile
```

You can then delete or change `myfile` and not affect the printout.

If you are printing a large file, `lpr` can take a long time to make the copy of the file (which it

doesn't really need to do, because it's already in a file in the first place, isn't it?). You can use `lpr -s` to tell UNIX to print from the original file to save time and disk space. If you use the `-s` option, be sure not to delete or change the file until it's printed.

You can tell `lpr` to delete the file when it has finished printing it. This capability is sometimes useful when you made the file in the first place only so that you could print it. Use the `-r` option to remove the file after printing, as follows:

```
lpr -r myfile
```

For large files, you can use `-r` and `-s` together, as in the following:

```
lpr -s -r myfile
```

This line means roughly, "Show me the status of all printers that are active." The lpstat program lists the status of all available printers, one per line, like this:

```
dj accepting requests since Thu Apr 25 13:43:50 1991
```

In this case, there is only one printer, whose name is `dj`. The listing also shows you the vital fact that it was installed on a Thursday afternoon in April 1991. Whoopee.

If you use the `lpr` command to print, try typing this line to get the same information:

```
lpq -a
```

The lpq program responds with a similar list, as follows:

```
lp:
      Rank    Owner  Job   Files          Total Size
      1st     johnl  7     longletter     4615 bytes
      ps:
      no entries
```

The lpq command stands for something like *l*ine *p*rinter *q*uery, and -a means *a*ll printers. In this case, there are two printers, named lp and ps, and something is printing on the first one.

Keep in mind that not every printer the lpstat and lpq commands report is usable. Frequently, system administrators put in the table of printers some test entries that don't really represent printers you can use.

Help! I've Printed and It Won't Shut Up!

The first time you print something large, you suddenly will realize that you don't really want to print the file, because you have found a horrible mistake on the first page. Fortunately, you can easily tell UNIX that you have changed your mind.

If you tell UNIX to print a file that does not contain text, such as a file that contains a program or a database, in most cases UNIX prints it anyway. In a classic example of Murphy's Law (anything that can go wrong, will go wrong), files like that tend to print about 12 random letters on each of 400 pages. Every page has just enough junk on it that you can't use that piece of paper again. As you might expect, people who print a lot of files like that tend to become unpopular, particularly with coworkers whose 2-page memos are in line behind the 400 pages of junk.

Cancel the order, System V

If you used lp to print the file in the first place, you use cancel (we don't know how that name slipped past the lazy typists) to cancel the print job. You have to give the cancel command the request ID that lp assigned to the job. If you're lucky, the lp command is still on your screen and you can see the request ID. If that information has vanished from your screen, remain calm. Remember that the lpstat command lists all the requests that are waiting for the printer. Type the following command:

```
lpstat
```

This command displays a list like the following:

```
dj-2620      john1  34895  Dec 23 21:12 on dj
```

This list tells you that your request was named `dj-2620`, that is was done on behalf of a user named `john1`, that the size of the file to be printed is 34895, and that the print command was given on December 23. You can cancel the request with the following command:

```
cancel dj-2620
```

UNIX responds with the following line:

```
request "dj-2620" cancelled
```

UNIX has a surprisingly convenient (surprising for UNIX, anyway) shortcut you can use. If you give the name of a printer, UNIX cancels whatever is printing on that printer. If you remember that the local printer is called `dj`, you can type the following line to cancel whatever `dj` is printing:

```
cancel dj
```

Cancel the order, BSD

If you made your printing mistake with the `lpr` command, you use `lpq` to find out the request ID, which — to add confusion — is called a *job number* here. Just type the following command:

```
lpq
```

UNIX responds with a list of print jobs, as follows:

```
Rank    Owner    Job    Files     Total Size

1st     john1    12     blurfle   34895 bytes
```

You need to note the job number (12, in this case). Use that number with the `lprm` command, which, despite its name, removes the request to print something and not the printer itself:

```
lprm 12
```

TECHNICAL STUFF

Why you don't want to know about PostScript

You may have what's known as a PostScript printer. There are two general camps of laser-printer design: the Hewlett-Packard (HP) camp and the PostScript camp. Printers in the Hewlett-Packard camp are based on the design of HP's LaserJet line of printers. Printers in the PostScript camp use the PostScript programming language designed by Adobe Systems. LaserJet printers are said to speak PCL, but PCL is not nearly as complicated or flexible (depending on how you look at it) as PostScript. To add to the confusion, many laser printers produced in the past year or two speak both PostScript and PCL.

You may reasonably ask, "What does a programming language have to do with a printer?" If you send a file that contains the text *Your mother wears army boots* to the simpler LaserJet, the printer prints Your mother wears army boots. If you send the same file to a PostScript printer, the printer doesn't print anything. The reason is that a PostScript printer is a powerful computer with a built-in programming language (that's PostScript) that can print stuff sort of as a sideline. To make a PostScript printer print anything, you have to send it a program to do the printing. Fortunately, such programs are widely available.

This arrangement isn't quite as deranged as it sounds. To print simple files of text, it's a pain, but for fancy typeset documents with lots of typefaces and figures and line drawings and such things, PostScript is considerably more flexible than PCL, enough so that people use PostScript to typeset entire books (such as this one).

PostScript has two problems that may bite you. The first is sending a regular file to a PostScript printer. Usually, UNIX printer software is smart enough to figure out automatically that it must PostScript-ize the file in order to print it. If the printer software is not that smart, another program can do the PostScriptization. Adobe, the originator of PostScript, sells a widely used package called Transcript. Transcript includes a program called enscript that prints plain files. If the plain lp or lpr command doesn't work, try using the enscript command before you run for help.

The other problem you may encounter is that a file contains PostScript but prints like a regular file. PostScript files look like incomprehensible programs written in an obscure programming language, because that's what they are. The tip-off is that the first two letters on the first line are %!. To see what the file is supposed to look like, you must send it to a PostScript printer that can run the program in the file and print whatever the file contains. If your printer prints the PostScript program instead, most likely your printer doesn't speak PostScript.

Lacking a PostScript printer, you still may not be out of luck. A program from the Free Software Foundation called Ghostscript can read PostScript files and translate them into something that your local printer can print. Later in this chapter, we discuss Ghostscript and its cousin Ghostview, which lets you preview PostScript documents on-screen.

The lprm command usually reports something about "dequeued" lines; this information is meant to be reassuring, although it's not clear to whom. In response to the lprm 12 command, for example, UNIX displays this message:

```
dfB012iecc dequeued
        cfA012iecc dequeued
```

Some final words about stopping the printer

Most printers have something called an *internal buffer,* which is where data to be printed resides before the printer prints it. An internal buffer is good and bad: It's good because it keeps the printer from stopping and starting if the computer is a little slow in passing your file to it. It's bad because, after data is in the buffer, there's no way the computer can get it back. So, even after you cancel something you want to print, some of it may still be in the buffer: as much as 2 pages of normal text or about 20 pages of the junk that results from printing a nontext file.

There's no easy way to keep from printing the stuff in the printer buffer. One really bad idea is to turn the printer off in the middle of a page: This method tends to get the paper stuck and, on laser printers, lets loose a bunch of black, smeary stuff that gets all over your hands and on the next 1,000 pages the printer prints. If you insist, press the printer's Stop or Off-line button and wait for the paper to stop moving. Then you can turn the printer off relatively safely.

After your print request is canceled, the printer probably still has half a page of your failed file waiting to print. You can eject that page by pressing a button on the printer labeled something like Form Feed or Print/Check, or even Reset.Prettying Up Your Printouts

If you send a file full of plain text to the printer, the result can look ugly: no margins, titles, or anything else. You can use the pr command to make your file look nicer. Use it only with plain text files, however, not with files full of PostScript, document files from your favorite word processor, or a desktop publishing program.

Titles and page numbers look so official

The simplest thing you can do with the pr command is to add titles and page numbers to your printout. By default, the title is the name of the file and the date and time it was last changed. You can use a pipe (defined in Chapter 7 as the vertical bar, |) to format with pr and print in a single line, as follows:

```
pr myfile | lpr
```

(Remember to use the `lp` command rather than `lpr`, if appropriate.) This command tells the `pr` program to pretty up the file and to pass the results to the `lpr` program.

You can set your own heading by using the `-h` option with the `pr` command, as shown here:

```
pr -h "My Deepest Thoughts" myfile | lpr
```

The `pr` command assumes that printer pages are 66 lines long. If that's not true for you, instead of the title appearing at the top of every page, it sort of oozes down from page to page. You can override the length of the standard page with the `-l` option. Suppose that the page length is 60 lines. You type the following line:

```
pr -l 60 myfile | lpr
```

If you want to use `pr` and not have any heading at the top of the page, use the `-t` option, as follows:

```
pr -t myfile | lpr
```

(This example doesn't do anything interesting to `myfile`. Later, however, you will see that it really is useful when you combine it with the margins and stuff.)

Marginally yours

You may frequently put printouts in three-ring binders. Normally, because printing starts very close to the left side of the page, the hole punch may put holes in your text and make the page difficult to read — not to mention make it look stupid. The `-o` option (that's a lowercase letter *o*, not a zero, for *offset*) pushes the stuff you print to the right, leaving a left margin. To leave five spaces for a left margin, for example, type the following command:

```
pr -o5 myfile | lpr
```

Sometimes, it's nice to leave a wider margin at the bottom of the page. You can do that by combining the `-l` option (described in the preceding section to set a page length) with the `-f` option that tells `pr` to use a special *form-feed character* to make the printer start a new page *now!* (Normally, the `-l` option uses blank lines to space to the next page, like a typewriter.) Use the following command if you find yourself in this situation:

```
pr -o5 -l 50 -f myfile | lpr
```

This command tells UNIX to print just 50 lines per page, indented 5 spaces. That should be enough space in the margin for anyone.

Seeing double

The `-d` option tells `pr` to double-space the printout. Type the command as follows:

```
pr -d myfile | lpr
```

This command also puts a title on every page. Use `-d` `-t` to avoid that, as shown here:

```
pr -d -t myfile | lpr
```

One column can't contain me

If the lines in your file are short, you can save paper by printing the file in multiple columns. To print your file in two columns, for example, type the following:

```
pr -2 myfile | lpr
```

Astute readers probably can guess what the options `-3`, `-4`, and up to `-9` do. (If you're not feeling that astute today, these options specify the number of columns you want.) Columns normally run down and then across the page, as they do in newspapers. If your file contains a list of items, one per line, and you want to print them in columns, you may want to change the order in which the lines print. If you want to print items across the page, and then move down to the next line, and so on (which is nowhere near as cool), use the `-a` option in addition to the `-2` or `-3` option.

For a truly baffling effect, you can arrange to print several files side by side with the `-m` option, as follows:

```
pr -m firstfile secondfile | lpr
```

This command prints the first line of every file on the first line of the printout, the second line of every file on the second line, and so on. You can specify as many as nine filenames and have them print side by side in skinny little columns. We never have been able to figure out much of a use for this option, but it is definitely a way to produce really odd printouts.

Troff, Nroff, Groff!

No, it's not a rabid dog. It's a typesetting program. The `troff` program is the "typesetter runoff" that's been part of UNIX since the 1970s. The `nroff` program is "new runoff" (new as of about 1972), which formats documents for simple printers without fancy fonts. The `groff` program is the GNU (see Chapter 2) version of `troff`, which, like every GNU program, does all the stuff the originals do and about 47 other things, too. Because `groff` is free, whereas `nroff` and `troff` are subject to expensive licenses from Bell Labs, `groff` is all you see these days.

All of the "roff" programs are what's known as *batch formatters*. In these, you type your document with formatting codes into a text file, and then you run it through `groff`, which produces a beautifully typeset version of your document, give or take all your typos and coding errors. Then you fix the document, re-`groff`, and so on. These programs are the antithesis of WYSIWYG (What You See Is What You Get) formatting.

People still use `groff`, partly because it's free and partly because you can do very fancy stuff with highly structured documents that's difficult or impossible with WYSIWYG formatters. We don't expect that you'll be writing a great many `groff` documents yourself, but you'll probably run into some on the Internet or in software packages, so here are a few hints on how to turn them into something legible.

Assuming that you have a PostScript printer available, type a command like this one:

```
groff filename
```

Replace *filename* with the name of the text file you want to print. The `groff` program interprets the typesetting codes in the text file and tells the printer how to print your document.

As you've probably figured out if you've gotten this far in this book, principle yields to hideous complication after you add in a few practical details. Here are some of the details and the ensuing complications.

Macro mania

Formatting a document using `troff` and its cousins requires rather low-level detailed instructions using incomprehensible two-letter codes in the documents, instructions so detailed that even UNIX weenies find them tedious (and that's saying a lot.) To relieve the tedium, most `troff` documents take advantage of *macro packages* that define higher level instructions, which people use rather than the low-level stuff. (These macro packages serve roughly the same function as style sheets in Microsoft Word.) The `troff` program has been around for more than 25 years, and many macro packages have come and gone, but a few have stood the test of time. All of them having been written by lazy typists, each has a cryptic two-or three-letter name, all starting with `-m`, the flag code that tells `groff` to read in the macro package. Table 9-1 lists a few popular macro packages.

Table 9-1	Macro Packages	
Name	**Description**	**Origin**
`-ms`	Manuscript macros	Bell Labs
`-mm`	Different manuscript macros	Another part of Bell Labs
`-me`	Eric's macros	Somebody's Ph.D. thesis at Berkeley
`-man`	Manual page macros	Same as -ms

To tell `groff` to format a document with, say, the -ms macros, you type the following:

```
groff -ms filename
```

It's different to tell *a priori* what macros were used in what document, unless the author took pity and gave you a clue by naming the file `mobydick.ms` or the like. Fortunately, the worst that will happen if you use the wrong macro package is that the document will look ugly (not totally illegible: The text will still be there, but it will be formatted incorrectly). You can try different macro packages and see which one works least badly. As a rule of thumb, documents from academia usually use the –me macro package, whereas those from industry usually use -mm or -ms. Documents about the UNIX system itself usually use -ms, because it was written by some of the same guys who did the original UNIX work, and pages from the on-line manual (what the `man` command shows you) use `-man`.

Let's sneak a peek

One of the nicest things about `groff` is that it's "device independent," which means that it can reformat your document for any of several output devices. To format your document and display it on a normal, text-only terminal, use the `nroff` command, as follows:

```
nroff -ms filename | more
```

Why UNIX succeeded

Back in the mid-1970s, the whole idea of computerized document formatting and typesetting was a lot less established than it is now. But within AT&T, `troff` and the UNIX system it ran on rapidly became the standard for document preparation. Why? Two words: line numbers. AT&T files a lot of patents, and patent applications must have every fifth line numbered. The `troff` program was the first text formatter that could do that. The patent typists embraced it (patent applications are revised and retyped about a thousand times before they're finally sent to the patent office), and the rest, as they say, is history.

(This command actually calls `groff`, but tells it to format for plain text output. Change the -ms to one of the other macro packages if necessary.) The `more` command makes the result display a screen at a time. Press space to move from screen to screen, or press Q when you've seen enough.

If you are running X Windows, you can tell `groff` to display a page at a time, beautifully typeset in an X window, by typing this command:

```
groff -TX75 -ms filename
```

In the window that `groff` creates, press space to move from screen to screen, or press Q when you've seen enough. If the type is too small to read, use -TX100 rather than -TX75 to make the text bigger. (You can't use any other numbers; X comes with one set of fonts for 75 dot-per-inch screens and another for 100 dot-per-inch screens, so that's what `groff` uses.)

Seeing Ghosts

Earlier in this chapter, we talked about PostScript, the fabulously complicated printer language that enables you to print fabulously complex documents on PostScript printers. But what if you don't have a PostScript printer?

These days, the short answer is "Get one." PostScript printers used to cost a lot more than other kinds of printers, but these days you can buy a perfectly decent PostScript laser printer for less than $1,000. Nonetheless there are still lots of PostScript-free sites, where Ghostscript comes to the rescue.

Ghostscript is a free, GNU (see "What's GNU?" in Chapter 2) version of PostScript, written by L. Peter Deutsch, a very skillful programmer from way back who surely should have been doing something else when he wrote it. When Ghostscript runs, it reads its PostScript input either from a file or from the keyboard (not very useful unless you're trying to learn PostScript), and produces its output on one of a zillion possible output devices. If you want to see what the PostScript document looks like, you can tell it to send its output to an X Windows System window. If you want to print the document, you can send its output to your printer.

Printing ghosts

If you're lucky, your system manager will have installed Ghostscript so that it's semiautomatically called when you print a PostScript file. You typically use the -v flag, something like this:

```
lpr -v floogle.ps
```

Failing that, to run Ghostscript, you type its name (gs) and the name of the PostScript file to display, as follows:

```
gs floogle.ps
```

If you just type that, Ghostscript opens a new X Window and display the first page of floogle.ps in that window — probably not what you want. (See the next section, "The friendly ghost," for that.) Press Ctrl+C once or twice to stop it. To get Ghostscript to do something useful, you need to use switches. Lots and lots of switches, as in the following:

```
gs -sDEVICE=deskjet -dNOPAUSE -sOutputFile=floogle.lj
            floogle.ps quit.ps
```

What's going on here is that we set the output device (DEVICE) to *deskjet*, a popular ink-jet printer. We tell it not to pause between pages, we tell it what output file to create, tell it which PostScript file to print, and then give it another file from the Ghostscript library (quit.ps). The quit.ps file contains a one-line command that tells Ghostscript that it's finished. You can tailor this as needed; run gs -h to see the available printers.

We expect that you'll find this all a wee bit complicated. In practice, unless your system manager has set up Ghostscript to run automatically, your best bet is to find a local expert who can tell you the exact command to use. Lacking an expert, you can still look at PostScript on the screen by using Ghostview.

Part III
Getting Things Done

In this part . . .

So far we have talked about the computer, files, mice, printers, the shell — you name it. But what about getting some real work done?

To do useful work, you need software. This part talks about using text editors, word processors, e-mail programs, and other useful programs. We also talk a bit about installing software and (for you Linux users) doing a tiny bit of system administration.

Chapter 10
Writing Deathless Prose

● ●

In This Chapter

▶ What is a text editor?

▶ What is a text formatter?

▶ What is a word processor?

▶ What is a desktop publishing program?

▶ How to use vi if you absolutely have to

▶ How to use ed if you don't have anything better

▶ How to use emacs, which is not that bad, really

▶ How to use pico, which is pretty nice

● ●

One Land, Many Programs

In the land of UNIX, many programs handle text. Where you come from, you may be accustomed to the idea of using a word processor when you want to type something and print it. Not in UNIX. There are four kinds of programs to do this, just to keep things interesting.

Just the text, ma'am

A text editor enables you to do the following things:

✔ Create a file full of text.
✔ Edit the text.

You can print the file by using the lp or lpr programs, described in Chapter 9, but text editors can't do boldface, headers or footers, italics, or all that other fancy stuff you need in order to produce really modern, overformatted, professional-quality memos.

You may want to use a text editor to write letters and reports. You certainly will use one to send electronic mail (see Chapter 17).

The most commonly used text editors in the land of UNIX are `ed`, `vi`, `emacs`, and `pico`. We have strong opinions about these editors, which become abundantly clear in the later sections of this chapter, where we tell you how to use each of them.

Text formatters aren't really editors

Text formatters are programs that read text files and create nice-looking formatted output. You use a text editor to make a text file that contains special little commands only the formatter understands; the `.IT` command, for example, makes something italic. When you run the text formatter, it reads the text file, reads the special little commands, and creates a formatted file that you then can print. You use `lp` or `lpr` to print the output of the text formatter.

The most common UNIX text formatter is `TeX`, pronounced "tecccccch" (like yecccccch), an arcane language popular among mathematicians and physicists because of its capability to format large, complex equations. A companion program, LaTeX, is designed to make TeX easier to use (relatively speaking, of course). Another common text formatter is `troff`. Some people use `nroff` (an older version of `troff`), or `groff`, a newer GNU version of the program. With luck, you will never have to use any of these.

Cuisinarts for text: word processors

Word processors combine the capabilities of text editors and text formatters. Most word processors are (or try to be) WYSIWYG (an acronym for *W*hat *Y*ou *S*ee *I*s *W*hat *Y*ou *G*et), which enables you to see on-screen how the documents (that's what they call their files) will look when you print them.

The most common word processor for UNIX is WordPerfect (available also for PCs and Macintoshes). Most UNIX users think that word processors are for wimps (*w*hat *y*ou *s*ee *is a*ll *y*ou've *g*ot), because they like the unintelligible and unmemorable commands used by text formatters and prefer to imagine what their text will look like when it is printed rather than be able to see it on-screen. Text formatters can do more complex things than word processors can, such as format complicated mathematical expressions, lay out multipage tables, and neatly organize sections and headers of huge, book-length documents. But that's probably not your problem.

Desktop publishing does it all

A desktop publishing (DTP) program resembles a very fancy word processor. It can do everything a word processor can, plus things you need only if you are printing a book, newsletter, or something else that looks fancy. DTPs include facilities for creating tables of contents and indexes, maintaining cross-references — you name it. For writing an occasional memo, a desktop publishing program is definitely overkill.

The two most common desktop publishing programs for UNIX are Interleaf (available for PCs also) and FrameMaker (available for PCs and Macintoshes also).

TeX and some versions of troff are available for free, which explains why they remain so popular (big surprise, eh?). All word processors and desktop publishers are commercial products that cost extra. Lots extra.

vi *and* emacs *and* pico *are your friends*

The rest of this chapter explains how to use each of the Big Three text editors (vi, emacs, and pico). Even if you use a word processor or desktop publishing program, you may need to use a text editor to do some things, such as the following:

- ✔ Write electronic mail (see Chapter 17)
- ✔ Create or edit text files called *shell scripts,* which enable you to create your own UNIX commands (see Chapter 12)
- ✔ Create or edit special text files that control the way your UNIX setup works (see Chapter 7)
- ✔ Write C programs (just kidding!)

Shy vi*, the Princess of Text Editors*

The vi text editor can claim a unique status among UNIX editors: Almost every UNIX system in the universe has vi. This makes it a good editor to know if you plan to be moving around from system to system, because you can always count on it being there. There are probably other reasons for using vi, too, but ease of use is not foremost among them.

To run vi, type **vi**, a space, the name of the file you want to edit, and press Enter.

If you get an error message when you try to run vi, talk to your system administrator. If the screen looks weird, your terminal type may not be set right — another reason to talk to your system administrator.

Editor à la mode

The most distinctive feature of vi (and the one that has spawned legions of vi-haters, along with a few devotees) is that it is a *modal* editor. The vi program is always waiting for one of two things: commands or text (a.k.a. input). When vi is waiting for a command, it is in *command mode*. When it is waiting for text, it is in *input mode*. Normally, it is up to you to figure out which mode vi is in at any particular moment — it doesn't give you a clue.

Most vi commands are one letter long. Some are lowercase letters, and others are uppercase letters. When you type vi commands, be sure to use the correct capitalization.

If you are in input mode and want to give a command, press the Esc key.

Whenever we tell you to type a command, it works only if you are in command mode. If you are not sure which mode you're in, press Esc first. If you are already in command mode, pressing Esc just makes vi beep.

To switch from command mode to input mode, you tell vi to add the text after the character the cursor (the point at which you are working) is on (by using the a command) or to insert the text before the current cursor position (by using the i command).

Emergency exit from vi

To escape from vi, do the following:

1. Press Escape at least three times. The computer should beep. Now you are in command mode for sure.

2. Type the following line and press Enter:

   :q!

   This line tells vi to quit and not save any changes.

Help! I need somebody!

The guy who wrote vi (remember Bill, the grouchy guy who's 6' 4" and in excellent physical condition? Same guy.) didn't believe in help, so there wasn't any.

Fortunately, vi has been used in so many introductory computing courses that Bill eventually relented and added a "novice" mode. Rather than type vi to run the editor, type vedit to get the same editor with some allegedly helpful messages. In particular, whenever you're in input mode rather than command mode, vi displays a message, such as INPUT MODE, APPEND MODE, CHANGE MODE, or OPEN MODE, at the bottom of your screen. All these messages mean the same thing (except to Bill, evidently): Text you type when these messages are visible is added to the file rather than interpreted as commands.

Easy text-entry techniques

Let's make a new file with some more deathless prose, so you can practice entering text in vi. Run vi with a new filename, as follows:

```
vi xanadu
```

To add text after the current position of the cursor, type the following (you do *not* press Enter after a command):

```
a
```

We tell you how to move the cursor in a minute, when there's some text to move around in. You can type a, for example, to add this text to the newly created xanadu file:

```
In Xanadu did Kubla Khan
A stately pleasure-dome decree:
Where Alph, the sacred river, ran
Through caverns measureless to man
Down to a sunless sea.
```

To get back to command mode, press Esc. Press Esc whenever you finish typing text so that you are ready to give the next command.

Other commands you can use to enter text include i to insert text *before* the current cursor position, A to add the text at the end of the line the cursor is on, and 0 to add the text on a new line before the current line.

The vi program shows you a full-screen view of your file. If the file isn't long enough to fill the screen, vi shows tildes (~) on the blank lines beyond the end of the file. Figure 10-1, for example, shows a text file called eating.peas (created in a later discussion about ed) as it would appear in vi.

Figure 10-1:
Tildes fill up the blank lines on the vi screen.

```
I eat my peas with honey,
I've done it all my life.
It makes the peas taste funny,
But it keeps them on my knife.
~
~
~
~
~
~
~
~
~
~
~
~
~
~
~
~
~
~
~
"eating.peas"  4 lines, 114 chars
```

The cursor appears at the beginning of the first line of the file.

All around the mulberry bush: Moving the cursor

You can use dozens of commands to move the cursor around in your file, but you can get to where you want with just a few of them, which are the following:

✔ The arrow keys (←, →, ↑, and ↓) usually do what you would expect: They move the cursor in the indicated direction.

Sadly, there are terminals on which vi does not understand the arrow keys. If this is true for you, use h to move left, j to move down, k to move up, and l to move right. Bill chose these keys on the theory that, because those keys are a touch typist's home position for the fingers on the right hand, you can save valuable milliseconds by not having to move your fingers. Really. In some versions of vi, arrow keys work only in command mode; in other versions, they also work in input mode.

✔ Enter or + moves the cursor to the beginning of the next line.

✔ The hyphen (-) moves the cursor to the beginning of the preceding line.

✔ G (the uppercase letter) moves the cursor to the end of the file.

✔ 1G moves the cursor to the beginning of the file. (That's the number *1*, not the letter *l*. Why ask why?)

A makeover for vi

To modify the text you have typed, follow these steps:

1. **Move the cursor to the beginning of the text you want to change.**

2. **To type over (on top of) the existing text, type the following line:**

   ```
   R
   ```

3. **Type the new text. What you type replaces what is already there. Press Esc when you finish replacing text.**

4. **To insert text in front of the current cursor position, type the following:**

   ```
   i
   ```

5. **Type the new text. What you type is inserted without replacing any existing text. Press Esc when you finish inserting text.**

Take a little off the top

To delete text, follow these steps:

1. **Move the cursor to the beginning of the text you want to delete.**

2. **To delete one character, type the letter x. To get rid of five characters, type xxxxx. You get the idea.**

3. **To delete text from the current cursor position to the end of the line, type an uppercase D.**

4. **To delete the entire line the cursor is on, type dd (the letter *d* twice).**

I liked it better the way it was

Like ed, vi has a way to "undo" the most recent change or deletion you made. Type the following to undo the change:

```
u
```

If you type the following (in uppercase), vi undoes all changes to the current line since you moved the cursor to that line:

```
U
```

Write me or save me, just don't lose me

To save the updated file, type the following (be sure that you have pressed Esc first so that you are in command mode):

```
:w
```

That's a colon and a *w*, and then press Enter. This command is the same one you use in ed to save (or write) a file. You should give this command every few minutes, in case the confusing nature of vi commands makes you delete something important by mistake.

Good-bye, vi

To leave vi, type the following:

```
ZZ
```

Be sure to press Esc a few times so that you are in command mode before giving this command. To quit and not save the changes you have made, type the following line:

```
:q!
```

Then press Enter. This means, "Leave vi and throw away my changes. I know what I'm doing."

Most other letters, numbers, and symbols are also vi commands, so watch what you type when you are in command mode. Table 10-1 lists the most common commands you use with vi.

Table 10-1	Commands in vi
Command	*Description*
Esc	Return to command mode
Enter	Move to beginning of next line
+	Move to beginning of next line
-	Move to beginning of preceding line
a	Add text after cursor
A	Add text at end of current line
dd	Delete entire current line
D	Delete from cursor to end of line
G	Move (go) to end of file
1G	Move to beginning of file
h	Move one space left
i	Add text before cursor
j	Move down one line
k	Move up one line
l	Move right one space
0	Add text on new line before current line
:q! (followed by Enter)	Quit vi, even if changes aren't saved
R	Replace text
u	Undo last change
U	Undo changes to current line
x	Delete one character
:w (followed by Enter)	Save (write) file
ZZ	Quit vi and save changes

I just love vi!

If you just love vi, try emacs or pico, and see if you still love vi.

Talk to Mr. ed

The vi editor may seem like a quaint throwback to prehistoric software, but there was a time in the early days of UNIX when even vi didn't exist. In the pre-CRT era of Teletype terminals, *line editors* ruled, and the standard among line editors was (and still is) ed. A line editor, such as ed, is one that assigns line numbers to the lines in the file. Every time you do something, you must tell ed which line or lines to do it to. If you have used the EDLIN program in DOS, ed should look familiar. The ed program has been a part of UNIX since the beginning of time. When you use it, you begin to appreciate how far software design has progressed since 1969.

If there is *any way* — repeat — *any way* you can get another text editor to use, do it. If you don't think that ed can really be that bad, just peruse the rest of this section and you will run screaming to your system administrator for vi , pico, or emacs (preferably pico or emacs).

Some systems have a program called ex that is similar to but not quite as horrible as ed. Try typing ex to see what happens.

To run ed, type this line:

```
ed important.letter
```

(Type the name of your file rather than *important.letter*.) If no file has the name you specify, ed makes one. UNIX responds to this command with a number, which is the number of characters (letters, numbers, punctuation, and spaces) in the file, just in case you are getting paid to write by the letter.

If you receive an error message when you try to run ed, talk to your system administrator. Congratulate her or him on getting rid of that Neanderthal text editor and find out which text editor you *can* use.

Hey, Wilbur, which command was that?

All ed commands are one-letter long (such as h).

Remember *not* to capitalize ed commands unless we specifically say to. ed commands are almost all lowercase letters.

Relatively recent versions of ed (since, oh, about 1983) have a P command (that's a capital *P,* one of the few uppercase commands) that turns on a prompt. If you type P and press Enter, ed prompts you with an asterisk when it's in command mode and waiting for a command. Is that incredibly user-friendly or what? Actually, this P command enables you to determine when you are in command mode! Must have snuck that one in when the lazy typists weren't looking.

> ## Emergency exit from ed
>
> To get the heck out of ed — in case someone used your computer and left it running — follow these steps:
>
> 1. Type a period on a line by itself and press Enter. This action gets you into command mode, in case you are in input mode. If you were already in command mode, a line of the file prints on-screen. Ignore it.
>
> 2. Type q and press Enter.
>
>   If changes to the file have been saved or if there were no changes, this action quits ed and you see a UNIX shell prompt. If
>
> changes to the file haven't been saved, ed displays a question mark, meaning, "Yo, you're about to throw away your changes. Are you cool with this?" Type q again and press Enter again. This time, ed exits. If someone has used your computer and run ed and didn't save the work, to heck with it. And if *you* ran ed by mistake and are fighting to get out, you probably don't want to save any changes anyway.
>
> In most versions of ed, you can also use the capital Q command, which means, "*Q*uit — and don't ask any questions!"

If you are in input mode and want to give a command, type this character:

```
.
```

That's just a single period on a line by itself. Typing this character switches ed to command mode.

In the remainder of this discussion about using ed, whenever we tell you to type a command, it works only if you are in command mode. If you are not sure, type a period and press Enter first.

If you are in command mode and want to type some text, you switch to text-input mode. But first you must decide whether you are going to *append* (by using the a command) after the current line the lines of text you will type or *insert* (by using the i command) the lines of text before the current line. More about the current line and the a and i commands in a minute.

Mr. ed *gets lunch*

Let's create a file and feed some text to it. Start the process by typing the following line:

```
ed eating.peas
```

You can name your file something other than `eating.peas` if you want. UNIX responds with a question mark, just to keep you on your toes. (This time, the question mark tells you that `ed` just created a new file for you.)

To add (append) new lines of text to the end of the file — in this case, the end of the file is the same as the beginning because the file is empty — type the following:

```
a
```

UNIX responds by saying absolutely nothing, which is your indication that `ed` is now in input mode and waiting for you to type some text. Type some pearls of wisdom, like this:

```
I eat my peas with honey,
I've done it all my life.
It makes the peas taste funny,
but it keeps them on the knife.
.
```

When you finish typing text, type a period on a line by itself to switch `ed` from input mode back to command mode. Not that `ed` gives you a hint that this is going on, unless you have used the P command to tell it to prompt you.

The lines of text are now in your file. This would be a good time to save the file, just in case you kick your computer's plug out of the wall in your frustration at having to use such a brainless program.

Save me from this stupid program!

The following command saves your text in a file with `ed`. If you are in input mode, remember to type a period on a line by itself to switch to command mode before giving this command:

```
w
```

That's `w` for *write*. UNIX responds with the number of characters now in the file. Be sure to give this command before leaving `ed` so that your deathless prose is saved in the file, in this case, `eating.peas` (or whatever filename you used when you ran `ed`).

What if ed commands end up in my text?

If you are in input mode and type an ed command, ed doesn't do the command. Instead, it thinks that you are typing text and stores the letter or letters of the command as just some more text in your file.

If this happens, delete the lines you don't want. (We explain how to delete lines later in this chapter.) The next time you want to enter a command, first be sure to type a period on a line by itself.

Show me the file, please

Now that you have text in the file, how can you see it or change it? By using the p (print) command. This command doesn't print anything on the printer; it just displays it on-screen — another example of superb software engineering. (Well, it printed on those old Teletypes.) If you type the p command by itself, as follows, ed displays the current line:

```
p
```

In the case of the sample eating.peas file, the current line is the last line in the file. You can also tell ed which lines to display by typing their line numbers. To display lines 1 through 4, for example, type the following line:

```
1,4p
```

You can also use the symbol $ to stand for the line number of the last line in the file (in case you don't know how many lines are in the file). The following command always displays the entire file:

```
1,$p
```

A miserable way to edit

You can change the contents of a line of text with ed, but it involves giving commands that look like this:

```
12,13s/wrong/right/
```

This command substitutes right for wrong in lines 12 through 13, inclusive. Totally primitive and painful, isn't it? For the amount of editing you probably do in ed, it is almost easier to delete the line with the typo and insert a new line. We recommend that you immediately ask your system administrator for a better text editor.

Make me better again, doctor

But wait — there is one useful, humane command in ed after all! The u command enables you to "undo" the last (and only the very last) change you made to the file. If you delete a line by mistake with the d command, for example, you can type this line to undo the deletion:

```
u
```

Be sure that you don't make any other changes before using the u command. It undoes only the very last thing you did.

Give my regards to Broadway, ed

When you finish making changes and you want to leave ed (or even if you're not finished making changes and you want to leave ed anyway), type the following:

```
q
```

If you are in input mode, first type a period on a line by itself to get into command mode. Then type q to quit.

If you haven't saved your work by using the w command, ed just doesn't quit. Instead, it displays a question mark to tell you that it was expecting a w command first. To save your changes, type these two commands, pressing Enter after each:

```
w
q
```

If you don't want to save the changes to the file, type q again at the question mark. This time, ed believes that you really want to leave and, thus, exits. Not a moment too soon!

As a review, Table 10-2 lists the commands you use most commonly with ed.

Table 10-2	Commands in ed
Command	*Description*
a	Add lines after the current line and enter input mode
d	Delete line or lines
h	Display extremely terse help message right now
H	Display terse help messages whenever anything goes wrong
i	Insert lines before the current line and enter input mode
n	Display line or lines with line numbers
p	Display line or lines
P	Display an asterisk whenever ed is in command mode
q	Quit the whole thing
Q	Quit regardless of whether changes have been saved
u	Undo last change
w	Write (save) the file

A Novel Concept in Editing: emacs *Makes Sense*

We don't want to get your hopes up, but emacs is much easier to use than ed or vi. The reason is that it doesn't have the mysterious modes that require to you remember at every moment whether the program is expecting a command or text.

On the other hand, commands in emacs aren't exactly intuitive. Still, we like them better. In case you are wondering, the name *emacs* comes from *editor macros,* because the original version of emacs was written as an extension to an early text editor called teco, an editor that makes ed look like the winner of the Nobel prize for user-friendliness. (Scary thought, isn't it?)

To run emacs, type the following line:

```
emacs eating.peas
```

You replace *eating.peas* with the name of the file you want, of course. If the file you name doesn't exist, emacs creates it. Like vi, emacs displays a full-screen view of your file (as shown in Figure 10-2). On the bottom line of the screen is the *status line,* which tells you the name of the file you are editing and other, less interesting information.

Figure 10-2:
The GNU
Emacs
display in a
text
console. At
the bottom
of the
screen,
emacs
displays the
filename
and other
mysterious
information
on the
status line.

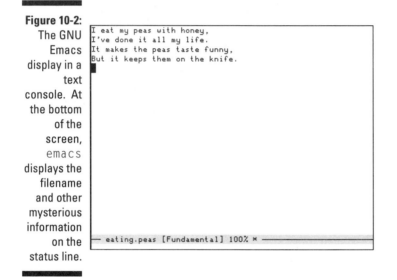

```
I eat my peas with honey,
I've done it all my life.
It makes the peas taste funny,
But it keeps them on the knife.




─── eating.peas [Fundamental] 100% *  ──────────
```

A tale of two emacs

Unlike vi, emacs does not normally come with UNIX. Because most versions of emacs are distributed for free, however, most systems have it or can get it. By far, the two most common versions of emacs are GNU Emacs and XEmacs. Despite the name, XEmacs runs under both X Windows and text-based consoles, and so does GNU Emacs. The basic commands are the same for both versions, and the most obvious differences between the two are the button-bars and more sophisticated 3-D look to the windows in XEmacs. (Compare the difference in Figures 10-3 and 10-4.) Other than that, it really doesn't matter which you use.

To run XEmacs on the eating.peas file, type the command xemacs eating.peas.

Figure 10-3:
The GNU
Emacs
display in
an X
Window
includes
pull-down
menus for
most
common
commands,
including
save,
search,
undo, and
help.

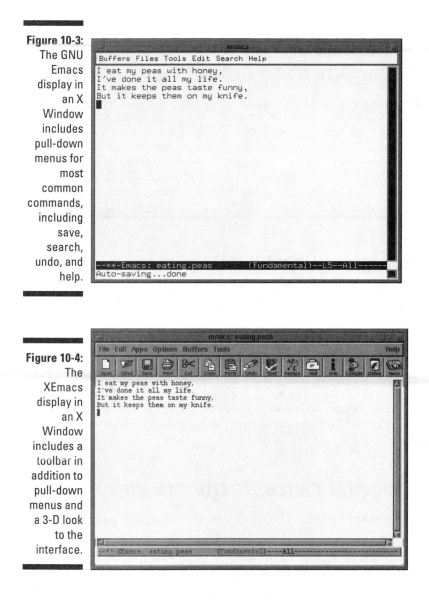

Figure 10-4:
The
XEmacs
display in
an X
Window
includes a
toolbar in
addition to
pull-down
menus and
a 3-D look
to the
interface.

✔ If you get an error message when you try to run emacs, ask your system administrator what's up. The emacs program may have another name on your system. If your system administrator says that you don't have emacs, plead with him or her to get it.

✔ If emacs looks or acts weird (weirder than usual, that is), your terminal type may not be set correctly. Again, ask your system administrator to straighten this out.

More than just a text editor

The emacs program is a cornucopia of bells and whistles, including two different mail packages, a newsreader, a file manager, color text highlighting, and countless other fun and unnecessary features. This makes it a far larger package than any other editor (it has been somewhat accurately called an operating system disguised as an editor), and has been known to cause some system administrators to balk at installing it on their UNIX machines. For others, it's almost a way of life, so whether or not you have access to emacs may depend on how strongly your system administrator feels about such things.

How to Meta-morphose emacs

Rather than have two modes, as do ed and vi, emacs treats normal letters, numbers, and punctuation as text and sticks them in your file when you type them. (Pretty advanced concept, huh?) Commands are usually given by pressing combinations of the Ctrl (Control) key and a letter. You also give some commands by pressing the Meta key and a letter.

On most computers, the Meta key is the Esc key. If your keyboard has an Alt key, it may be the Meta key. Try Alt to see if it works. If it doesn't, use Esc. Unlike Alt, if you use Esc, you must release the Esc key before you type the subsequent letter (Esc,release+letter). In the following section, we tell you to press Esc.

Another novel concept: type to enter text

To enter text, just start typing! The text is inserted wherever your cursor is.

Tripping hither, tripping thither

To move the cursor around in your text, use the following keys:

✔ Arrow keys usually move the cursor up, down, left, and right.

In a few situations, emacs doesn't understand the arrow keys. If this is true for you, use Ctrl+B to move backward one character, Ctrl+F to move forward one character, Ctrl+P to move to the preceding line, and Ctrl+N to move to the next line. At least they tried to make them mnemonic.

- ✔ Ctrl+A moves to the beginning of the line.
- ✔ Ctrl+E moves to the end of the line.
- ✔ Esc+< (press Esc and then hold down Shift and press the comma key) moves to the beginning of the file.
- ✔ Esc+> (press Esc and then hold down Shift and press the period key) moves to the end of the file.

A small change

Even though emacs is a better text editor, you still make typos, change your mind, and think of brilliant improvements to your text. To change text, follow these steps:

1. **Move the cursor to the beginning of the text you want to change.**

2. **Type the new text. The text is inserted wherever the cursor is.**

3. **Delete any text you don't want.**

It's that simple. No weird commands required.

More than one way to delete a character

emacs has several commands for deleting stuff:

- ✔ To delete the character the cursor is on, press Ctrl+D. Or press the Delete key on many terminals.
- ✔ To delete text from the cursor to the end of the word (up to a space or punctuation mark), press Esc and then D.
- ✔ To delete from the cursor to the end of the line, press Ctrl+K.

Emergency exit from emacs

To stop using emacs, press Ctrl+X followed by Ctrl+C.

This command doesn't save any changes you made to the file in emacs. It just gets you out. Some versions of emacs may ask whether you want to save the file the editor was looking at, or say something like "Buffers not saved. Exit?" (Translation: "Do you really want to quit without saving your changes?") Press Y for yes or N for no, as appropriate. If you just want to get out, press N to the "Do you want to save" question or Y to the "Buffers not saved" question.

TIP

Moving text in emacs

Although this discussion is beyond the scope of this quick introduction to emacs, here's how to move text from one place to another in the file. It turns out that when you use Ctrl+K to kill the text from the cursor to the end of the line, it stores the killed information in a temporary place called the *kill buffer*. You can copy the information from the kill buffer back into your file by pressing Ctrl+Y (*yank* it back into the file). To move some text, kill it with Ctrl+K, move the cursor to the new location, and press Ctrl+Y to insert the text where your cursor is. ("Kill" and "yank" in emacs-ese correspond to "cut" and "paste" in the regular world.)

Someone saved my file tonight (sorry, Elton!)

To save the text in the file, press Ctrl+XS (press and hold down the Ctrl key, press XS, and then release the Ctrl key). You should save your work every few minutes. Even though emacs isn't as frustrating as ed or vi, lots can still go wrong.

Bidding emacs *adieu*

When you finish editing and want to leave emacs, press Ctrl+XC (press and hold down the Ctrl key, press XC, and then release the Ctrl key). You leave emacs and see the UNIX shell prompt.

If you didn't save your work, emacs politely points out that your "buffers" (the stuff you have been working on) aren't saved and asks whether you really want to exit. It suggests N as the safe default in case you want to return to emacs to save the file. To leave without saving, press Y and then Enter.

It takes many fewer emacs commands to make a file and type some stuff, make a few changes, and then save the file and leave than it does with ed or vi. The emacs program has tons of commands, most of which are utterly useless. Table 10-3 lists the commonly used emacs commands.

Table 10-3	Commands in emacs
Command	**Description**
Ctrl+A	Move to the beginning of the line
Ctrl+B	Move back one space
Ctrl+D	Delete one character
Ctrl+E	Move to the end of the line
Ctrl+F	Move forward one space
Ctrl+K	Delete to the end of the line
Ctrl+N	Move to the next line
Ctrl+P	Move to the preceding line
Ctrl+XC	Leave emacs
Ctrl+XS	Save the file
Esc+<	Move to the beginning of the file
Esc+>	Move to the end of the file
Esc+D	Delete to the end of the word

A Peek at pico

One other editor has become popular — pico. As the Pine mail program has spread like wildfire, the editor that comes with it, pico, has taken off, too. pico is the easiest to use of the four text editors we describe in this chapter, if not the most powerful. It was written by folks at the University of Washington.

To run pico, type this command:

```
pico eating.peas
```

As usual, type the name of the file that you actually want to edit, instead of *eating.peas*. If you type a filename that doesn't exist, pico makes a file by that name just for you.

Your system may not have pico — if not, ask your system administrator if she or he could get it for you. Assure her or him that if she or he doesn't, you'll be pestering her or him ten times a day for the next year for help with ed or vi.

The `pico` screen looks like that shown in Figure 10-5. Amazing — `pico` actually shows you a menu of the most commonly used commands at the bottom of the screen! What will they think of next?

Figure 10-5:
The `pico`
editor is
actually
easy to use,
with a small
menu at the
bottom of
the screen.

You're my type

Typing text into a file using `pico` is a breeze. Just type. That's all. No modes, commands, or anything strange.

You move me

If your cursor keys work in `pico`, great. If not, you can use Ctrl+F to move forward one character, Ctrl+B to move back one character, Ctrl+N to move to the next line, and Ctrl+P to move to the previous line. The following keys also move you around the screen:

- ✔ Ctrl+A moves to the beginning of the line.
- ✔ Ctrl+E moves to the end of the line.
- ✔ Ctrl+V moves forward one screenful of text (F8 also does this).
- ✔ Ctrl+Y moves back one screenful of text (as does F7).

You're a big help

To get help with `pico`'s commands, press Ctrl+G. If your keyboard has an F1 key, that should work, too. You see pages of helpful information about the program. Press Ctrl+V to see more, or Ctrl+X to return to `pico`.

Time for a change

It's also easy to edit your text in `pico`. Whatever you type is inserted wherever the cursor is. You can use these commands to edit stuff:

- ✔ Ctrl+D deletes the character the cursor is on.
- ✔ Ctrl+^ (that's Ctrl+Shift+6) marks the beginning of some text that you want to work with. You use this command to select a bunch of text to delete or move.
- ✔ Ctrl+K (or F9) deletes ("cuts") the text from the mark to the current cursor position. Blammo! — the text is gone and stored in an invisible holding tank somewhere.
- ✔ Ctrl+U (or F10) "uncuts" or "pastes" the last text that you cut, making it reappear where the cursor is now.

Thanks for saving my file

To save the text in a file, press Ctrl+O (or press F3). `pico` asks for the filename to write the text into, suggesting the filename you used when you ran `pico` in the first place. You can change the name, so that the text is written out to a new file, or leave it as is, to update the existing file. When you press Enter, `pico` writes the information into the file.

I'm outta here

When you have finished editing and want to leave `pico`, just press Ctrl+X. If you haven't already saved your file, `pico` asks if you really want to leave, because leaving will lose any changes you made to the file since you last saved it. Tell it that you do. Then you're out, and you see the shell prompt.

`pico` doesn't claim to be an editor with the power of `emacs` or `vi`. After all, you can't edit ten files at once, read your mail, and rename files from `pico`. But who cares? It's a nice, easy program for editing text. Isn't that what a text editor is supposed to be for?

Table 10-4 lists the top pico commands.

Table 10-4	Commands in pico
Command	*Description*
Ctrl+A	Move to the beginning of the line
Ctrl+B	Move back one character
Ctrl+D	Delete one character
Ctrl+E	Move to the end of the line
Ctrl+F	Move forward one character
Ctrl+G (or F1)	Get help (display on-line help information)
Ctrl+K (or F9)	Kill (delete) selected text (text between the mark and the cursor)
Ctrl+N	Move to the next line
Ctrl+O (or F3)	Output (save) the file
Ctrl+P	Move to the previous line
Ctrl+U (or F10)	Uncut (paste) the last text that was deleted using the Ctrl+K command
Ctrl+V (or F8)	Move down one screenful of text
Ctrl+X (or F2)	Exit from pico
Ctrl+Y (or F7)	Move up one screenful of text
Ctrl+^ (Ctrl+Shift+6)	Mark the beginning of selected text

Chapter 11

Umpteen Useful UNIX Underdogs

● ●

In This Chapter

▶ A grab bag of useful programs

▶ Sorting and comparing files

▶ Stupid calendar tricks

▶ Squashing files to make them smaller

▶ Some other odds and ends

● ●

A dictionary defines an *underdog* as a victim of injustice or persecution. We certainly have been persecuting UNIX in this book. But UNIX actually has some fairly handy programs lying around. In this chapter, we look briefly at some of them. All these programs have a severe case of what is known as Feature Disease (closely related to the greasy fingerprints mentioned in Chapter 2): They all are bristling with features and options. Most of the features and options aren't worth mentioning, however, so we won't.

Comparing Apples and Oranges

When you have used your UNIX machine for a while, you have piles of files (say that six times quickly) lying around. Often, many of the files are duplicates, or near duplicates, of each other. Two programs can help sort out this mess: cmp and diff.

The simplest comparison program is cmp; it just tells you whether two files are the same or different. To use cmp to compare two files, type the following line:

```
cmp onefile anotherfile
```

You replace onefile and anotherfile with the names of the files you want to compare, of course. If the contents of the two files are the same, cmp doesn't say anything (in the finest UNIX tradition). If they're different, cmp tells how far into the files it got before it found something different. You can compare any two files, regardless of whether they contain text, programs, databases, or whatever, because cmp cares only whether they're identical.

A considerably more sophisticated comparison program is `diff`. This program attempts to tell you not only whether two files are different but also how different they are. The files must be plain text, not word processor documents or anything else, or else `diff` becomes horribly confused. Here's an example that uses two versions of a story one of us wrote. We compared files `tse1` and `tse2` by typing the following command:

```
diff tse1 tse2
```

Enter the name of the older file first and the name of the new, improved file second. The diff program responds with the following:

```
45c45

< steered back around, but the sheep screamed in panic
and reared back.

—

> steered back around, but the goats screamed in panic
and reared back.
46a47

> handlebars and landed safely in the snow.
```

The changes between `tse1` and `tse2` are that, in line 45, the *sheep* changed to *goats,* and a new line 47 was added after line 46.

In its first line of output, `45c45`, `diff` reports that there are changes (that's what the *c* stands for) in lines 45 through 45 (that is, just line 45). Then it displays the line in the first file, starting with a <, and the line in the second file, starting with a >. We think of this as `diff`'s way of saying that you took out the lines starting with < and inserted the lines starting with >. Then `diff` reports that there is a new line between lines 46 and 47 of the original file, and it shows the line that was inserted. This is a great way of seeing what changes have been made when you get a new revision of a document you have written.

BSD versions of `diff` (including the version that usually runs under Linux) can compare two directories to tell you which files are present in one and not in the other and to show you the differences between files with corresponding names in the two directories. Run `diff` and give it the names of the two directories.

Assorted Files

Computers are really good at putting stuff in order. Indeed, there was a time when a third of all computer time was spent sorting. UNIX has a quite capable sorting program, cleverly called `sort`, that you may remember meeting briefly in Chapter 7. Here, we talk about some other ways to use it.

The `sort` command sorts the lines of a file into alphabetical order. From `sort`'s point of view, a line is anything that ends with a carriage return (that is, you pressed Enter). If you have a file containing a list, with one item per line, this command alphabetizes the list.

The easiest way to use `sort` is to sort one file into another. In other words, you take the original file and tell `sort` to place the sorted version in another file. This way, you don't risk screwing up the original file if the sort runs amok. To sort the original `myfile` into a second file called `sortedfile`, type the following command:

```
sort myfile > sortedfile
```

Although you can sort a file back into itself, you can't do it in the obvious way. The following line, for example, doesn't work:

```
sort myfile > myfile
```

The problem with this command is that the UNIX shell clears out `myfile` before the sort starts (with the result that, when `sort` tries to sort something, it finds that `myfile` is empty). You can use the `-o` (for *o*utput) option to tell `sort` where to put the results, like this:

```
sort myfile -o myfile
```

This command works because `sort` doesn't start to write to the output file until it has read all its input.

Normally, `sort` orders its results based on a strict comparison by the internal ASCII code the computer uses. The good news is that this command sorts letters and digits in the correct way, although there are some peculiarities: Normally, uppercase letters sort before lowercase letters, so *ZEBRA* precedes *aardvark*. You can use the `-f` (for *f*old cases together) option to sort regardless of uppercase and lowercase letters, as follows:

```
sort -f animals -o sortedanimals
```

Although we could have used the > redirection symbol here, with `sort` it's safer to use `-o`. You can use several other options also to tell it to sort:

-b   Ignore spaces at the beginning of the line.

-d   Use dictionary order and ignore any punctuation. You usually use this option with `-f`.

-n   Sort based on the number at the beginning of the line. With this option, 99 precedes 100 rather than follows it, as it does in usual alphabetical order. (Yes, the normal thing the computer does is pretty dumb. Are you surprised?)

-r   Sort in the reverse order of whatever would have been done otherwise. You can combine this option with any of the others.

We find sorting to be particularly useful in files in which every line starts with a date. For example:

```
0505       Tonia's birthday
1204       Meg's birthday
1102       Zac's birthday
0318       Sarah's birthday
```

We can type `sort -n` to sort this file by date. Notice that we wrote May 5 as 0505 (not 55, for example) so that a numeric sort would work.

You can do much more complex sorting and treat every line as a sequence of "fields" that `sort` uses to decide the final sorted order. If you really need to do this, talk to someone who knows something about sorting.

Time Is Money — Steal Some Today!

All UNIX systems have internal clocks. You can ask it what the date and time are with the `date` command, as follows:

```
date
```

UNIX responds with the following information:

> Thu Dec 4 15:43:50 EST 1997

Many options enable you to tailor the date format any way you want. Don't waste your time. UNIX has an idea about the time zone, too, and even does daylight savings time automatically.

You can schedule things to be done later by using the `at` command. You say something like the following:

```
at 5:15pm Jul 4
sort -r myhugefile -o myhugefile.sort
pr -f -2 myhugefile.sort | lp
```

Then you press Ctrl+D to indicate that you've finished giving commands.

You give the `at` command and specify a time and date. Then you enter the commands you want to run at that date and time. Press Ctrl+D on a separate line to tell UNIX that you're finished listing tasks. In this example, we sort a huge file and then print it in two columns, all on the Fourth of July when presumably no one will be around to complain that it's taking too long. If you omit the date, UNIX assumes that you mean today if the time you give is later than the current time; otherwise, UNIX assumes that you mean tomorrow.

Any output that normally would go to the terminal is sent back to you by electronic mail, so you should at least skim Chapter 17 to find out how to read your mail.

Squashing Your Files

One problem that is common to all UNIX systems — indeed, to nearly all computer systems of any kind — is that there is never enough disk space. UNIX comes with a couple of programs that can alleviate this problem: `compress` and `pack`. They change the data in a file into a more compact form. Although you can't do anything with the file in this compact form except expand it back to the original format, for files you don't need to refer to very often, it can be a big space saver.

You use `compress` and `pack` in pretty much the same way. To compress a file called `confidential.doc`, for example, type the following line:

```
compress -v confidential.doc
```

The optional `-v` (for *verbose*) option merely tells UNIX to report how much space it saved. If you use it, UNIX responds with the following information:

```
confidential.doc: Compression: 49.79% — replaced with
confidential.doc.Z
```

The `compress` program replaces the file with one that has the same name with `.Z` added to it. The degree of compression depends on what's in the file, but 50 percent compression for text files is typical. On a few files, the compression scheme doesn't save any space, in which case, `compress` is polite enough not to make a `.Z` file.

To get the compressed file back to its original state, use `uncompress`:

```
uncompress confidential.doc.Z
```

This command gets rid of `confidential.doc.Z` and gets back `confidential.doc`. You can also use `zcat`, a compressed-file version of the `cat` program, which sends an uncompressed version of a compressed file to the terminal, without storing the uncompressed version in a file. It is rarely useful by itself but can be quite handy with programs such as `more` or `lp`. Use it as follows:

```
zcat confidential.doc.Z | more
```

This command enables you to see one page at a time what's in the file. Unlike `uncompress`, `zcat` does not get rid of the `.Z` file.

The GNU crowd weighed in with their own `compress`-like program called `gzip`. It works the same way that `compress` does, but uses a different slightly better compression scheme. The `gzip` program is analogous to `compress`. `gunzip` and `gzcat` uncompress stuff. Use them as shown here:

```
gzip -v confidential.doc
gunzip confidential.doc.z
zcat confidential.doc.z | more
```

Note that the files end with lower case z rather than upper case Z.

Fortunately, `gzip` knows how to uncompress files produced by `compress`, as well as those produced by several other compression programs, so you can use `gunzip` as your one-stop uncompression utility.

A similar but older program that uses a different compacting scheme is `pack`. To use it, type the following line:

```
pack confidential.doc
```

UNIX responds with the following information:

```
/usr/bin/pack: confidential.doc: 37.1% Compression
```

You get packed files back with `unpack`.; you can look at packed files with `pcat`. Packed files end in `.z` (that's a lowercase *z,* the same as `gzip` uses, to confuse the innocent). Like compress, pack leaves the file untouched if packing doesn't save any space. In most cases, pack doesn't save as much space as compress does, although it occasionally does better. Sometimes it's worth it to try both.

Zippedy day-tah

WinZip and PKZIP are widely used compression programs among Windows and DOS users to create *ZIP* files containing one or more files compressed together. You may run into ZIP files if you get information from the Internet or on a diskette from a DOS or Windows system. Fortunately, a number of volunteers (led by a perfectly nice guy who goes under the enigmatic handle of Cave Newt) have written free zipping and unzipping programs called zip and unzip. They're both available for free over the Internet, so no UNIX system should be without them.

To unzip a ZIP file, you use unzip, as follows:

```
unzip video-list.zip
```

The unzip command has a whole bunch of options, the most useful of which is -l, which tells the program to list the contents of the ZIP file without actually extracting any of the files. To find out what all the options are, run unzip with no arguments.

If you need to create a ZIP file, you can use the equally boringly named zip program, as shown here:

```
zip video-list *.txt
```

This command says to create a file called video-list.zip (it adds the .zip part if you don't) containing all the files in the current directory whose names end in .txt. The zip program has a lot of options, the most useful of which are -9, meaning to compress as well as possible even though it's slow (-1 means as fast as possible; other digits give results in between), and -k, which means to make the file look just like one created on a DOS system, not using any lowercase filenames or other UNIX-isms. We use zip -9k to create ZIP files to copy to DOS systems.

Incidentally, gzip bears only the vaguest connection to zip and unzip. gzip compresses single files, whereas zip compresses multiple files into a single archive.

What's in That File?

Sometimes you have a bunch of files and no recollection of what they contain. The `file` command can give you a hint. It looks at the files you name on the command line and makes its best guess about what's in the files.

To have `file` try to figure out what's in the files in the working directory, type the following line:

```
file *
```

UNIX responds with the following bunch of seemingly incomprehensible information:

```
sleuth1.doc: data

sleuth1.ms: [nt]roff, tbl, or eqn input text

tse1: ascii text

tse2.Z: compressed file - with 16 bits
```

This mess says that `file` figured out that the `sleuth1.ms` file is a text file coded for input to the `troff` text formatter (those other programs are some of `troff`'s helpers), that `tse1` contains text, and that `tse2.Z` is compressed. (The "16 bits" stuff tells basically which version of `compress` was used; it doesn't really matter, because current versions of `compress` can read any compressed file.) The `file` program guesses "data" whenever it has no idea what's in a file. The first file, `sleuth1.doc`, was a Microsoft Word document, something `file` doesn't know about, so it guesses that it's data.

How does compress work?

Normally, every character in a file is stored as a byte by using 8 bits (binary digits, 1s and 0s, the smallest unit of data a computer can handle). In 1952, David Huffman explained how to use the fewest bits for a particular message. Ever since then, this kind of code has been known as *Huffman coding*.

`compress` uses a dictionary-compression scheme. Frequently occurring groups of bytes are encoded as a single dictionary entry, or *token*. `compress` doesn't include the dictionary in the compressed file — `uncompress` can deduce the contents of the dictionary from the sequence of tokens in the compressed file. Clever, no?

Chapter 12

I Can't Install Software!

In This Chapter

▶ Where does software comes from (the software stork)?

▶ Where to put software

▶ Writing shell scripts, or files full of commands

▶ Writing aliases for your favorite commands

*H*ey, calm down. No, we're not about to train you to be a system programmer. Every user has a few favorite programs, and you will wear out your welcome quickly if you go off to your local wizard every time you want to use a new program. In many cases, installing new programs is easy enough that you can do it yourself.

If you are a Windows or Macintosh user, you probably are thinking just the opposite: "Sure, I can install new programs. What's the big deal? I just stick in a floppy disk and type INSTALL, right?" No. In UNIX, it's not that simple, of course. There are issues of paths, permissions, and other technical-type stuff we have been protecting you from.

The Software Stork

Interesting software comes from many places:

✔ Some other user on the same machine already has it for his or her own use and you want to use it too.

✔ Some other machine on the network has a program you want for yourself. See Chapter 21 for the gory details of copying it from other machines on the network.

✔ Someone sends you programs through e-mail. (Yes, it's possible.)

✔ You create files that contain frequently used commands so that you don't have to type them repeatedly. In UNIX-speak, these files are called *shell scripts.* In essence, you make your own multipurpose UNIX commands.

First, let's talk about where you should put your own software. Then we can go into more detail about the mechanics of putting it there.

You've bin *Had*

Every UNIX user should have a bin directory. It's just a directory called bin in your home directory. If it's not there, you can make it by going to your home directory and typing the following line:

```
mkdir bin
```

The thing that's special about bin is that the shell looks for programs there. Most system administrators automatically set up a bin directory for users. If not, and you had to create it yourself, you may have to do some fiddling to tell the shell to look for programs there. See the sidebar entitled "Your search path" for the bad news.

To put programs in your bin directory, you just copy them there by using the cp command. Alternatively, you can move them there by using the mv command, a text editor, or any other way to create or move a file.

A bin *of Shells*

You can make your own commands (that is, shell scripts) and put them in your bin directory. A shell script is a text file that contains a list of shell commands — the same commands you type at the shell prompt. You can store a list of commands as a shell script, and run the commands any time by typing the name of the shell script. The following sections tell you how.

Why is it called bin?

Early on, *bin* was short for *bin*ary, because most programs that people put there were, in fact, compiled binary code. In the late 1970s, a famous professor of cognitive science at the University of California published a paper called "The Trouble with UNIX," in which he complained bitterly about how difficult it was to use UNIX. One of the items on his list was that bin was difficult to remember. One of the UNIX guys at Bell Labs published a witty rebuttal and pointed out that many of the allegedly "more natural" command names the professor suggested were merely the names the computer system at his university used. The UNIX guy reported that many Bell Labs users thought that a bin was the obvious place to stash their programs. So, it's still a bin.

The famous professor has come around somewhat and is reputed to even use UNIX now and then, although he probably shuts his office door so that no one can see.

You, too, can be a scriptwriter

To create a shell script, use any text editor (see Chapter 10). Enter the commands one per line, just as you would type them at the shell prompt. Save the file in your bin directory.

Here's an example — if you frequently search for files with names that begin with *budget,* you probably are tired of typing the following command over and over:

```
find . -name budget* -print
```

(Check out Chapter 8 to see how the find command works.) Instead, you can put this command in a shell script and perhaps call the script findbud. To do this, create a text file named findbud that contains just one line: the command.

First you move to your bin directory, because that's where your programs live, as follows:

```
cd bin
```

Then you use a text editor to create a text file containing the commands you want in your script. In this example, we use ed, a creepy editor, but you can use the editor of your choice instead. Type the following:

```
ed findbud
```

UNIX responds with the following line:

```
?findbud
```

or maybe

```
findbud: No such file or directory
```

Either way, you are editing the findbud file. Type the following command:

```
a
```

This command tells ed to start appending text to the end of the findbud file. (Remember that, because you're using ed, you have to type weird commands.)

Then type these two lines:

```
find . -name budget* -print
.
```

The dot on a line by itself tells ed to return to command mode. To save the file, type the following:

```
w
```

UNIX responds with the information that you have saved a file with 29 (or so) characters:

```
29
```

Quit ed by typing this command:

```
q
```

You see the shell prompt again. Great! You've created a shell script!

Making a screenplay from a text file

Now you must tell UNIX that the text file you have created is executable — that it's more than a mere text file. To do this, type the following line:

```
chmod +x findbud
```

This line marks the findbud file as *executable* (it's a script the shell can run).

Take 1

To run the shell script, just type its name, as follows:

```
findbud
```

Voilà! You have just created your own UNIX command! UNIX runs the find command to look for your budget files.

You're not quite finished, though. Observe what happens when you go to another directory. Type the following two commands to go to your home directory and give the `findbud` command there:

```
cd
findbud
```

UNIX may respond with this message:

```
findbud: Command not found.
```

If so, type the following command to get UNIX to do what you want:

```
rehash
```

Now when you type `findbud`, it works.

What's going on? Well, it's Mr. too-smart-for-his-own-good Shell. Because programs don't appear and disappear very often, when the shell starts up, it makes a list of all the commands it can access and where they are. Because there are frequently five or six command directories, this process saves considerable time (the alternative is to check every directory for every command every time you type one). The `rehash` command tells UNIX to rebuild its list (known in geekspeak as a *hash table*) because you have added a new command (the `findbud` file is really a command, remember?). If the command still doesn't work, you will have to fiddle with your search path — not a pretty job. See the sidebar titled "Your search path."

Type **rehash** to tell the shell that you have added a new command and that you want it to rebuild its list of available commands to include this one. If you don't give the `rehash` command and you change directories, you can't use the newly created shell script during this login session.

We could write an entire book about shell scripts (others have). The finer points naturally vary depending on which shell you use, but this explanation gives you the general idea. Shell scripts aren't limited to one line: They can be as long as you want, which is handy when you have a long list of commands you want to run regularly.

Your search path

You can ignore this section unless you have put a command in your `bin` directory and the shell can't find it. Still reading? Sorry to hear it. The shell has a list of directories that contain commands; this list is known as the *search path*. On any sensible UNIX system, the `bin` directory is already in your search path. If it's not, you have to put it there. There are two stages: putting it in once and putting it in permanently.

To see what your current search path is, type the following line if you are using the C shell:

```
echo $path
```

If you have BASH or the Bourne or Korn shell, type this line:

```
echo $PATH
```

Yes, one's uppercase and one's lowercase. Arrgh! The C shell responds with something like this:

```
/bin /usr/bin /usr/ucb/bin /
usr/local/bin
```

BASH or the Bourne or Korn shell shows something like the following:

```
/bin:/usr/bin:/usr/ucb/bin:/
usr/local/bin:.
```

What you have to do is add your bin directory to the path.

If you use the C shell, type this magical incantation:

```
set path=($path ~/bin)
```

That's a tilde (~) in the middle. This tells the C sheet to set the path the same as the current path ($path), plus the bin subdirectory of your home directory (~).

If you use BASH or the Bourne or Korn shell, type this even more magical incantation:

```
PATH=$PATH:$HOME/bin
export PATH
```

Note that the second time you type PATH and HOME in the first command, you include a dollar sign ($) in front of them. This tells the Bourne or Korn shell to set the path the same as the current path ($PATH), plus the bin subdirectory of your home directory ($HOME). Same song, different words.

Now you should be able to run your new script regardless of which directory you're using.

This new, improved path lasts only until you log out. To put your bin directory on the path every time you log in, you must add the incantation to the end of the shell script that runs automatically whenever you log in. If you use the C shell, add it to the .login file. If you use the Bourne or Korn shell, add it to the .profile file.

Yes, these filenames begin with periods. Filenames that start with periods usually don't show up in file listings, which is why you haven't noticed these files in your home directory. Type the following line to list all your files, including these hidden ones:

```
ls -a
```

In principle, you only have to edit the file, go to the end, and add the necessary lines. In practice, it's easy to screw up, so — unless you're feeling particularly brave — you're probably better off asking for expert assistance.

Don't give me any arguments!

Shell scripts can be complete programs. Every shell program has lots of swell programming features you don't want to know about. But one is so useful that we're going to tell you anyway: Your shell scripts can use information from the command line. That is, if you type `foogle dog pig`, your script called `foogle` can see that you ran it saying `dog` and `pig`. The things on the line after the name of the command are called *arguments*. The word *dog* is the first argument, and *pig* is the second one. In shell scripts, the first argument is called `$1`, the second `$2`, and so forth. In shorthand, `$*` means "all the arguments."

Suppose that you want to write a script called `2print` that prints files in a two-column format. (You do that by using the `pr` command, described in Chapter 9.) Create a file called `2print` that contains the following line:

```
pr -f -2 $* | lp
```

Then use the `chmod` and, if necessary, `rehash` commands to make `2print` an executable script. If you want to print several files, one right after the next, in two-column format, you can type the following line:

```
2print onefile anotherfile
yetanotherfile
```

In reality, you are saying this:

```
pr -f -2 onefile anotherfile
yetanotherfile | lp
```

This line prints all three files in two-column format. (Note that you may need to use `lpr` rather than `lp` in this shell script. Refer to Chapter 9.)

Borrowing Other People's Programs

Lots of times, someone else has a cool program you want to be able to use. There are two approaches to getting what you want, and both are pretty easy. Suppose that your friend Tracy has a program called `pornotopia` in the `bin` directory. (No, we don't know what it does, either.) How can you run it?

The long way

If you use the C shell, you can run the program from Tracy's directory by typing this line:

```
~tracy/bin/pornotopia
```

If you use BASH or the Bourne or Korn shell, you can type this line:

```
/usr/tracy/bin/pornotopia
```

The easier way

It is a pain to type this long string of letters and symbols every time you want to run the program. A better way is to put in your `bin` directory a *link* to the cool program so that you can run it directly. (Links are described in Chapter 8.) You use the `ln` command to create a link, which makes the file appear to be in your own `bin` directory, too.

Try the direct approach. Move to your home directory and create a link, as follows:

```
cd
ln ~tracy/bin/pornotopia bin/pornotopia
```

With any luck, this method will work, creating a link from Tracy's file to your `bin` directory. Give or take a quick `rehash`, you're all set.

The `ln` command doesn't work, however, if you and Tracy have files on different disks. (This is all explained in Chapter 8 and 21.) In this case, you may get this unhelpful message:

```
ln: different file system
```

If you get this message, it's time for Plan B. Most UNIX systems have things called *symbolic links* that work across different disks (these are explained in Chapter 8, too). Try the following line:

```
ln -s ~tracy/bin/pornotopia bin/pornotopia
```

If it works, it makes a symbolic link to the file you want. You're all set: The link to `pornotopia` refers to Tracy's version. After a `rehash`, you're ready to go.

Using an alias

Well, if you were named pornotopia, you probably would want an alias, too. Fortunately, the BASH, Korn, and C shells give you the ability to invent a short name for a long command. (Bourne shell users: you are out of luck. Skip to the next section.)

In the BASH and Korn shells, type this line:

```
alias dobudget='/usr/tracy/bin/pornotopia'
```

This line tells the shell that, when you type `dobudget`, you really want to run Tracy's program. Heh, heh. To avoid inadvertent ease of use, the C shell's `alias` command works in almost the same way, but it is punctuated slightly differently, as follows:

```
alias dobudget '/usr/tracy/bin/pornotopia'
```

(In both cases, the quotes are optional if the command doesn't contain any spaces or special characters, but it never hurts to use them.)

You can define aliases for any frequently used one-line command. The alias can contain spaces, pipes, and anything else you can type on a command line. In BASH, for example, you can type the following:

```
alias sortnprint='sort -r bigfile | pr -2 | lpr'
```

This line makes the new `sortnprint` command sort your `bigfile` in reverse alphabetical order, format it in two columns with `pr`, and send the result to the printer. Aliases can also be useful if you are subject (as we are) to chronic miswiring of the nerves in your fingers. We always type `mroe` when we mean `more`, so the following alias fixes it:

```
alias mroe=more
```

(That's the BASH version; the C shell would have a space rather than an equal sign between `mroe` and `more`.)

Aliases you type directly to the shell are lost when you log out. If you want them to be available permanently, you must put the `alias` commands in your `.login` or `.profile` file, in the same way we mentioned earlier, in the "Your search path" sidebar.

The last resort

If this method doesn't work either, try Plan D to use Tracy's program: a one-line shell script. Although we use the `ed` program because it's easier to show, you should use a real editor. Start by revving up `ed`, as follows:

```
ed bin/pornotopia
```

You get the following helpful response, or something like it:

```
?bin/pornotopia
```

Now tell `ed` to add some text to the file, by typing the following command:

```
a
```

You are now in append mode. Type the command line you want to include in the shell script, followed by a dot (period) on a line by itself:

```
/usr/tracy/bin/pornotopia
.
```

The dot on a line by itself switches back to ed's command mode. Then type this command:

```
w
```

This writes the new shell script file and prints the size of the file. Then type the following to quit ed:

```
q
```

Type the next command to make your new shell script runnable, as follows:

```
chmod +x pornotopia
```

If necessary, give this command to tell UNIX to redo its hash table:

```
rehash
```

Now your script named pornotopia will run Tracy's original program called pornotopia. At least one of these three plans should work for any program lying around anywhere on your system.

We don't even discuss software copyrights, licenses, and ethics here, but if you use a copyrighted program, you should pay for it unless you like to think of yourself as a thief.

Stealing Software from the Network

If you are on the Internet, zillions of programs are free for the taking. You can get copies of programs in the same way you get copies of anything else on the Internet — using FTP. See Chapter 20 for the inside scoop on FTP.

On many UNIX systems, this is the most common way to get new software. Most of it is shareware or freeware, but even some commercial outfits are now selling their programs to be downloaded from the Internet.

Tar pits

When you download UNIX software from the Internet, nine times out of ten, the filename will end in either `.tar`, `.tar.Z`, or `.tar.gz`. (We get to the most common exception in the next section.) These are called, oddly enough, *tar files*. They don't have anything to do with black, goopy paving material; *tar* is short for *tape archive*. You use this command for backing up (what used to be called "archiving," in the days when people went out of their way to make computers look important) UNIX systems onto tape. (We discuss this use of `tar` in Chapter 23).

Here, though, you're seeing `tar` in its other role, where it moonlights as a software packaging command. The people who distribute the software use `tar` to gather all the files that make up the software package (it can be anywhere from just a few up to hundreds of files), and glom them into one big tar file. This way, you only need to download one big file instead of hundreds of little files. Because tar files are generally so big, the software distributors then squish them even further, using either the `compress` command (which results in a file ending in `.tar.Z`) or the `gzip` command (which results in a file ending in `.tar.gz`). Using `compress` used to be the standard, but because `gzip` results in smaller files, it's the compression program that most people use these days.

If you're familiar with the Microsoft Windows world, you may have come across "zip files," which end in `.zip`. These are the Windows equivalent of tar files, except that zip combines the glomming and squishing phases into one command, an example of efficiency that true UNIX die-hards would never stand for.

By way of example, suppose that you've found a really cool editor that you've decided you can't live without, and you've downloaded the tar file. It will probably look like `really_cool_ed_unix_v.3. 4pl6.tar.gz`. To unpack your newly acquired tar file, first you need to unsquish it. If the file ends in `.tar.Z`, type the following command:

```
uncompress really_cool_ed_unix_v.3.4p15.tar.Z
```

Otherwise, type this command:

```
gunzip really_cool_ed_unix_v.3.4p15.tar.gz
```

Either way, you get a file called `really_cool_ed_unix_v.3.4pl6. tar`. Notice that the .Z or .gz is gone? This file is much bigger now that it's unsquished.

Now you *untar* the file. This step blows up your tar file into potentially hundreds of little files and puts them into whatever your current directory is. Make sure that your current working directory is the directory where you really want all those files to be, rather than someplace where you'll have to move them later. (It's easier to move one tar file where you want it, rather than waiting until after you've blown it up into multitudes of files.) Type the following command:

```
tar xvf really_cool_ed_unix_v.3.4p15.tar
```

The *x* in *xvf* stands for extract, the *v* means verbose (you can see all the files being created), and *f* is for file, and is followed by the name of the tar file.

There's still more to do. Included in the bunch of files you've just created should be a file called README or INSTALL. This file has the rest of the installation instructions specific to the package you've just downloaded.

Revving up RPM

For years, tar has been the only game in UNIX-land for distributing software over the Internet. For UNIX administrators, it has worked just fine. A growing number of disgruntled users have clamored for an easier way. Their calls were answered by Red Hat Linux, which came up with the Red Hat Package Manager (RPM).

RPM is a software management system that is a substitute for tar. Instead of downloading a file ending in `.tar.gz`, you download one that ends in `.rpm`. The RPM utility unpacks the file, puts all the resulting little files in their correct places, and updates a database of installed software on the computer. If you later want to install an upgrade, RPM remembers that an older version is already installed, and saves any existing configuration files while upgrading the necessary files.

You can only install software with RPM if you are the system administrator. RPM is not restricted to Linux; we've heard of people using it on other UNIX systems.

Sneaking Software through the Mail

It is possible to disguise programs as mail messages so that you can mail them around. This method is often the only way to do samizdat software distribution when networks and system administrators are uncooperative.

Sneaky shar

For short programs and shell scripts, send a *shar message*. It's a shell script that recreates the files. (If you care, shar is lazy-typist-ese for *sh*ell *ar*chive.) Shar files are also a convenient way to mail groups of text files.

Shar messages usually start with lines like the following:

```
#!/bin/sh
# This is a shell archive (produced by shar 3.49)
# To extract the files from this archive, save it to a
# file, remove everything above the "!/bin/sh" line
# above, and type "sh file_name."
#
# made 01/05/1997 19:41 UTC by johnl@iecc
# Source directory /usr/johnl/bin
```

Recovering the files is a three-step process:

1. Save the message in a file, something like `new-shar`. (See Chapter 17.)

2. Use any text editor to delete all the lines from the beginning of the file to the first line that starts with a #.

3. Feed the edited file to the shell by typing the following line:

```
sh incoming-shar
```

This command creates the program files or whatever else is in the shar file. (Most shar messages start with a manifest of the files in the file.) When you see the UNIX prompt, it is finished. Delete the `new-shar` file and move its output files it to the appropriate place, probably to your `bin` directory.

Shar files are security gaps. Nothing stops them from harming your system Run shar files only if you know the sender. Uuencoded files are far safer.

Sneaky you-you

Shar files don't work well for binary programs, so `uuencode` disguises them as text. If you receive a file coded in `uuencode` file, the message looks like:

```
begin 775 pornotopia
M3'$$'!C?&RRRN:4@"0',"!P"P"P"P":"Y":":":":":":":":":"$"-"""<
```

Recovering the binary file from the uuencode file is a two-step process:

1. Save the message in a file with a name along the lines of uu-incoming.

2. Feed the file to the uudecode program by typing the following line:

```
code uu-incoming
```

Don't delete the first lines in the file; uudecode ignores them for you. When you see the UNIX prompt, it is finished. Then get rid of the uu-incoming file and move to the appropriate place the binary file that is created.

Making your own sneaky e-mail

Want to send a program or other binary file by e-mail? Use the uuencode program. Just follow these steps to create uuencoded files:

1. Type the following command:

```
uuencode pornutopia strange-program > temp
```

In this command, replace pornutopia with the file you want to uuencode, strange-program with the name that you want the file to have when it is uudecoded, and temp with any temporary filename (junk is another favorite). This command creates a uuencoded file named temp that, when uudecoded, will create a file named strange-program with the same contents as your pornutopia file.

2. Include this uuencoded file at the end of an e-mail message. The message should say that it contains a uuencoded file and what it's for. (See Chapter 17 for how to send e-mail.)

Real Software Installation

There are official installation procedures for software. To install, you log in as root (the superuser, who can clobber anyone's files anywhere) and run a program called install. The install program directs you to load tapes, CD-ROMs, or diskettes, and asks configuration questions, such as "Does this system support DES-protected NFS mounts across router boundaries?" We suggest that you leave this procedure to trained professionals.

Chapter 13

How to Run a Bunch of Programs at a Time

In This Chapter

▶ What processes are

▶ Where processes come from

▶ What is a background program?

▶ Shuffling background programs around

▶ Hints about windows and background programs

• •

*1*f you have a plain old terminal with no windowing system, you may be envious of users with fancy window systems who can pop up a bunch of windows and run umpteen programs at a time.

Well, don't. Any UNIX system enables you to run as many programs simultaneously as you want. Nearly all the systems let you stop and restart programs and switch around among different programs whenever you want.

If you're used to an old-fashioned, one-program-at-a-time system, such as DOS (without Windows) or the pre-System 7 Mac, you might not see the point of doing several things at a time. Suppose, however, that you're doing something that takes a while and that the computer can manage with little or no supervision from you, such as copying a large file over a network (which can take 10 or 15 minutes). There's no reason for you to sit and wait for that process to finish — you can do something useful while the copy runs in the background.

Or, suppose that you're in the middle of a program and you want to do something else: You're writing a memo in a text editor and need to check some e-mail you received to make sure that you spelled someone's name right. One way to do that is to save the file, leave the editor, run the mail program, leave the mail program, start the editor again, return to the same place in the file, and pick up where you left off. What a pain. UNIX enables you to stop the editor, run the mail program, and resume the editor exactly where you left it. For that matter, you can run *both* the editor and the mail program and flip between them as necessary.

In the interest of fairness, we must point out that *job control,* the feature that enables you to flip back and forth, was written by Bill, the same guy who wrote the C shell, vi, and NFS. In contrast to our opinion of some of his other efforts, we think that job control is pretty cool.

If you have a process that has run amok, see Chapter 24 to find out how to kill it.

So What Is a Process, Anyway?

All the work UNIX does for you is done by UNIX *processes.* When you log in, the shell is a process. When you run an editor, the editor is a process. Pretty much any command you run is a process.

Processes called *daemons* lurk in the background and wait to do useful things without manual intervention. When you use lp or lpr to print something, for example, a daemon does the real work of sending the material to the printer.

Normally, all this process stuff happens automatically and you don't have to pay much attention to it. But sometimes a program gets stuck and you can't make it go away. If you use a personal computer running DOS or a Macintosh, the usual response to a stuck program is to restart the computer. When you run UNIX, resetting the computer is a little extreme for a single stuck program. For one thing, other running programs and other people who are logged in do not appreciate having their computer kicked out from underneath them. Also, it can take UNIX a while to restart from a forced reboot (it takes our system about 20 minutes to check all the disks), and you run the risk of losing files that were being updated.

Lots of X Windows

If you're running Motif or any other X Window graphical user interface (GUI), you've probably already figured out how to run many programs at once — open several xterm windows and run a program in each one. You create a new window by moving the mouse outside of any window, holding down the left mouse button to get a menu, and selecting New Window or something similar.

But read this chapter anyway, particularly the sidebar later on called "Do windows and job control mix?"

Why processes are not programs and vice versa

Programs and processes are similar, but they're not the same. A *process* is, more or less, a running program. Suppose that you're using X Windows or Motif, have two windows on-screen, and are running vi in both of them. Although the same program is running in both windows, they're different processes doing different things (in this case, editing different files).

To add to the confusion, some programs use more than one process apiece. The terminal program cu, for example, uses two processes: one to copy what you type to the remote computer, and the other to copy stuff from the remote computer back to your screen. Sometimes, there are "hidden" processes: Many programs have a way you can execute any UNIX command from inside the program. (In ed, for example, you type ! and the command you want to run.) In addition to the command, a shell process usually interprets the command.

In most cases, it is easy enough to tell in a list of processes which one is which, because each one is identified by the command that started it.

Any Processes in the House?

The basic program you use to find out which processes are around is ps (for *process status*). The details of ps (wait! — how did you know?) vary somewhat from one version of UNIX to another, but there are two main kinds of ps: the System V kind and the BSD kind. (SVR4 uses the System V kind of ps, even though SVR4 has a lot of BSD mixed in. Linux uses a ps that looks more or less like BSD.)

Mind your ps (and qs)

If you run plain ps, no matter which version of UNIX you have, you get a list of the processes running from your terminal (or window, if you're using X Windows). The list looks something like the following:

```
PID TTY       TIME COMMAND

24812 ttyp0   0:01 -csh

25973 ttyp0   0:00 ps
```

The PID column gives the *process identification,* or *process ID.* To help keep processes straight, UNIX assigns every process a unique number as an identifier. The numbers start at 1 and go up. When the PIDs become inconveniently large (about 30,000 or so), UNIX starts over again at 1 and skips numbers that are still in use. To get rid of a stuck process, you need to know its PID to tell the system which process to destroy.

The TTY column lists the terminal from which the process was started. In this case, ttyp0 is the terminal, which happens to be pseudo-terminal number 0. (Because UNIX systems were written by and for nerds, they tend to start counting at 0 rather than at 1.) A *pseudo-terminal* is what UNIX uses when you're logged in from an X window or from a remote system through a network rather than through a real, actual, drop-it-on-your-foot-and-it-hurts terminal. For our purposes, all terminals act the same, be they real, pseudo, or whatever.

The TIME column is the amount of time the computer has spent running this program. (The time spent waiting for you to type something or waiting for disks and printers and so forth doesn't count.)

The COMMAND column shows the name of command that started the process, more or less. If the process is the first one for a particular terminal or pseudo-terminal, the command name starts with a hyphen.

The Linux ps

Linux's ps command has one additional column, as shown here:

```
PID    TTY    STAT    TIME    COMMAND

1797   pp5    S       0:00    -bash

1855   pp5    R       0:00    ps
```

The STAT column shows the status of the process. According to the man page for the command, *R* means runnable, *S* means sleeping, *D* means uninterruptible sleep, *T* means stopped or traced, and *Z* means a zombie process. Wow! For our purposes, *R* means it's a command you ran, and other stuff doesn't matter much.

Fancier ps *(and qs)*

The System V version of ps has lots of options, most of which are pretty useless. One of the more useful is -f, which produces a "full" listing, as in the following example:

```
UID     PID    PPID   C   STIME      TTY     TIME   COMMAND

johnl   11764  3812   0   14:06:02   ttyp3   0:00   /usr/ bin/emacs

johnl   11766  11764  0   14:06:05   ttyp3   0:00   /bin/ sh -i

johnl   11769  11766  10  14:06:15   ttyp3   0:00   ps -f

johnl   3812   3804   0   Jan 18     ttyp3   0:04   -sh
```

(We did this from a different window, which you can tell because the PID of the shell is different.)

This listing has a few more columns than does the basic ps listing, and a few columns are different. The UID column is the user name — just what it looks like. PPID is the *parent PID,* the PID of the process that started this one. We had run emacs from the shell and then had told emacs to start another shell to run a ps command.

The parent PIDs reflect the order in which the processes started each other: The login shell process (number 3812) is the parent of emacs, which in turn is the parent of the shell /bin/sh, which is the parent of ps. (We could explain why the processes aren't listed in order, but, trust us — you don't want to know.) All processes in a UNIX system are arranged in a genealogical hierarchy based on which process started which. The grand ancestor of them all is process number 1, which is named init. You can trace the ancestry of any process back to init. "Hark! I am yclept Ps, son of Bourne Shell, daughter of Emacs, son of Dash-shell (or is that Dashiell?), great-great-grandson of the ancient and holy Init!"

The C column is a totally technoid number relating to how much the process has been running lately. Ignore it. STIME is the *start time,* the time of day the process began. If it began more than 24 hours ago, this column shows the date. TTY is the name of the terminal the process is using. If you run a GUI, such as X Windows or Motif, and you run the xterm program in a window (as we did here), the entry for TTY doesn't show the terminal you are using. Instead, it lists the "pseudo-terminal" assigned to the window (a completely useless piece of information). Sometimes the TTY column shows a ?, which means that the process is a daemon that doesn't use a terminal.

The COMMAND column shows the full command that began this process, including (in some cases) the full path name of the program. (Standard system programs live in the directories /bin and /usr/bin, so you see them alot in ps listings.)

If you're logged in on several terminals or in several windows, you may want to see all your processes, not just the ones for the current terminal. With the System V version of ps, you can ask to see all processes for a given user by using the following command:

```
ps -u tracy
```

This command lists all processes belonging to user tracy. You can ask to see any user's processes, not just your own. You can get a full listing for that user, too, as follows:

```
ps -fu tracy
```

System V has other, less useful, switches for ps, notably -e, which shows every process in the entire system.

Berkeley ps (and qs)

The basic report from the BSD version of ps looks like the following example:

```
PID     TT     STAT    TIME     COMMAND

7335    p4     S       0:00     -csh (csh)

7374    p4     R       0:00     ps
```

The PID, TIME, and COMMAND columns are the same as those you already know about. (In the COMMAND column, the true name of the program is listed in parentheses if a dash or something is in the regular name.) The TT column lists a short form of the terminal name (pseudo-terminal 4, in this case). STAT lists the status of the process: R means that the process is running right now; anything else means that it isn't. Usually, you don't care unless you have a stuck process and you wonder whether it's sitting there waiting for you to type something (then its status is I or IW) or running off into the woods (then its status is R).

Adding the -u switch gives a user-oriented report, although perhaps they had a different kind of user than you and us in mind, as you might gather from the following example:

```
USER    PID   %CPU  %MEM  SZ    RSS   TT   STAT  START  TIME   COMMAND

john1   7375  0.0   0.9   196   436   p4   R     14:59  0:00   ps -u

john1   7335  0.0   0.6   196   316   p4   S     14:56  0:00   -tcsh
                                                                (tcsh)
```

The %CPU and %MEM columns list the percentage of the available central processor time and system memory the process has taken recently (these numbers are usually close to 0). RSS is Resident Set Size, a measure of how much memory the process is using right now, measured in thousands of bytes (abbreviated as K). The ps command, for example, takes 436K bytes (which is horrifying when you consider that the *entire* UNIX system used to fit into 64K total bytes). The START column lists the time of day the process began.

You can ask for a particular terminal's process list by using the -t option, as in this example:

```
ps -tp4
```

With the -t option, you have to use the same two-letter terminal abbreviation ps uses. Have fun guessing it. Try the two-letter abbreviations that appear in the TT column of the ps listing.

There are lots of other useless options for the BSD version of ps, including -l for a *long* technoid listing; -a for *all* processes, not just yours; and -x to show processes not using a terminal. There's no way to ask for all processes belonging to a particular user.

To see all the processes that you started, type the following incantation:

```
ps -aux | grep tracy
```

Replace Tracy's name with your own user name. This redirects the output of the ps command to the grep command (described in Chapter 8), which throws away all the lines except those that contain your user name.

Why cd isn't a process

People always ask us (well, someone asked once) why the cd command doesn't always act the way they expect it to. The problem is what is called in erudite circles *Lamarckian Heritability,* but what we call "you look like your mother."

When a parent process creates a child process, the child inherits many characteristics from its parent, such as the user name, the terminal, and (this is important) the current directory. The child, ungrateful for its heritage — as all children are — can change many of these things. Inheritance goes only one way, so changes in the child don't affect the parent. Suppose that you create a new process (type sh to start a new shell as the second process). Then go to some directory other than the one you were using, such as /tmp, by typing cd /tmp. Then type pwd to make sure that you are in /tmp. Leave the new shell by typing exit, and then type pwd back in the old shell to prove that you're back in the original directory.

This example proves that cd can't be a normal command executed in its own process. If it were, the new directory would apply only to that process. As soon as the process was finished, you would be back in the shell with the directory unchanged.

The authors of the various shells finessed this problem using what's technically known as a *kludge* (something that works but that you're not proud of; it rhymes with "huge," not with "fudge.") The kludge checks especially for the cd command and handles it itself in the shell. The exit and logout commands also are handled in the shell for the same reason.

Here's an example of where you may run into this: If you make a shell script (see Chapter 14) that contains a cd command, the cd affects only subsequent commands in that script. After your shell script has finished running, you find yourself back in the original directory as though the cd had never occurred. Although it's possible to write a script that does change the directory, it's so complicated that even wizards shrink from the task.

Starting Background Processes

Starting a background command is simplicity itself. You can run any program you want in the background: When you type the command, stick a space and an ampersand (&) at the end of the line just before you press Enter.

Suppose you want to use troff to print a file (even though we warned you not to use it). This is bound to take a long time, for example, so typing the ampersand to run it in the background is wise, as shown here:

```
troff a_really_large_file &
```

The shell starts the command and immediately comes back to ask you for another command. It prints a number, which is the *process ID* (or PID) assigned to the command you just started. (Some shells print a small number, which they call the *job number,* and a larger number, which is the PID.) If you know the PID, you can check up on your background program with the ps command. If you get tired of waiting for the background process, you can get rid of it with the kill command and the PID, as you will see in Chapter 24.

You can start as many programs simultaneously as you want in this way. In practice, you rarely want more than three or four. Because only one computer is switching back and forth among the various programs, the more simultaneous things you do, the slower each one runs.

When your background program finishes, the C, Korn, BASH, and SVR4 Bourne shells tell you that it's finished; older versions of the Bourne shell say nothing.

If you know that a program is going to take a long time (a program that crunches for a long time to produce a report, for example), you can use the nice command with that program. The nice command tells the program to run in a nice way so that it gets a smaller share of the computer than it would otherwise. The niced program takes longer to run, but other programs run faster, which is usually a good trade-off if the niced program was going to take a long time anyway. To use it, you just type nice followed by the command to run:

```
nice genreport Tuesday.raw &
```

You almost always use nice to run programs in the background, because it would take an inexplicably saintly user to want to slow down a program he or she was going to sit and wait for.

If you want to wait for background programs to finish, the wait command waits for you until they're all finished. If you become impatient, you can interrupt wait by pressing Ctrl+C (or Del, depending on your system). These keystrokes interrupt only the wait and leave the background processes unmolested.

The Magic of Job Control

Quite a while ago (in about 1979), people (actually, our pal Bill) noticed that, many times, you run a program, realize that it's going to take longer than you thought, and decide that you want to switch it to a background program. At the time, the only choices you had were to wait or to kill the program and start it over by using an & to run it in the background. Job control enables you to change your mind after you start a program.

The job-control business requires some cooperation from your shell. In SVR4, all three shells handle job control. In some earlier versions of UNIX, only the C shell, or sometimes the C shell and Korn shell, handled job control.

Suppose that you start a big, slow program by typing the following line:

```
bigslowprogram somefile anotherfile
```

The program runs in the foreground because you didn't use an ampersand (&). Then you realize that you have better things to do than wait, so you press Ctrl+Z. The shell should respond with the message Stopped. (If it doesn't, you don't have a job-control shell. Sorry. Skip the rest of this chapter.) At this point, your program is in limbo. You can do three things to it:

- ✔ You can continue it in the foreground as though nothing had happened, by typing fg (which stands for *f*oreground).
- ✔ You can stick it in the background by typing bg (for *b*ackground), which makes the program act as though you started it with an & in the first place.
- ✔ You can kill it if you decide that you shouldn't have run it at all. This method is slightly more complicated. Details follow.

Take this job and . . .

UNIX calls every background program you start a *job*. A job can consist of several processes (which, as you know, are running programs). To print a list of all your files in all your directories with titles, for example, you can type this line:

```
ls -lR | pr -h "My files" | lp &
```

This command lists the files with ls, adds titles with pr, and sends the mess to the printer with lp, all in the background. Although you use three different programs and three separate processes, UNIX considers it one job, because each of the three programs needs the other two in order to get work done.

Every regular command (those you issue without an &) is also a job, although, until you use Ctrl+Z to stop it, that's not a very interesting piece of information. You can use the jobs command to see which jobs are active. Here's a typical response to the jobs command:

```
[1]     - Stopped (signal) elm

[2]     + Stopped     vi somefile
```

This listing shows two jobs, both of which have been stopped with Ctrl+Z. One is a copy of elm, the mail-reading program; the other job is the vi editor. (The difference between Stopped (signal) and plain Stopped is interesting only to programmers, so we don't discuss it much.) One job is considered the *current job* — the one preceded by a plus sign (+); it's the one most recently started or stopped. All the rest are regular background jobs, and they can be stopped or running.

. . . Stick it in the background

You can tell any stopped job to continue in the background by using the bg command. A plain bg continues the current job (the one marked by a plus sign) in the background. To tell UNIX to continue some other job, you must identify the job. You identify a job by typing a percent sign (%) followed either by the job number reported by jobs or by enough of the command to uniquely identify it. In this case, the elm job can be called %1, %elm, or %e, because no other job used a command starting with an *e*. As a special case, %% refers to the current job. Some other % combinations are available, but no one uses them. Typing bg %e, for example, continues the elm job in the background.

. . . Run it in a window in the foreground

To put a process in the foreground, where it runs normally and can use the terminal, you use the fg command. Continuing a job in the foreground is such a common thing that you can use a shortcut: You just type the percent sign and the job identifier. Typing %1 or %e, for example, continues the elm job in the foreground. Typing %v or %%, however, continues the vi editor in the foreground.

. . . Shove it

To get rid of a stopped or background job, use the kill command with the job identifier or (if it's easier, for some reason) the PID. You can get rid of the vi editor job by typing this line:

```
kill %v
```

Typically, you start a job, realize that it will take longer than you want to wait, press Ctrl+Z to stop it, and then type bg to continue that process in the background.

Alternatively, you interrupt a program by pressing Ctrl+Z, run a second program, and, when the second program is finished, type fg or %% to continue the original program.

You don't often `kill` a program, but it's nice to know that you can put a nasty program to sleep for good. Chapter 24 talks more about it.

What happens when two programs try to use the terminal?

Suppose that a program running in the background tries to read some input from your terminal. Severe confusion can result (and did, in pre-job-control versions of UNIX) if both the background program and a foreground program — or even worse, two or three background programs — try to read at the same time. Which one gets the stuff you type? Early versions of UNIX did the worst possible thing: A gremlin inside the computer flipped a coin to decide who got each line of input. That was not very satisfactory.

With the advent of job control, UNIX enforced a new rule: Background jobs can't read from the terminal. If one tries, it stops, much as though you had pressed Ctrl+Z. Suppose that you try to run the `ed` editor in the background by using the following command:

```
ed some.file &
```

UNIX responds:

```
[1]    + Stopped (tty input)     ed
```

As soon as `ed` started and wanted to see whether you were typing anything it should know about, the job stopped. You can continue `ed` as a foreground program by typing `fg` or `%%` if you want to type something for `ed`. You can kill it (which is all that `ed` deserves) by typing `kill %%`.

Full-screen programs and job control

Programs that take over the entire screen, notably the `vi` and `emacs` editors and mail programs such as `elm`, treat the Ctrl+Z interrupt in a slightly different way. Just stopping the program and starting it again later isn't adequate; the screen would show the results of what you did in the meantime. To solve this problem, full-screen programs make arrangements with UNIX to be notified when you press Ctrl+Z, and again when you continue them so that they can do something appropriate, such as redraw the screen when you continue. This process generally is all automatic and obvious, although people occasionally are confused when the screen is magically returned after they give the `fg` command.

Chapter 14

Linux Taming — The Reluctant System Administrator

In This Chapter

▶ A few basics for the reluctant system administrator

▶ How is a Linux system structured?

▶ Where to get help

*Y*eah, we know it's pronounced linn-ux or leen-ux, not line-ux, but it still needs taming, and if you look around the office and find nobody but yourself to fix things, you're the Linux tamer.

Congratulations! You're a System Administrator!

Using Linux is no different from using any other UNIX, as long as it's on someone else's computer, and they have set you up with an account. But when it's *your* computer that's running Linux, and *you* are responsible for maintaining it, then things become a lot more complicated. There is no way to teach all the complexities of UNIX system administration in a book like this. But we can describe a few key points to get you started.

Running Linux, by Welsh and Kaufman (published by O'Reilly & Associates), has most of the information you need to *really* administer a Linux system. Also, the World Wide Web is awash in sites devoted to Linux. A good place to start is the Linux home page at http://www.linux.org/. (See Chapter 18 for more information on the World Wide Web if you're uncertain what this means.)

The root of all UNIX

UNIX is a multiuser world: Lots of people can use the computer at the same time, by connecting from remote locations. The first thing you need to know about administering a Linux system is the difference between the user called *root* and every other user. Root (also grandly called the *superuser*) is the system administrator. This account has all the privileges to change things on the system. If you want to add users, install some software, or even turn off the computer, you must be logged in as root. If you're logged in as someone other than root, and you try to do anything related to system administration, you find your computer responding with a barrage of "permission denied" messages. It's nothing personal, really. It's just the computer's way of telling you that in a multiuser environment, it doesn't want just *anyone* messing around with it — only the one person it trusts, which is root.

Fine, you say. I'll just log in as root all the time, and not have to worry about running into those pesky permission problems. Bad idea! Using the root account to do non-system-administration tasks is dangerous, because sometime — eventually, when you least expect it — you will type a command that you really didn't want to — oh, say, deleting all the files on the hard disk (it happens more frequently than you might think). If you're logged in as someone other than root, the computer will reply with a simple "permission denied." If you're root, though, the damage is done, and UNIX does not have an "undelete" command! Remember: permissions are your friends!

Adding a user

Assuming you're convinced about not logging in as root unless you really must, you'll need to add a user account for yourself (or for others) to use for everyday tasks. Say you want to create the user name "bobbyjoe" for yourself. To add this user, log in as root (because adding users is one of those special, privileged tasks that only root can perform) and type the command `adduser bobbyjoe`. The computer creates the new user, and then reminds you to set the password for the new user. You add the password by typing `passwd bobbyjoe`. Then enter the password when the computer asks for it (it will ask you to enter it twice, just to make sure that you typed it in correctly).

How do I turn this thing off?

UNIX is very sensitive to impolite treatment on the part of the operator. If you just log out and turn the machine off with the power switch, it will remind you of this rude treatment with a flood of error messages when you next restart the computer. To turn the machine off, you first must execute the `shutdown` command. While logged in as root, enter the command `shutdown now` to turn the machine off gracefully. If other users are logged in and you want to give them some warning, you can type in the number of minutes until shutdown: `shutdown +10`, for example, waits 10 minutes before shutting down and warns any users that are logged in. To reboot the computer, `shutdown -r now` (-r for reboot) shuts down the machine and then restarts it. Some Linux systems also let the "three-finger salute" (Ctrl+Alt+Del, familiar to DOS and Windows users) serve as a shortcut for `shutdown -r now`.

A Trio of Linuxes

Complete Linux systems are packaged into "distributions," which don't really describe how Linux is distributed, but rather how the operating system and the GNU programs are bundled together. Three distributions are in common use: Slackware, Red Hat, and Debian. All three are available for free via the Internet or for a small charge on CD-ROM. As a user, it doesn't really matter which distribution you use, because they all behave pretty much the same way. As a system administrator, though, there are important differences among the distributions that you should consider.

Slackware is the oldest of the three, and has been around since the beginning of Linux. It is the most "traditional" distribution (traditional in UNIX sense, as in not particularly user-friendly), and has little in the way of utilities to facilitate the management of a Linux system. For this reason, it tends to be favored by those who have been around UNIX systems for a while. Red Hat Linux is fast becoming the most popular distribution. It features plenty of tools to make the life of the system administrator easier, most notably the Red Hat Package Manager (RPM), which eases the installation, upgrade, and deletion of software packages, and even the operating system itself. The Debian distribution, like Red Hat, also provides an interface that eases the task of the system administrator. Although it is currently not as popular as Slackware or Red Hat, its popularity is growing quickly. If you really enjoy editing lots of configuration files and moving them around "by hand," the old-fashioned way (believe it or not, there are some people like that), then you should go with Slackware. Everyone else will find life easier with Red Hat or Debian.

I Need Help!

What happens when there's a problem with Linux? (It has been known to happen.) Unlike other operating systems, there is no technical support hot line to call when things go wrong. There *is* a huge base of Linux users around the world, though, most of whom have access to the Internet. Usenet is the best place to find help on Linux (see Chapter 19). For someone accustomed to calling a commercial entity on the phone for tech support, the idea of posting questions on Usenet may seem foreign, even hopelessly naive. Generally, though, questions are read by so many thousands of people that the odds are overwhelming that someone familiar with your problem will read the question and respond, usually within a day or so. (In fact, many people claim that Usenet-based support is faster and more reliable than some technical support hot lines!) So far, the Linux community as a group still maintains an attitude of "we're all in this together," and the Usenet support system has mostly worked. The Linux groups tend to be some of the most active computer groups on all of Usenet. They are listed at the end of Chapter 27.

Linux goes commercial

The freely available, "alternative" image of Linux discouraged commercial enterprises from adopting Linux in its early days. Understandably, many companies did not want to deal with an operating system that did not have a corporate entity standing behind it, no matter how reliable or trouble-free the product. To fill this need, two companies have stepped in to provide commercial support for Linux. Red Hat Software, Inc. provides a commercial version of its Linux distribution, in addition to the free version. This means that organizations that purchase the commercial Red Hat distribution can turn to Red Hat for support instead of (or in addition to) Usenet. Another company, Caldera, Inc., also provides support for commercial users. Purchasers of Caldera's Linux package get user support from Caldera, as well as some additional commercial software packages that Caldera includes. The Caldera package is based on the Red Hat distribution.

Chapter 15

The Windows-to-UNIX Rosetta Stone

- -

In This Chapter

▶ The UNIX programs that do the same things as the Windows programs you wish that you could use

- -

*F*or those of you who have used Windows, this chapter provides a map to steer you from your favorite Windows programs to the equivalent (sort of) UNIX commands. For those of you who have stayed far away from Windows, skip this chapter.

For each commonly used Windows program, we explain how to get UNIX to do the same thing, more or less. Unless we indicate otherwise, we're talking about Windows 95, by the way. In the Windows descriptions, we tell you what Windows program we are referring to (Windows Explorer, My Computer, or whatever), and we may list specific commands. When we do, a ⇨ means that you are choosing a command from a menu. For example, File⇨Exit means that you choose the File menu, and then you choose the Exit command from the File menu that appears.

The Most Important Differences

Slashes! You know how you finally learned to type backslashes (\) in Windows pathnames? It's time to flip them all around, because UNIX uses regular slashes (/) in its pathnames instead. This difference takes months of getting used to, but there's no way around it.

On the other hand, it surely is nice that filenames can be longer in UNIX than they could be in Windows 3.1. Windows 95 finally approaches UNIX filenames by allowing long names, too. You're not limited to eight little characters with a three-letter extension. Go nuts with your filenames. Name your next file in the following way:

```
terrific.file.name.possible.in.UNIX
```

Although we are talking about filenames, remember that, even though Windows doesn't care about capitalization, UNIX does. In UNIX, uppercase and lowercase letters are considered different letters, so be consistent and don't mix them up.

System Maintenance

Windows 95 (and 3.1) come with a bunch of programs you use for keeping track of your computer, printer, screen, and files. UNIX does, too — except you use a lot more different commands in UNIX.

Windows Explorer and My Computer

For Windows 3.1 users, we're talking about File Manager. Windows Explorer and My Computer let you copy, delete, and rename files and folders. In UNIX, you use the following commands:

- cp to copy files
- rm to delete files
- mv to rename files or directories or move them to other directories
- mkdir to create directories
- rmdir to delete directories

See Chapters 5 and 6 for details on how to carry out these common tasks.

Control Panel

The Control Panel is where you tell Windows 95 about new hardware, install new software, or change many of the settings for Windows 95 itself.

UNIX systems are resolutely unhelpful in that regard. User names are in /etc/passwd. Software you've installed tends to be in /usr/local/bin and /usr/local/lib. Hardware drivers are hidden away in some place specific to the version of UNIX you're using. Fortunately, most versions of UNIX come pre-configured with drivers for all the commonly used hardware, so you don't have to worry about it. Much.

ScanDisk and Disk Defragmenter

The Windows 95 ScanDisk program checks the current disk for logical problems. Its Disk Defragmenter program rearranges files on the disk to speed up access.

On UNIX, unless you are the system administrator, you should try not to think about the possibility of your disk having logical problems. To find out how much space is free on your disk, type the following command:

```
df
```

This command shows the free space on all disks (see the section "What's NFS?" in Chapter 21), so you have to figure out which disk is yours by looking for the one that matches the beginning of your home directory name (the one that pwd displays).

You can also type the following command to find out how much space your files use:

```
du
```

The du command (for *d*isk *u*sage) reports the amount of space used by the files in each directory and subdirectory. (If a directory has subdirectories, the space used in the subdirectories is included in the amount for the directory.)

If your disk really is screwed up, the disk fixing program is called fsck.

Help

We mean the Help command on the Start menu in Windows 95. Most versions of UNIX don't have a help command, but all have a man command that you can use to see a sometimes incomprehensible online manual. See Chapter 27 for further explanation.

Batch files

If you remember how to use DOS (the system that runs underneath the surface of Windows), you may remember how to make *batch files,* text files that contain a list of DOS commands, one per line. To run the list of commands, you run the batch file.

You can use similar things, called *shell scripts,* in UNIX. Amazingly, a UNIX shell script is a text file that contains a series of UNIX commands, one per line. In DOS, batch files have names that end with the BAT extension. In UNIX, you can name a shell script anything you want. See Chapter 12 for some hints about writing shell scripts.

In DOS, if you have a batch file named AUTOEXEC.BAT in the root directory of the disk you load DOS from, DOS runs that batch file automatically whenever you start DOS (that is, whenever you start or restart the computer). UNIX has a similar shell script.

If you are using the Bourne, Korn, or BASH shell and have a file called .profile in your home directory, this file is executed automatically whenever you log in. The C shell equivalent file is .login. You can edit these files with a text editor. Your system administrator probably already has given you a .profile or .login file full of stuff to set up your local environment. Don't take anything out without consulting your system administrator. If you want to add commands, add them at the end of the file.

The DOS CONFIG.SYS file contains information about your hardware and software configuration. When you turn on your computer, after it loads DOS but before it runs the AUTOEXEC.BAT file, the system looks in this file to configure DOS for your system.

UNIX configuration is entirely different and, in most cases, is not your problem. In most cases, UNIX systems automatically adapt themselves to whatever hardware is attached to the computer (pretty advanced concept, eh?).

Shut Down

Before you turn off a computer running Windows 95, you have to choose Start⇨Shut Down from the Task bar. In UNIX, you also need to warn the computer that you are planning to turn it off.

The best idea is never to turn your computer off — most UNIX users leave their computers on all the time.

If you must turn your computer off, use the shutdown or halt command.

Application Programs

An *application program* is a program that actually gets some useful work done, like writing documents, sorting mailing lists, or playing Minesweeper.

Netscape and Internet Explorer

Good news for you Web enthusiasts! The Netscape Navigator Web browser is available for UNIX, too, if you've got a windowing system. Otherwise, forget about graphics and check out Lynx. See Chapter 18 to learn more about both Lynx and Netscape.

You may also use Netscape (or Internet News or Free Agent) for reading Usenet newsgroups. In UNIX, you can use one of a number of powerful (if ugly) newsreaders, including trn, nn, and tin. See Chapter 19 for a discussion of newsgroups.

Eudora, Microsoft Exchange, and other e-mail programs

UNIX has a number of e-mail programs, too. We recommend Pine, although elm is good, too. Take a look at Chapter 17 for details.

Microsoft Word, WordPerfect, and Lotus Word Pro

If you use WordPerfect, you're in luck — versions of WordPerfect run under UNIX, too. WordPerfect for UNIX is the closest thing to a Windows-style word processor you're going to find. If you just need to push some words around, consider using a text editor, such as pico, emacs, or vi (again, see Chapter 10). If you want to make beautiful documents, there's the groff text formatter (mentioned in Chapter 9), but it has what's known as a steep learning curve, so we'd stay away from it unless you have a groff wizard handy to help you out. (groff and its predecessor, troff, are quite powerful — enough so that we've published entire books by using them.)

Microsoft Excel and Lotus 1-2-3

There are a couple of respectable UNIX spreadsheets called sc and oleo (the latter allegedly having less fat than the leading spread.) Both are freeware, so your system manager can install them easily enough, but neither is a drop-in replacement for Excel or 1-2-3.

Microsoft Schedule, Microsoft Outlook, and other personal information managers

A Personal Information Manager (PIM) includes a calendar with which you can schedule appointments, an address book, and a list of things to do. There are lots of them for Windows.

In UNIX, things are simpler. You can put your appointments in your calendar file, and UNIX will remind you of your daily activities each morning (see Chapter 11). For anything else, UNIX users tend to use plain old text files, which they search with the simple but extremely fast and powerful search program grep (mentioned in Chapter 8).

Paint, Paintbrush, Paint Shop Pro, and other graphics editors

These programs let you view, edit, and create pictures stored in various graphics formats. In UNIX, the popular xv program offers image viewing under Motif and other X Window GUIs, as well as limited image editing.

Freecell, Hearts, Minesweeper, and Solitaire

UNIX is the home of one of the most popular games of all time: rogue. It's the classic multi-level dungeon program, and even though its graphics are feeble, people have wasted months or years mastering it. Most windowing systems also come with xsol, Solitaire, and mille, a version of Parker Brothers' Mille Bornes card game, which we've found quite adequate for time wasting.

Zillions of other UNIX-based games are available, but we'll do your boss a favor and not tell you about them.

Part IV
UNIX and the Net

In this part . . .

Most computers that run UNIX are connected to other computers. Many are parts of office-wide networks, many have telephone connections to UNIX systems in other places, and an increasing number are connected to the biggest network of all: the Internet.

This part of the book reveals how to use your UNIX system to send and receive e-mail, browse the World Wide Web, read articles in Usenet newsgroups, transfer files, and log into other computers over the Internet.

Chapter 16

Who's Out There?

In This Chapter

▶ Find out who else is using your computer

▶ Communicate with them

rom the beginning, UNIX was designed as a multiuser system. In the early years of UNIX computing, it was considered greedy to keep to yourself an entire PDP-11/45 (a 1972 vintage minicomputer about the speed of a PC AT but the size of a trash compactor). It was also kind of expensive. These days, the cost argument is much less compelling — unless your computer is a Cray supercomputer or the like — but UNIX remains multiuser partly because it always was and partly because multiuser systems make it easier to share programs and data.

Even if you have your own workstation but are attached to a network, your machine is potentially multiuser, because other people can log in to your machine over the net (as we technoids call a network). (On the other hand, you can log in to their machines, too. See Chapters 19 and 20 for details.)

Of course, in this day and age, all anyone ever talks about is the Internet. If your computer is attached to the Internet, there are literally millions of computers that you can talk to.

In this chapter, you see how you can nose around and find out who's on your system and on other systems on the network. Then you can look into getting in touch with them.

If you are the only person who ever uses your computer and you don't have a network or a phone line (your computer is all alone in the world), skip this chapter — in fact, skip this entire part of the book.

Finding Out Who's on Your Computer

There are two main commands you can use to find out who's using your machine: who and finger. The simple way to use either one is just to type who.

The typical response is something like the following:

```
root        console     Dec 29  20:16
john1       vt01        Dec 21  15:19
john1       ttyp2       Jan 6   16:36
john1       ttyp1       Jan 6   17:20
john1       ttyp0       Jan 6   16:36
```

You see the user, the terminal, and the login time. User `john1` is logged in five times because he has a bunch of X terminal windows, each of which counts as a login session. The exact output from `who` varies from one version of UNIX to another, but it always contains at least this much. You can also type `who am i`, and UNIX prints just the line for the terminal (or terminal window) in which you typed the command.

A considerably more informative program is `finger`, because it produces a more useful report than `who` does, as shown in the following:

```
Login   Name                TTY  Idle   When        Office
root    0000-Admin(0000)    co   1:11   Tue 20:16
john1   John R. Levine      vt   1:11   Mon 15:19   x3712
john1   John R. Levine      vt   1:35   Tue 16:47   x3712
john1   John R. Levine      p2   1:11   Wed 16:36   x3712
john1   John R. Levine      p1          Wed 17:20   x3712
john1   John R. Levine      p0          Wed 16:36   x3712
```

Although `finger` reports the same stuff as `who` does, it also looks up the user's real name (if it's in the user password file) and tells you how long the terminal has been idle (how long it's been since the user last typed something). If the system adminstrator has entered the information, it also usually gives an office phone number, room number, or other handy info about where the user works.

You can also use `finger` to ask about a specific user, and UNIX looks up some extra info about that user. Here, we used it to look up one of the authors, as follows:

```
finger john1
```

UNIX returned the following information:

```
Login name: johnl     In real life: John R. Levine
Directory: /usr/johnl  Shell: /bin/sh
On since Dec 21 15:19:45 on vt01 1 hour 27 minutes Idle Time
Project: Working on "UNIX for Dummies, 3rd Ed."
Plan:      Write many books, become famous.
```

The Project and Plan lines are merely the contents of files called .project and .plan in the login directory. (Yes, the filenames start with periods.) It has become customary to put a clever remark in your .plan file, but please don't overdo it. If the user is logged in on more than one terminal or terminal window, finger gives a full report for each terminal. The finger johnl command we gave, in fact, reported five times — one for each login — but we edited it to save paper.

Finding Out Who's on Other Computers

If your machine is on a network, you can use rwho and finger to find out about other machines. You type the system name you want to check up on after an @ (at sign). (Chapter 17 has more information about system names.) We can check a nearby system, as in the following example:

```
finger @spdcc
```

The spdcc machine turns out to be not very busy, as shown here:

```
[spdcc.com]
Login  Name            TTY  Idle  When       Office
uucp   Uucp Daemon     02         Wed 20:13
johnl  John R. Levine  03         Wed 20:44  Rm 418
dyer   Steve Dyer      p0   1     Wed 08:13
```

You can also ask about an individual by putting that user's name in front of the @, as follows:

```
finger johnl@spdcc
```

This command gives the same sort of report as a local `finger` does:

```
[spdcc.com]
Login name: johnl    In real life: John R. Levine
Directory: /var/users/johnl   Shell: /bin/csh
On since Jan 6 9:22:45 on tty02     2 minutes Idle Time
Plan: no plan
```

If you're on the Internet, you can finger any machine on the Internet. Because there's no rule that says machines must answer when you call, however, in many cases, you get a "connection refused" response or no response.

Some systems at universities have set up `finger` to return user-directory information. Suppose that you ask who's at MIT, as follows:

```
finger @mit.edu
```

You get an introduction to the MIT on-line directory, such as the following:

```
[mit.edu]
Student data loaded as of Dec 15, Staff data loaded
as of Dec 19. Notify the Registrar or Personnel as
appropriate to change your information.

Our on-line help system describes

How to change data, how the directory works,
where to get more info.

For a listing of help topics, enter finger help@mit.edu.
Try finger help_about@mit.edu to read about how the di-
rectory works. Please see help_url@mit.edu for questions
about the new URL field.
```

You can try to finger a particular individual at MIT, too, as shown here:

```
finger chomsky@mit.edu
```

Now you can see the public data on that individual:

```
[mit.edu]
... There was 1 match to your request.    name:
Chomsky, Noam A
email: CHOMSKY@MIT.EDU
```

```
phone: (617) 555-7819
address: ZZZ-219
department: Linguistics & Philos
title: Linguistics, Institute Professor
alias: N-chomsky
```

You can engage in wholesale nosiness by using rwho. This command attempts to compile a list of all the people using all the machines in the local network.

Chatting with Other People on Your Computer

After you figure out who is on your computer, you may want to send them a message. There are two general schools of message sending. The first is the real-time school, in which the message appears on the other user's screen while you wait, presumably because it's an extremely urgent message. The write and talk commands enable you to do that. Excessive use of real-time messages is a good way to make enemies quickly, however, because you interrupt people's work all over the place.

The second school is electronic mail, or e-mail, in which you send a message the other user looks at when it's convenient. E-mail is a large topic in its own right, so we're saving that for Chapter 17.

Real-time terminal communication has been likened to talking to someone on the moon, because it's so slow: It's limited by the speed at which people type. Here on Earth, most of us have telephones, so the most sensible thing to do is to send a one-line message asking the other user to call you on the phone.

The simpler real-time communications command is write. If someone writes to you, you see something like the following on your screen:

```
Message from johnl on iecc (ttyp1) [ Wed Jan 6
20:28:42 ] ...
Please call me at extension 8649
<EOT>
```

Usually the message appears in the middle of an editor session and scrambles the file on your screen. You will be relieved to know that the scrambling is limited to the screen — the editor has no idea that someone is writing to you. The file is okay.

In either `vi` or `emacs`, you can tell the editor to redraw what's supposed to be on-screen by pressing Ctrl+L. (If you're in input mode in `vi`, press Esc first.)

To write to a user, use the `write` command and give the name of the user to whom you want to talk, as follows:

```
write dguertin
```

After you press Enter, `write` tells you absolutely nothing, which means that it is waiting for your message. Type the message, which can be as many lines long as you want. When you are finished, press Ctrl+D (the general end-of-input character) or the interrupt character, usually Ctrl+C or Delete. `write` copies every line to the other user's screen as you press Enter, so reading a long message sent by way of the `write` command is sort of like reading a poem on old Burma-Shave signs as you drive by each one.

You want to send an important message, so you type these lines:

```
write dguertin
Yo, Dave, turn on your radio. WBUR is rebroadcasting
Terry Gross's interview with Nancy Reagan!
```

You press Enter at the end of each line. After the last line, you press Ctrl+D.

I'm talking — where are you?

Sometimes `write` tells you that the user is logged in on several logical terminals, as in the following example:

```
dguertin is logged on more than one place.
You are connected to "vt01".
Other locations are:
ttyp1
ttyp0
ttyp2
```

The `write` command is pretty dumb. If the person you are writing to is logged in on more than one terminal — or, more typically, is using many windows in X — `write` picks one of them at random and writes there. You can be virtually certain that the window or terminal `write` chooses is not the one the user is viewing at the time. To maximize the chances that the user sees your message, use the `finger` command to figure out which terminal is the most active (the one with the lowest idle time) and write to that window. Remember the results of the `finger` command, for example, from a few pages back:

```
Login      Name                TTY Idle  When       Office
root       0000-Admin(0000)    co  1:11  Tue 20:16
dguertin   David S. Guertin    vt  1:11  Mon 15:19
```

The best candidates to send a message to are `ttyp1` and `ttyp0`. (The `finger` command cuts out the `tty` from terminal names.)

To write to a specific terminal, give `write` the terminal name after the user name, as follows:

```
write dguertin ttyp1
```

If you are writing back to a user who just wrote to you, you should use the terminal name that was sent in the user's `write` message. (In this case, it was also `ttyp1`.)

Can we talk?

You can have a somewhat spiffier conversation with the `talk` command, which allows simultaneous two-way typing. You use it the same way you use `write`, as in the following example:

```
talk margy
```

The other user sees something like this:

```
        Message from Talk_Daemon@iecc at 20:47 ...
        talk: connection requested by john1@IECC
        talk: respond with: talk john1@IECC
```

If someone tries to talk to you and you're interested in responding, type the `talk` command it suggests. If you're in the middle of a text editor or other program, you must exit to the shell first.

While `talk` is running, it splits your screen and arranges things so that what you type appears in the top half and what the other user types appears in the bottom half. Unlike `write`, `talk` immediately passes what you type — without waiting for an Enter — which means that you can see all the other user's typing mistakes and vice versa. Exit by pressing Ctrl+D.

Chatting with Other People on Other Computers

The `talk` command is designed to talk to users on other computers. If the other computer is a long way away, typing rather than talking can make sense. As the Internet stretches around the world, you may find yourself "talking" with someone for whom English is not a native language. In that case, typing can be faster than trying to understand someone with a strong accent across a noisy phone connection.

Computers have *machine names* (more on this in Chapters 20 and 21). To talk to someone on another computer, give `talk` the user name and machine name:

```
talk zac@greattapes.com
```

After you're connected, `talk` works just like talking to a local user, except that sometimes it can take several seconds for characters to get from one machine to another on an intercontinental link.

If you want to talk to a lot of other people, use a system called Internet Relay Chat (IRC). You can read about it on our Web site at the following address:

```
http://net.dummies.net/irc
```

If you don't know how to read a Web site, see Chapter 18.

Reading the Writing on the Wall

A program called `wall` blats what you type to every single terminal and window on your entire computer. You use it much like `write`, as shown here:

```
wall
Free pizza in the upstairs conference room in 5 minutes!
```

As with `write`, you tell `wall` that you're finished by pressing Ctrl+D. Be sparing in your use of `wall` unless you want a bunch of new enemies.

`wall` affects the people who use your computer, not everyone on your network.

Chapter 17
Automating Your Office Gossip

● ●

In This Chapter
▶ What is e-mail?

▶ What are e-mail addresses?

▶ Where is your mailbox?

▶ How to use the Pine program

▶ How to use the `elm` program

▶ How to use the `mail` program

▶ How to use Netscape to read your mail

▶ How to organize your mail into neat piles

● ●

*E*lectronic mail (or *e-mail*) is the high-tech way to automate interoffice chatter, gossip, and innuendo. Using e-mail, you can quickly and efficiently circulate memos and other written information to your coworkers, including directions to the beer bash this Saturday and the latest Dave Barry column. You can even send and receive e-mail from people outside your organization, if you and they use networked computers.

If your organization uses e-mail, you probably already have some. In fact, there may be vitally important but unread mail waiting in your mailbox at this very moment. Probably not, but who knows? You can tell whether unread messages are in your mailbox because UNIX displays this message when you log in:

```
You have mail.
```

What You Need in Order to Use E-Mail

Any UNIX system handles e-mail for users on that system. To exchange e-mail with the outside world, your computer must be on a network — or at least have a phone line and a modem. You definitely don't want to know how to set up a mail network or make connections to other computers — if your computer doesn't already have e-mail on it, it's time to talk to a UNIX wizard.

In the great tradition of UNIX standardization, there are about 14 different mail-sending-and-receiving programs. (Fortunately, they can all exchange mail with each other.) To find out whether your computer can do e-mail, try using the simple `mail` program to see whether you have any mail waiting. Just type this line:

```
mail
```

UNIX says `No mail` if no mail is waiting, or it blats a copy of the first unread message onto your screen. In the latter case, if you don't want to read your mail right now, type x (for exit) and press Enter to get out. We talk more about reading your mail later in this chapter.

Addressing the Mail

E-mail, like regular mail (usually referred to by e-mail advocates as *snail-mail*) needs an address, usually called a *net address* or *e-mail address*. To send mail to a person, you send it to his or her user name. (See Chapter 1 for information about logging in with a user name.) If the other user uses a different computer than the one you use, the mail system has to know which computer the other person is on — and the address becomes more complicated.

Sending mail to people on your computer

For people who use the very same computer you do (that is, you both use terminals connected to the same computer running UNIX), the mail address is just their user name. If you enter `georgew` for your user name, that's your mail address, too. Make sure that you don't use uppercase letters in the mail address unless the user name also does.

Sending mail to people on other computers

You can send mail to people who use other computers if your computer is connected to their computer on a network. For people who use other computers, you send mail by telling the mail system which computer they use.

Computers have names, too, you know. They sometimes have boring names that indicate what they are used for, such as `marketing` or `corpacctg`. Sometimes all the computers in an organization are named according to a more interesting scheme, such as naming them all after fish, spices, or cartoon characters. It's traditional in UNIX networks to give the computers tasteful yet memorable names. One company we worked for had computers named haddock, cod, and flounder. The next company used basil, chervil, dill, fennel, and ginger. At Internet for Dummies Central, they're called chico, astrud, xuxa, tom, and ivan, after some of our favorite Brazilian singers.

When you are writing to someone on another computer on your network, include the computer name in the mail address by using an at sign (@) to indicate where they are "at." If your friend Nancy, for example, has the user name nancyb and uses a computer named ginger, her mail address is nancyb@ginger.

A skillful system administrator can automatically note which computer each user in an organization uses. With luck, you can merely send mail by user name, and the system automatically figures out which computer to send it to.

If you have trouble with addresses, the easiest way to send a message to someone is to wait until that someone sends a message to you and then reply to it. All mail programs have a command (usually r) that replies to the message you just read. Messages almost always have return addresses, and the r command enables you to send a message without typing an address.

Sending mail to people "out there"

If your computer network has phone connections to the outside world, you can probably also send mail to people out in the wide world of The Internet: the invisible network of UNIX and other computers that extends worldwide. Check with your system administrator or other e-mail users to find out if your organization is "on the Net" (connected to the outside world).

To correspond with people on the outside, you need an Internet address for the person you want to send mail to. After you have it, type it in *exactly* the way she wrote it. Internet addresses tend to look like the following:

        ellenz@persimmon.abc.com

The part in front of the @ is the person's user name. The rest of the address is the name of the computer and other information about where the computer is, usually the name of the company. The computer name, company name, and so on are connected by periods. The last three letters frequently tell you what kind of organization it is: com is for companies, for example, and edu is for educational institutions. Sometimes the parts of the address spell out the city, state, and country where the computer is located. It's all very well organized, really.

If your computer is on the Internet, you can also exchange mail with users of commercial services, such as CompuServe and America Online (AOL). For details, see the sidebar about sending mail to on-line services.

When you are typing Internet addresses, keep these points in mind:

✔ Be sure that you don't type any spaces in the middle of the address. There are no spaces in user names or computer names, or on either side of the @ or a period.

✔ Don't capitalize anything unnecessarily. Check the capitalization of the person's user name and computer name. Most addresses are entirely in small letters.

✔ Don't forget the periods that separate the parts of an Internet address.

If your computer is on the Internet and you want to try out network mail, send a message to the authors of this book, at `unix3@gurus.com`, and tell us what you think of the book. Our computer will send you an automatic reply, and we'll read your message, too. (If you can get that address right, you're already halfway to being a mail wizard.)

It's dead, Jim

If you get an address wrong, you will usually get the message back within a few hours (for mail on your own computer or your own network), or a few days (for mail that has bounced around the Internet). The dead letter usually has all kinds of cryptic automated error messages in it, but the gist is clear — the message wasn't delivered. Check the address and try again. Generally, the safest way to address a message is to reply to someone else's message.

Sending Stuff Other than Text

These days, e-mail is getting to be such a widespread thing that you may want to send things other than plain old short text messages. For example, we e-mailed most of the chapters in this book as Microsoft Word documents to our long-suffering editor. Most mail programs now have commands for attaching files to e-mail messages, or at least including text files in messages.

If you want to send a text file by e-mail, just include the text file as part of your message. Note, however, that UNIX e-mail was designed for sending text, not for sending programs, graphics, or formatted word processing files.

Sending mail to people who use on-line services

You can send mail to people who don't use UNIX computers. By using the Internet, you can usually send mail to anyone who uses CompuServe, MCI Mail, and other services.

To send mail to a CompuServe user, do the following:

✔ Find out his or her CompuServe user ID. It is a nine- or ten-digit number with a comma somewhere in the middle, such as 71234,5678. Most CompuServe user IDs begin with a 7, for reasons we don't claim to understand. Probably because of its mystical significance.

✔ For purposes of sending mail from UNIX, replace the comma in the CompuServe user ID with a period, as in 71234.5678. Because Internet addresses aren't allowed to contain commas, you have to do this.

✔ Tack @compuserve.com to the end of the number and, voilà! — you have the person's Internet address, as in the following example:

71234.5678@compuserve.com

To send mail to an America Online (AOL) user, you do more or less the same thing as for a CompuServe user:

✔ Find out the AOL screen name, such as Steve Case.

✔ Take out any spaces and tack @aol.com to the end of the number. Voilà! — you have the person's Internet address, as shown here:

stevecase@aol.com

For users of Prodigy Classic, use the Prodigy username followed by @prodigy.com, as in the following:

XYZ666Q@prodigy.com

For users of Prodigy Internet, use the Prodigy username followed by @prodigy.net, as in the following example:

furdle@prodigy.net

Luckily, several ways of cheating have been developed, so that the e-mail system doesn't realize that e-mail messages actually contain stuff other than text. The two most widely used methods are:

✔ Uuencoding, which involves using a uuencoding program to convert the file to text and a uudecoding program to convert the text back to the original file. We described uuencoding a bit in Chapter 15, section "Sneaky you-you."

✔ MIME (*M*ultipurpose *I*nternet *M*ail *E*xtensions), which is much easier to use than uuencoding, because many newer mail programs handle it automatically.

When we describe mail programs, we tell you whether they work with MIME. All UNIX mail programs work with uuencoding, because *you* have to do the work.

Before sending a file using a uuencoded or MIME attachment, you might want to send a plain, old, nonattached e-mail to the intended recipient, asking whether the recipient can handle uuencoding or MIME.

A Mailbox with Cardinals and Pheasants on It

To receive mail, you need a mailbox. (Not one of those tasteful roadside mailboxes, in this case. It's an invisible mailbox made up entirely of electronic data.) Your system administrator can make (or already has made) one for you if your organization uses e-mail. The mailbox comes in the form of a file called something like /var/mail/yourusername. It contains your unread mail and any mail you choose to leave lying around. You may also have a directory called mail or Mail (some systems capitalize it, some don't — sigh) in your home directory that you can use to sort your mail into piles and keep it for historical reference.

To read the mail in your mailbox and send mail, you use a program such as mail or elm or Pine. If you use Motif, you can use a fancy X Windows mail program, such as xmail.

Exchanging Gossip Using Pine

Pine was originally a cut-down version of elm (which we describe next, for pineless users) intended for novice users, which makes it even easier to use than elm. Now it's become a lot more powerful than elm ever was. It has lots of nice menus to remind you of what to do next, and it even uses pico, a simple editor, for composing mail.

To run Pine, just type pine. You see a display like the one shown in Figure 17-1.

If you are using UNIX by way of a communications program, watch out for which terminal you are emulating. Pine works fine if your program emulates a VT100 terminal, but not so well if it emulates an ANSI terminal. You can usually change which terminal your program emulates.

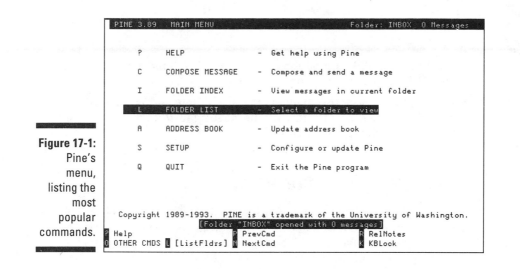

```
 PINE 3.89   MAIN MENU                           Folder: INBOX  0 Messages


          ?     HELP                -  Get help using Pine

          C     COMPOSE MESSAGE     -  Compose and send a message

          I     FOLDER INDEX        -  View messages in current folder

          L     FOLDER LIST         -  Select a folder to view

          A     ADDRESS BOOK        -  Update address book

          S     SETUP               -  Configure or update Pine

          Q     QUIT                -  Exit the Pine program



     Copyright 1989-1993.   PINE is a trademark of the University of Washington.
                      [Folder "INBOX" opened with 0 messages]
 P Help                            P PrevCmd                       R RelNotes
 O OTHER CMDS L [ListFldrs]        N NextCmd                       X KBLock
```

Figure 17-1:
Pine's menu, listing the most popular commands.

Figure 17-1 is Pine's *main menu,* with a list of its favorite commands. Like elm, Pine uses one-letter commands. Note that one of the commands is highlighted — you can also choose commands by pressing the up- and down-arrow keys to move the highlight and then pressing Enter.

The commands you are most likely to use are the following:

✔ Type **c** to compose (write a new message).

✔ Type **i** to see a list of your messages.

✔ Type **q** to exit from Pine.

✔ Type **?** for lots of helpful on-line help.

Into the postbox

To use Pine to send mail, type c. Pine runs pico, a nice simple editor that we described in more detail in Chapter 10. Instead of starting with a blank file, you see the headers ready for you to fill in — To, Cc, Attchmnt (for attaching files to a message — skip that one for now), and Subject. Use pico to type the header information and the text of your message. Then press Ctrl+X to leave pico. Pine sends the message and displays the main menu again.

If you decide not to send the message after all, you can press Ctrl+C to cancel it.

TIP

This list shows you some cool things you can do while you are writing your message:

✔ For lots of helpful information about how to use Pine, you can press Ctrl+G. Pine has complete on-line help.

✔ You can even check the spelling of your message — just press Ctrl+T. Pine checks all the words in your message against its dictionary and highlights each word it can't find.

I'm pining for some mail

To read your mail, type i to see the index of messages (Figure 17-2). The messages are numbered, with codes (*N* for new messages you haven't read, *D* for messages you have deleted, and *A* for messages you have answered) in the left margin. One of the messages is highlighted.

```
  PINE 3.89    FOLDER INDEX                Folder: INBOX  Message 1 of 3 NEW

+ N 1    Apr  6 Margy Levine Young     (695) How about lunch?
+ N 2    Apr  6 To: John R Levine      (474) Trying out some software!
+ N 3    Apr  6 Margy Levine Young     (710) It's budget time again...


















? Help          M Main Menu    P PrevMsg      - PrevPage    D Delete     R Reply
O OTHER CMDS    V [ViewMsg]    N NextMsg      Spc NextPage  U Undelete   F Forward
```

Figure 17-2: A list of your messages, in Pine.

To read a message, move the highlight to it, using the up- and down-arrow keys or by typing **p** (for previous) and **n** (for next). Then type v to view the message.

When you are looking at a message, here are some things you can do:

✔ Forward the message to someone else by typing **f**. Pine lets you start composing a message, with the text of the original message included in the text of this message.

✔ Reply to the person who sent the message by typing **r**. Pine automatically addresses the message to the person who sent the original one.

- Delete the message by typing **d**. The message doesn't disappear right away, but it is marked with a D on the list of messages. When you exit from Pine, your deleted messages really are deleted. (If you change your mind, you can undelete a message by typing **u**.)

- Move on to the next message by typing **n**, or move back to the preceding one by typing **p**.

- Return to Pine's main menu by typing **m**.

Send this file, too

Pine can handle MIME attachments with great ease and flair — there's nothing to it. To attach a file in Pine, move the cursor to the Attchmnts: line and press Ctrl+J while you are composing the message. When Pine prompts you for the filename, type it and press Enter. That's all it takes!

Creating your own address book

If you use Pine to send messages to Internet addresses, it can certainly be annoying to type long, complicated Internet addresses. That's a good reason to let Pine do it for you — set up an address book.

When you type **a** at the Pine menu, you switch to *address book mode*. (It even says ADDRESS BOOK at the top of the screen.) If you have already entered some addresses, Pine lists them.

When you finish fooling with your address book, type **m** to return to Pine's main menu.

To create an entry in your address book when you are in address book mode, follow these steps:

1. **Type** a.

   Pine asks for the full name of the person.

2. **Type the person's last name, then a comma, and then the first name, and then press Enter.**

   Pine asks for a nickname (the name you type when you address mail).

3. **Type the nickname. (Make it short but easy to remember.)**

   Finally, Pine asks for the person's e-mail address.

4. **Enter the e-mail address just as you would when you address a message.**

Sign here

You can make a *signature file,* a file that contains text for Pine or elm to include at the end of every message. The file must be called .signature and be in your home directory.

Use your text editor to make a signature file. Keep it short (no more than three lines long) and include your name, your e-mail address, other address information you want everyone to know, and (if there's room) a pithy or philosophical message that characterizes you.

After you've created a signature file, you don't have to type this stuff at the end of every message. To test it, send a message to yourself and see how the signature looks. The signature appears at the bottom of the message when you compose it. To omit the signature information from a message, just delete it.

Pine stores the entry in your address book and lists it on the address book screen.

If you make a mistake, you can edit an entry later. Just highlight it on the list of addresses and type **e** to edit it.

 You can also create an address book entry directory from the address of a message. If you are looking at a message from someone whose address you want to save, just type **t**. Pine prompts you for the person's full name (it might even suggest it, if it's part of the message header), nickname, and e-mail address. (Pine suggests the address of the sender of the current message.)

Saving messages

Pine enables you to create lots of folders in which to put your messages so that you can save them in an organized manner. To save a message in a folder, type **s** when you are looking at it or when it is highlighted on the list of messages.

If you save a message to a folder that doesn't exist, Pine asks whether you want to create it. Type **y** to do so. When you move a message to a folder, Pine automatically deletes it from your inbox. Very tidy.

What's all this junk at the beginning of the message?

An e-mail message has a *header* that the mail program (mail, elm, Pine, or whatever) creates automatically. The header consists of the following pieces:

- ✔ The To address (the person to receive the mail)

- ✔ The From address (the return address)

- ✔ The Cc addresses (the addresses to send copies to)

- ✔ The Bcc address (the addresses to send blind copies to)

- ✔ The subject

- ✔ Optional information you rarely use, such as expiration date, priority, which mailer mailed the message, and sometimes (for incoming messages) the arcane route that the message took to get to you

Don't worry if the header looks like gobbledy-gook — it is. On incoming mail, there can be all sorts of extra glop in the header that reports on which systems have passed it along, which program was used to send the mail, and lots of other useless stuff.

You can specify cc addresses, subject, and other information for messages you send.

Looking in a folder

After you've put messages in folders, you may want to look at them later. When you see Pine's main menu, you can type **l** (the lowercase letter *L*) to select which folder to look in. Pine automatically makes several for you, including the ones in this list:

- ✔ **INBOX:** Your incoming messages. Messages remain here until you delete or move them.

- ✔ **sent-mail:** Messages you've sent.

- ✔ **saved-messages:** A place to save messages before you send them.

Move the highlight to the one you want and then press Enter. Pine lists the messages in the folder.

You can make more folders by moving messages into them (as described in the preceding section).

Exchanging Gossip Using elm

The elm mail-reading program is a heck of a lot easier to use than is either version of the mail program (which we describe later, for the desperate), although it's not as nice as Pine. The elm program even tells you what is going on once in a while. Like Pine, it also helps you organize your mail into folders if you plan to save your messages.

To read your mail, send mail, or peruse mail you left lying around the last time, type the following line:

```
elm
```

The elm program displays a list of your mail messages (see Figure 17-3).

Figure 17-3:
elm mail-
message
list.

```
Mailbox is '/usr/mail/margy' with 3 messages [ELM 2.3 PL11]
    1   Dec 22 John R. Levine      (49)    a few troff hints
O   2   Dec 23 Jordan M. Young     (12)    Bye, bye, Brazil!
N   3   Dec 23 Meg Young           (10)    Hi, cutie
```

This display is called the *mail index.* The listing shows the date the mail was received, who sent it, the number of lines in the message, and the subject. Below the index are instructions, including the one-letter commands you use to read and send mail, which are as follows:

- ✔ Use the ↑ and ↵ (or type **j** and **k**) to highlight the message you want to read, reply to, delete, or whatever.
- ✔ Press Enter to read the highlighted message.
- ✔ Type **d** to delete a message.
- ✔ Type **u** to undelete a message you didn't want to delete.
- ✔ Type **m** to send (mail) a message.
- ✔ Type **r** to reply to a message.
- ✔ Type **f** to forward a message to someone else.
- ✔ Press > or type **s** to save the message in a folder or text file.
- ✔ Type **p** to print the message.
- ✔ Type **q** to quit the elm program.
- ✔ Type **?** for more help.

Just put a stamp on it

To use elm to send mail, type **m**. The program asks you for the address, the subject of the message, and addresses to send copies to. Then it runs a text editor, usually vi. (You can arrange for elm to run another editor if you loathe vi as much as we do — see the tip in the next section.) Use the editor to type the text of the message. When you finish, save the message and exit from the editor. (If you are forced to use vi, press Escape and type **ZZ** to save the message and exit from vi.)

Tell the world!

Next, elm gives you a chance to edit the message (perhaps to add a P.S.), fool with the header (useful if you decide that your message is so fascinating it should be sent to a wider audience), forget the whole thing, or send the message off.

Type **h** to edit the header for the message. elm displays all the components of the header, including the addressee and the subject line. You can change most of them, or add names of people to receive copies of the message (cc's).

To change each of these things, press the letter shown before the parenthesis. For example, to add cc's, type **c**. elm asks you for the list of addresses to send copies to. Enter the addresses, separated by at least one space, and press Enter. If elm recognizes the address, it displays the person's actual name in parentheses after the e-mail address. Otherwise, it shows just the address you typed.

When you have finished fooling with the header, press Enter to indicate that you are finished. elm asks what to do with the message, as follows:

```
And now: s
Choose e)dit message, !)shell, h)eaders, c)opy file, s)end, or f)orget.
```

Type **s** to send it. You can also type e to go back and edit some more or **h** to change the headers (To, Cc, Bcc, and Subject, for example). There are also some less useful choices you don't have to worry about.

You can change the editor elm uses for writing and editing mail messages. (Thank goodness, because otherwise you might have to use vi!) When you are using elm and looking at the mail index, do the following:

1. Type **o** to look at the elm options.

2. Type **e** to change the editor you use.

3. Type the name of the editor you usually use to edit text files. (We like `emacs` and `pico`.)

4. Press > to save this change.

5. Finally, type **i** to see the mail index again.

Old friends say hello

To read a message, highlight its line in the mail index and press Enter. The `elm` program displays the message — or the first screen of it if it is a long message.

When you finish reading the message, you can do several things with it:

- Delete it. (Type **d**.)
- Forward it to someone else. (Type **f** and tell `elm` the address to forward it to.)
- Reply to it. (Type **r**.)
- Save it. To leave it hanging around in your mailbox, press spacebar to leave the current message and go to the next message, or type **i** to leave the current message and return to the mail index. In either case, the message remains unaltered. Alternatively, you can save the message in a folder or text file. (See the following sections.)

Saving your mail for a rainy day

If you like to save mail messages, you can save them with `elm` in folders, one folder per topic or one folder per sender. You can have lots of folders — each one is just a text file in your `Mail` directory. (Note the initial uppercase letter.)

To save a message to a folder, either highlight the message in the mail index or display the message. Then press > or type **s**. The `elm` program asks for the name of the folder you want to save the message to. For some reason, folder names begin with = (an equal sign). The `elm` program suggests a folder with the name of the person who sent the message, assuming that you want to save messages organized by sender. But you can type any name you want (no space, and no funny characters other than the = at the beginning).

To see the messages in a folder, return to the mail index and type **c** to change folders. Type the name of the folder you want to use (or type **?** to see a list of your folders). Be sure to type the = at the beginning of the folder name. You see a list of messages just like the mail index of your original mailbox.

All the same commands work in a folder that work in your regular mailbox. For example, after you highlight a message, you can read it by pressing Enter, forward it by typing **f**, or delete it by typing **d**.

To return to your regular mailbox, type **c** again and then type **!** when elm asks for the name of the folder. (Don't ask us why.)

Mail for word processors

You can also save a message in a text file so that you can edit it later or include it in a word processing document. Use the > or s command to move the message, but rather than type a folder name (which always begins with an =), type a filename (such as message.text). The elm program creates the file in your home directory and puts the message there. If the file already exists, elm adds the message to the end of the existing file so that you can save a series of messages to a single text file.

Taking it with you

To print a message on the printer, highlight the message in the mail index or display the message. Then type **p** to print it.

Attaching stuff using elm

Unfortunately, most versions of elm can't attach files to e-mail messages by using the popular MIME system described earlier in this chapter. Bummer, but there it is.

If you want to send a text file, just include it in your e-mail message. The pico command to include another file in a message is Ctrl+R, and the emacs command is Ctrl+XI (just plain I).

If you want to send a file that contains something other than text, you can do it with uuencoding. Follow these steps:

1. Create a uuencoded version of the file you want to send, by typing this command to the shell:

```
uuencode file-to-send new-name > temp
```

In this command, replace file-to-send with the file you want to uuencode, new-name with the name that you want the file to have when it is uudecoded, and temp with any temporary filename (junk is another perennial favorite).

2. Run elm and compose a new message. Address it as usual.

3. At the beginning of the message, explain that you are sending a uuencoded message.

4. At the end of the message, include the file you created in Step 1 (which is called temp, or whatever you typed in place of *temp*). If you use pico as your editor, press Ctrl+R to include the file. If you use emacs as your editor, Press Ctrl+XI to include the file.

5. Send the message.

Dealing with uuencoded stuff

If you receive a message that contains a uuencoded file, here's what to do.

1. Tell elm to run the message through the uudecoder, by typing the following command:

```
|uudecode
```

That's a vertical bar and then the name of the command uudecode.

2. The original file should be reconstituted.

So what's the new file called? Look on the *begin* line of the uu-incoming file (or the original e-mail message that contained the file) — it shows the length of the file in bytes and the name the uudecoded file will have.

Exchanging Gossip Using mail

The basic mail program comes with every brand of UNIX and is an acceptable way to read and send mail. Not great, but acceptable if there's nothing else. It can't deal with MIME attachments, if you're wondering.

Take a letter

Assuming that you want to send mail to your friend Nancy B., you can send a message with the mail program by typing this line:

```
mail nancyb
```

Some versions of mail prompt you to enter a subject line for the message; others respond by doing absolutely nothing. You can tell that something is afoot because you don't see a UNIX shell prompt such as $ or % anymore. The mail program is waiting for you to type the message. So type something, as many lines long as you want, such as the following:

```
Yo, Nance! I've figured out how to use e-mail on this
        thing!
Send a message so I can see if my mailbox works. Thanks...
```

Press Enter when the line reaches the right end of the screen (or window) to make it easier to read. Otherwise, your line wraps around to another line, and UNIX may put the line break in the middle of a word.

When you finish typing the message, type a period on a line by itself to tell the mail program that you are finished. The mail program confirms that it has sent the message by doing absolutely nothing except displaying a UNIX prompt. (Some particularly ancient versions of mail don't understand the dot, so you have to press Ctrl+D to tell it that you are finished.)

Because the mail program is so helpful, you may want to consider using a better program, such as elm or Pine. If you have to use mail, send yourself a test message to make sure that it is working. System V computers usually have a really old and awful mail program called mail and a somewhat better one called Mail. (These guys really had a lot of fun thinking up names for these programs.) If you can use Mail rather than mail, do so, because it's more likely to work the way it's supposed to. (Often, mail doesn't even understand Internet mail addresses.)

What's in my mailbox?

To read your mail, reply to letters, and do other mail-related stuff, type this on a line by itself:

```
mail
```

The mail program starts by showing you your unread mail. Some versions print the first unread message or show a list of incoming messages. Then the program displays the following prompt:

```
?
```

As you doubtlessly found intuitively obvious from that prompt, the mail program understands many commands and is ready for you to type one.

If it hasn't already showed you a list of messages, type **h** to tell mail to show you a listing of the messages in your mailbox (if there are any).

Figure 17-4 shows what you might see when you start the mail program. The little > shows you which message mail is working with (the *current message*).

```
3 letters found in /usr/mail/margy, 0 scheduled for deletion, 0 newly arrived
    >   3    283       tonias        Wed Dec 23 11:51:57 1997
        2    365       jordany       Wed Dec 23 11:51:45 1997
        1    1738      johnl         Tue Dec 22 23:58:50 1997
    ?
```

Talking to `mail`

The `mail` program understands lots of commands, including these:

✔ Press Enter to see the current message (the one the > points to).

✔ To move to a different message, type the message number (the first thing on the line in the list of headers).

✔ Type **d** to delete the current message (usually after you have read it).

✔ Type **u** to undelete a message you didn't want to delete.

✔ Type **m** and type *mailaddress* to send (mail) a new message. (Use a real user name or mail address rather than `mailaddress`.)

✔ Type **r** to reply to the current message.

✔ Type **z** to see more message headers if there are too many to fit on-screen.

✔ Type **p** to print the current message.

✔ Type **q** to quit the `mail` program.

✔ Type **?** for further help.

What does it say? What does it say?

To read a message, type its message number (the number at the beginning of the line). To read the current message (the one with the >), just press Enter. The `mail` program displays the message — or the first screen of it if it is a long message.

When you finish reading the message, you can do several things with it:

✔ Delete it. (Type **d**.)

✔ Reply to it. (Type **r**.) Then type a message (like the preceding one to Nancy). End the message by typing **.** (a period) on a line by itself.

✔ Save it. (See the following section.)

Messages accumulate in a file called mbox, which gets pretty big if you don't edit it.

Saving your letters for posterity

You can save a message in a text file. To save the current message (the one you are reading or have just finished reading), type the following line:

```
s filename
```

Replace filename with the name of the text file you want to create. If the text file already exists, mail adds the current message to the end of the file. You can save a series of messages to a single text file in this way.

Run that by me again

To print a message (on the screen, not on the printer), type **p**. You will want to do this when you are looking at a list of messages and you want to see the contents of one of them. If you want to see a message other than the current one, put the message number (shown in the list of headers) after the p, as follows:

```
p 5
```

To quit mail, type **q**. You see the UNIX prompt.

It Slices, It Dices, It's Netscape

Netscape Navigator includes a mail program. We don't like it, but it works. If you're familiar with Netscape on Windows or Mac, the UNIX version works almost identically. Two versions of Netscape are popular at this point: the older 3.0 Navigator and the new (and very buggy) 4.0 Communicator.

Navigating with Netscape 3.0

After you have Netscape running, select Window⇨Mail to read or send mail. A three-part window lists the names of your mailboxes (usually Inbox and Trash), the titles of the messages, and the contents of the current message.

To send a message, click the New Mail Message button on the toolbar. (You can do this in any Netscape window, not just the mail window.) Netscape opens a new message window. Type the recipient's name in the To field, the message subject in the Subject field, and the body of the message in the large, otherwise empty window. Then click Send to send your message.

To read mail with Netscape, click the Get Mail button on the toolbar to retrieve any waiting mail. (You may have to enter your login password again.) Your Inbox displays the sender and subject of each message.

After the mail is in your Inbox, click on a message to display its contents. After you've displayed a message, you can click on Delete, Reply, Reply All, or Forward. You step through the messages in your mailbox by clicking the Next and Previous buttons, and print a message with the Print button.

Communicating with Netscape 4.0

After people had figured out how Netscape 3.0 worked, the Netscape developers invented Netscape Communicator. Although the screens have changed, the functions are pretty much the same. Now there are fancy ways to format your mail. Don't use them. The 95 percent of the world that doesn't use Netscape 4.0 mail will see only garbage in your messages.

To start Messenger, select Communicator⇨Messenger Mailbox. The layout of the window has changed, so now the top half lists the messages in the current mailbox, and the bottom shows the current message. To send a message, click the New Msg (New Message) button on the toolbar. The window that opens is chock-full of incomprehensible icons you can ignore. First, you have to enter the name of your recipient. At the top of the window are a couple of lines. Near the left end of the line may be an entry that says To or Cc or Bcc. If it says anything other than To, click the little arrow to the left of the Cc or Bcc and switch it to To. Your recipient's address in the right half of your updated To line. Should you have other recipients, you can enter them into the next lines, one per line. (It creates new lines as needed.)

Now move on to the subject. Type the subject into the Subject box. Now, you can enter your message into the rest of the window.

Don't use Messenger formatting unless you are sure that your recipient uses Netscape 4.0. Anyone else will see glop and will throw your message away.

After you have created your message, click on the Send button. If you've used any of the formatting features, or even if you haven't, Netscape warns you that your recipient may not be able to handle the beautiful formatting and gives you some options. Pick Send in Plain Text Only and click Send.

To see your new mail, click the Get Msg button on the toolbar. (You may be prompted for your login password, depending on your mail setup.) Once there's mail in your mailbox, double-click on a message in the message listing to see that message in a new window. Again, the Reply, Forward, Next, and Previous buttons do what they look like they should.

Chapter 18

Websurfing for UNIX Users

The What?

The World Wide Web (WWW, or just the Web) is the zoomiest, coolest Internet facility around. It contains lots of information, including pictures and other nontext stuff, in the form of *hypertext*. As you read through the information, therefore, you can click (or otherwise select) words, pictures, or buttons to zoom right to related information. These clickable words, pictures, and buttons are called *links*.

The amazing thing about all these linked pages is that a page might be stored on any Internet host computer in the world. If you are looking at a page stored on a computer in Brookline, Massachusetts, a link on that page might jump you to a page stored in Basel, Switzerland. You never even notice, unless you look carefully at the names of the Web pages.

You read the World Wide Web by using a *browser*. If you're stuck with a plain, old text-based terminal (for example, if you have connected to a remote UNIX host with telnet), you can use a text-only browser named Lynx. "Text-only" means that you don't get to see any of the cool pictures, animations, and sounds that have made the Web the phenomenally popular success that it is. If you use X Windows, you can use a graphical browser such as Netscape, currently the most popular browser for UNIX. With a graphical browser, you get to see all the cool stuff as well as the text. (Does this make the browsing experience any more educational or enriching? Well, in some cases, maybe, but mostly it just makes it more fun.) This chapter describes both Netscape and Lynx in addition to giving you some pointers to some great Web pages.

When you start Netscape or Lynx, you can begin with the Web page it suggests and find your way to the information you want by following the hypertext links. (Don't worry — we tell you how.) Alternatively, you can jump directly to a Web page if you know its name. These names are called *URLs* (for Uniform Resource Locators) — see the nearby sidebar about them.

URL!

The World Wide Web brought us the extremely useful concept of Uniform Resource Locators, or URLs. The point of a URL is to have a simple and consistent way to name Internet resources that tells you both the type of the resource and where to find it. A URL consists of a resource type, a colon, and a location. URLs look horrendous. In most cases, the location is two slashes, the host name where the resource can be found, a slash, and a filename on that host.

Commonly used resource types are shown in the following list:

http: A HyperText Transfer Protocol document; that is, something in native Web format

ftp: A directory or file on an FTP server

news: A Usenet news item (unsupported by many Web browsers)

gopher: A gopher menu (an early hypertext system that is dwindling as quickly as the Web is expanding)

Here's a typical URL:

```
http://net.gurus.com/
toc-u4d3.html
```

The reason that most URLs look more like run-on typos than actual locations is that they were originally designed to be read by computers rather than actual human beings. Still, there is an underlying order to their structure, and understanding that order helps to demystify them (a little). The sample URL is a Web document. Reading backwards, the part after the last slash is the filename: `toc-u4d3.html`. The part following the two slashes is the host name of the computer: `net.gurus.com`. Finally, back at the beginning, we see `http:`, which just tells the browser to use the `http` resource type (the Web) to view this file.

Although URLs were originally intended as a way for computers to pass around resource names, they've also become widely used as a way to tell people about Internet resources, and that's how we use them in this section of the book. It's unfortunate that they are so difficult to type!

There's no place like home . . .

You hear a lot these days about *home pages*. Everyone who is anyone has a home page. So what are they?

A *home page* is a page on the World Wide Web that serves as a starting point for information about something. If, for example, you want information about our *...For Dummies* books, you might want to start at the Internet for Dummies Central Home Page, which is at `http://net.gurus.com`.

Home pages generally contain introductory information about the entity whose home page it is, along with lots of links to other pages. Many home pages for organizations have URLs such as `http://www.something`, where *something* is the Internet domain name for the organization. Guess whose home page is `http://www.microsoft.com`?

A Day on the Lynx

Lynx is a boring-looking, character-based, graphics-impaired Web browser, but by gosh, it works. For most UNIX users (except those with GUI interfaces), Lynx is the only browser they can use. It was created at the University of Kansas. This chapter describes Version 2.7.

If your UNIX system doesn't have Lynx, you (or your system administrator) can get it for free by anonymous FTP from `ftp2.cc.ukans.edu` in the `pub/lynx` directory. For up-to-date information about Lynx, you can subscribe to the Lynx mailing list by sending the message `subscribe lynx-dev <your-name>` to `listserv@ukanaix.cc.ukans.edu`.

Coming and going

To run Lynx, just type **lynx**. You see a Web page (for example, the page shown in Figure 18-1). This particular page is the home page of The World, a Boston-based Internet provider.

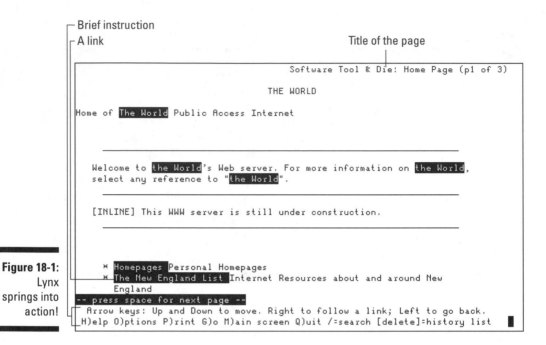

Figure 18-1:
Lynx
springs into
action!

When you are in Lynx, you can exit at any time by pressing **q**. Lynx asks whether you really want to leave — press **y**.

If you don't want Lynx to ask you if you really, really, truly want to leave, press **Q** (capitalized) or press Ctrl+D to quit.

Anatomy of a page

Lynx tells you the name of the Web page (in words, not the URL) in the upper-right corner of the screen. The bottom two lines of the screen comprise a cryptic little menu that reminds you about which keys do what. The third line from the bottom displays various helpful messages. In Figure 18-1, it tells you that this Web page is too long to fit on the screen, as well as how to see the rest of it. And the rest of the screen is the Web page itself.

A Web page can contain text, links, pictures, sounds, and movies. Unfortunately, Lynx can deal with only text and links. Text looks (not surprisingly) like text. Hypertext links (things you can click to view a related Web page) are displayed in reverse video. Graphics, sound, and movies aren't displayed at all. Instead, Lynx shows you something such as [INLINE] or [IMAGE]. This is Lynx's way of saying, "Nyaah, nyaah, nyaah! There's a picture here, but I'm not going to show it to you!"

Skating the Web

Each *link* (highlighted word or phrase) on the Web page connects to another page on a related topic. The links that say The World, for example, connect to a page that describes Software Tool & Die's World Internet service. The Homepages link connects to a list of home pages about individual people.

One of the links appears in a different color on the screen. (This color difference doesn't show up worth a darn on paper, so in Figure 18-1, you can't tell that the first link is displayed in white letters on black and that the others are in yellow on black. Your colors may differ.) This link is the selected link. To select a link, follow these steps:

1. **Press the arrow keys so that the link you want is selected.**

2. **Press the right-arrow key or Enter to jump to the linked page.**

The linked page appears (sometimes after a short delay while Lynx retrieves the page over the Internet).

So that's it! To "surf the Web," you just move from page to page until you find something interesting. Here are some surfing pointers:

- The links you see may be numbered — if they are, you can choose a link by typing its number and pressing Enter.

- To return to the page you were looking at previously, press the left-arrow key.

- To return to the first screen you saw when you started Lynx, you can press **m** at any time. Lynx calls this first screen your *main screen*.

- To display a good starting point for surfing, press **i** for index. The Web page that Lynx displays depends on the one your system administrator chose. One popular index page is the Welcome to the World-Wide Web page at CERN, the laboratory near Geneva, Switzerland, where the Web was invented (see Figure 18-2).

- Sometimes a link doesn't take you to a different Web page. Sometimes it takes you to another part of the same page. It is common (and convenient) for long Web pages to contain a table of contents at the top of the page, with links to the major headings.

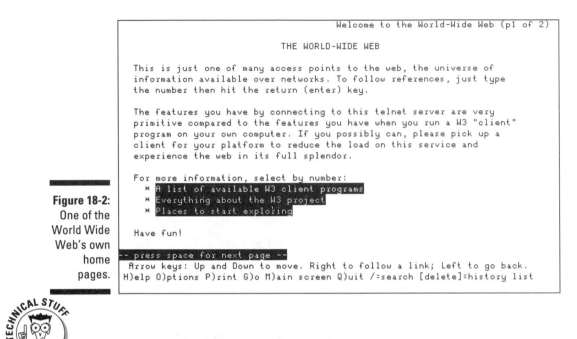

```
                                        Welcome to the World-Wide Web (p1 of 2)
                        THE WORLD-WIDE WEB

     This is just one of many access points to the web, the universe of
     information available over networks. To follow references, just type
     the number then hit the return (enter) key.

     The features you have by connecting to this telnet server are very
     primitive compared to the features you have when you run a W3 "client"
     program on your own computer. If you possibly can, please pick up a
     client for your platform to reduce the load on this service and
     experience the web in its full splendor.

     For more information, select by number:
       * A list of available W3 client programs
       * Everything about the W3 project
       * Places to start exploring

     Have fun!

  -- press space for next page --
     Arrow keys: Up and Down to move. Right to follow a link; Left to go back.
     H)elp O)ptions P)rint G)o M)ain screen Q)uit /=search [delete]=history list
```

Figure 18-2:
One of the
World Wide
Web's own
home
pages.

Where do all these pages come from?

Web pages don't all come from any one source. Lots of universities and companies have Web pages — in fact, right now it's the in thing for anyone and everyone to have a Web page about themselves (so much for humility). Most Internet providers run *Web servers* (programs that store Web pages and make them available to any Web browser that wants to display them). If you get the urge to have your own Web page, contact your Internet provider to find out whether the people there can help you.

Web pages are stored as ASCII text files. In addition to the text that is displayed by the Web browser, special instructions are written in a language called HTML (HyperText Markup Language), which is discussed in another sidebar in this chapter. These instructions include marking headings and lists, links to other pages, and information about nontextual stuff, such as pictures and sounds. Several books are available that tell you how to write Web pages in HTML, including our *MORE Internet For Dummies,* 3rd Edition (IDG Books Worldwide, Inc.).

But before you rush to create your own Web page, with a picture of your dog and a list of your kids' latest cute utterances, consider this question: How are people going to find your page? Sure, your friends will see your page after they type the URL you proudly give them. But will anyone else ever see it? Remember that the way most people display most pages is by selecting a link to the page. Will any other pages contain links to your page? Probably not.

Handling long pages

Some Web pages just fit on the screen, and others are miles long (or they seem like it). You can press the PgUp and PgDn keys to move around the page one screenful at a time. Pressing the Home and End keys (if your keyboard has them) moves you to the very top and the very bottom of the page. (We'll let you guess which does which.)

If you are looking for something in particular on a very long page, you may want to try Lynx's search commands. The page shown in Figure 18-2, for example, is 14 screens long and can be tedious to look through for a specific topic.

Instead, press the slash key (/) to begin a search. Lynx says `Enter a search string`. Type a word or phrase and press Enter. Lynx skips to the part of the page that includes the word or phrase, if it occurs in the page.

Getting help

If you want help, you can see hypertext help pages by pressing **H**. (Be sure to capitalize it.) You see a page like the one shown in Figure 18-3.

The help pages are themselves Web pages, so move around them as you would any Web page. Of course, if you need help navigating the Web, this may not be so easy!

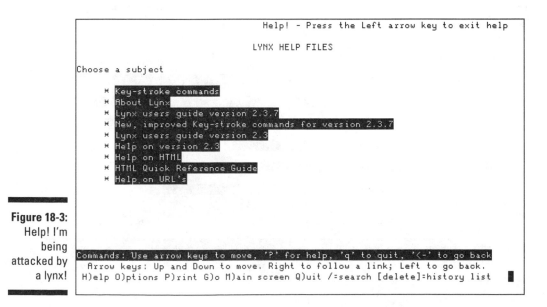

```
                         Help! - Press the Left arrow key to exit help

                              LYNX HELP FILES

Choose a subject

        *  Key-stroke commands
        *  About Lynx
        *  Lynx users guide version 2.3.7
        *  New, improved Key-stroke commands for version 2.3.7
        *  Lynx users guide version 2.3
        *  Help on version 2.3
        *  Help on HTML
        *  HTML Quick Reference Guide
        *  Help on URL's




Commands: Use arrow keys to move, '?' for help, 'q' to quit, '<-' to go back
  Arrow keys: Up and Down to move. Right to follow a link; Left to go back.
 H)elp O)ptions P)rint G)o M)ain screen Q)uit /=search [delete]=history list
```

Figure 18-3:
Help! I'm being attacked by a lynx!

Where have I been?

Lynx keeps a list of the pages you have seen, in order. It needs this list to make the left-arrow key back you up through the pages. You can also see the list of pages by pressing the Delete key. (If it doesn't work, try the Backspace key.) You see the Lynx History Page, as shown in Figure 18-4.

The pages you've seen are listed, and you can jump to any of them by choosing the link and pressing the right-arrow key. (If the links are numbered, you can also type the number and press Enter.)

Going right to a URL

If you know the URL of the Web page you want to see, and if you have the stomach to attempt to type it, press **g** (for *goto*). Type the URL, and be careful about both the punctuation and the capitalization (yes, capitalization counts). Then press Enter. Lynx gets the page you want.

Printing or saving good stuff

What if you want to print what's on a Web page? If you press **p**, you see the Lynx Printing Options page, which looks something like that shown in Figure 18-5. The exact options on this page depend on your Lynx installation.

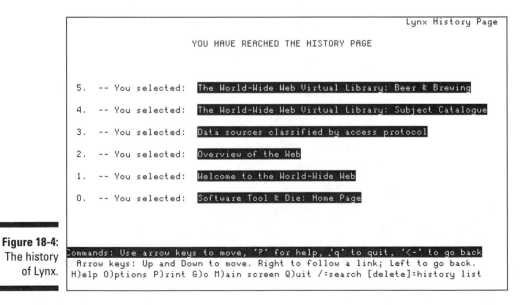

Figure 18-4:
The history
of Lynx.

```
                                                      Lynx History Page

                        YOU HAVE REACHED THE HISTORY PAGE


  5.  -- You selected: The World-Wide Web Virtual Library: Beer & Brewing

  4.  -- You selected: The World-Wide Web Virtual Library: Subject Catalogue

  3.  -- You selected: Data sources classified by access protocol

  2.  -- You selected: Overview of the Web

  1.  -- You selected: Welcome to the World-Wide Web

  0.  -- You selected: Software Tool & Die: Home Page



Commands: Use arrow keys to move, '?' for help, 'q' to quit, '<-' to go back
  Arrow keys: Up and Down to move. Right to follow a link; Left to go back.
  H)elp O)ptions P)rint G)o M)ain screen Q)uit /=search [delete]=history list
```

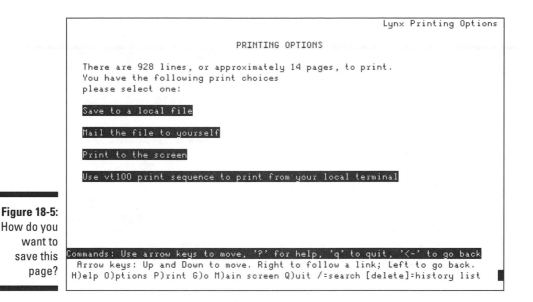

```
                                              Lynx Printing Options
                        PRINTING OPTIONS

      There are 928 lines, or approximately 14 pages, to print.
      You have the following print choices
      please select one:

      Save to a local file

      Mail the file to yourself

      Print to the screen

      Use vt100 print sequence to print from your local terminal




Commands: Use arrow keys to move, '?' for help, 'q' to quit, '<-' to go back
   Arrow keys: Up and Down to move. Right to follow a link; Left to go back.
 H)elp O)ptions P)rint G)o M)ain screen Q)uit /=search [delete]=history list
```

Figure 18-5:
How do you
want to
save this
page?

Some of the options on this page enable you to save the text of the page in a file rather than print it.

Here's HTML in your eye!

As you may know, Web pages are written in a language called *HTML,* which includes instructions to tell the browser about text, headings, links, graphics, and anything else a Web page might contain. Each browser reads the HTML information about a page, formats it tastefully, and displays it. Different browsers use different formatting.

If you want to see the actual HTML version of a page, just press the backslash (\) key. You see something like the following:

```
<HTML>
  <HEAD>
  <TITLE>Great Tapes for Kids!
www.greattapes.com </TITLE>
  <!— Changed by: Margy Levine
Young, 6-Dec-1997 —>
  </HEAD>
```

```
<BODY BGCOLOR="#FFFFFF"
  BACKGROUND="back.gif">


<CENTER><IMG SRC="title.gif"
  HEIGHT=30 WIDTH=500></CENTER>


<H1>Great Tapes for Kids: A
  Catalog of the Best
  Children's Video and Audio
  Tapes</H1>
```

Have you ever seen a terrific, educational tape at a friend's house, a tape that your kids loved, and then never been able to find the tape for sale? Many of the best kids' video and audio

(continued)

(continued)

> tapes aren't in your local video store, but you can order them here!
>
> All those brackets surround HTML markings, which tell Lynx (and other Web browsers) about how to format the text and where to put pictures and links. If you want more information about HTML, the Lynx help system includes an introduction to HTML. There are also links to HTML introductory documents on the CERN home page.

Fake Web pages

As you wander around the Web, you may stumble across a Usenet newsgroup, telnet session, or list of files on an FTP server. How did that stuff sneak onto the Web, you may ask. Lynx, like most Web browsers, can display not only Web pages but also information from other Internet services. Lynx makes the information look like a Web page, but it's not.

This is a wonderfully clever way to make lots of information about a topic accessible by way of a single program (your browser). Lynx can display Usenet newsgroups, FTP sites, Gopher menus, and telnet sessions for you. How convenient!

News of the weird

Figure 18-6 shows you how a Usenet newsgroup looks in Lynx. It lists the latest 30 or so articles, with a link at the top of the page to display earlier articles. (See Chapter 19, for background information about Usenet.)

To read an article, just select its link, and you see something like Figure 18-7. Lynx shows you all the newsgroups to which the article was posted and enables you to jump to them.

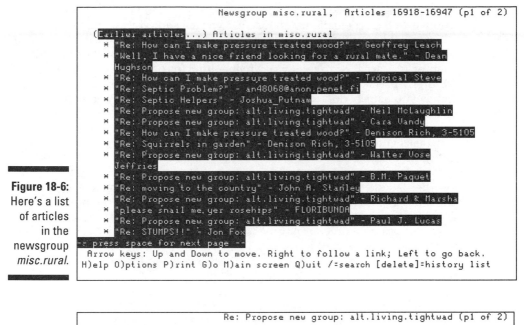

Figure 18-6:
Here's a list of articles in the newsgroup *misc.rural.*

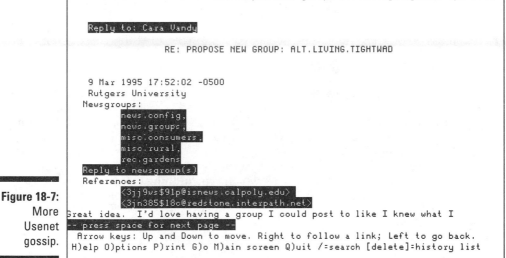

Figure 18-7:
More Usenet gossip.

The first link, `Reply to: author`, enables you to send e-mail to the person who wrote the article. If you choose it, Lynx asks for your name, e-mail address, and the subject of the e-mail, and then it runs an editor so that you can type your post. (See the section, "Controlling your Lynx," later in this chapter to learn how to tell Lynx which editor to run.) If you specified an editor, Lynx runs the editor and enables you to type the message. Save and exit as you usually do, using that editor. If you didn't specify an editor, Lynx enables you to type the lines one line at a time, and lets you type a period on a line by itself to signal that you are finished. After you type the message, Lynx asks you whether you really want to mail it. If it's angry, petty, or not funny, think again.

Another link, `Reply to newsgroup(s)`, posts a follow-up article. If you choose it, Lynx asks for your e-mail address, the subject of the post, and whether you want to include the original message, and then it runs an editor to enable you to type your post. After you type the message, Lynx asks you whether you really want to post it. Think twice — will it really be of interest to lots of people in the newgroup, not just to you and the person who wrote the post to which you are replying?

Although Lynx is a pretty good Web browser, it's a lousy news program. If you spend much time reading news, switch to a real news program, such as `trn`, `nn`, or `tin`. See Chapter 19 for details.

Files via Lynx

With Lynx, you don't need a separate FTP program for downloading files. If a Web page contains a link to an FTP server and you choose that link, you see the message `Retrieving FTP directory`, and Lynx displays the files on the FTP server as a Web page, similar to the one shown in Figure 18-8.

You see one directory on the FTP server. For each item in the directory, Lynx displays its date and time, which type of thing it is (directory or file), its name, and its size. For files, it guesses which type of file it is. Follow these steps:

1. **Move to the directory that contains the file you want.**

   If you select a directory, you see the contents of the directory. All directories except the root (/) have a link that enables you move up to the directory's parent directory.

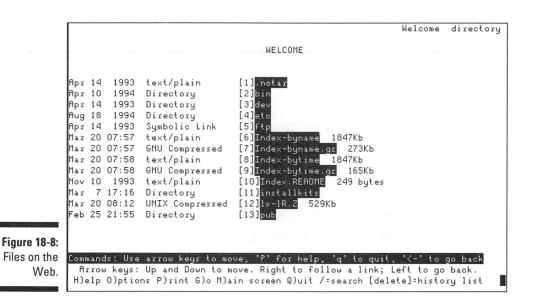

Welcome directory

WELCOME

Apr 14	1993	text/plain	[1].notar
Apr 10	1994	Directory	[2]bin
Apr 14	1993	Directory	[3]dev
Aug 18	1994	Directory	[4]etc
Apr 14	1993	Symbolic Link	[5]ftp
Mar 20	07:57	text/plain	[6]Index-byname 1847Kb
Mar 20	07:57	GNU Compressed	[7]Index-byname.gz 273Kb
Mar 20	07:58	text/plain	[8]Index-bytime 1847Kb
Mar 20	07:58	GNU Compressed	[9]Index-bytime.gz 165Kb
Nov 10	1993	text/plain	[10]Index.README 249 bytes
Mar 7	17:16	Directory	[11]installkits
Mar 20	08:12	UNIX Compressed	[12]ls-1R.Z 529Kb
Feb 25	21:55	Directory	[13]pub

Commands: Use arrow keys to move, '?' for help, 'q' to quit, '<-' to go back
  Arrow keys: Up and Down to move. Right to follow a link; Left to go back.
 H)elp O)ptions P)rint G)o M)ain screen Q)uit /=search [delete]=history list

Figure 18-8:
Files on the
Web.

2. **When you see the file you want, select it.**

   If the file is a text file or contains a Web page, Lynx displays it. You are finished.

   If the file is anything else (not text), Lynx says that this file can't be displayed on this terminal. True enough. You don't want to display it — in fact, you want to store it in a file on your system. Lynx asks what you what to do with it — download it to a file or cancel.

3. **Press** d **to download the file.**

   Lynx displays the menu shown in Figure 18-9.

4. **Choose one of the options for downloading a binary file.**

   (We recommend the last option on the menu, downloading by using ZMODEM to download a binary file, because it's the fastest.)

   Lynx asks for the name to give the file on your system. It suggests the same name the file now has, but you can change it.

5. **Type the filename and press Enter when you are finished.**

   The download begins! That is, Lynx and FTP begin transferring the file to your disk. You see various messages, depending on which type of transfer you chose in Step 4.

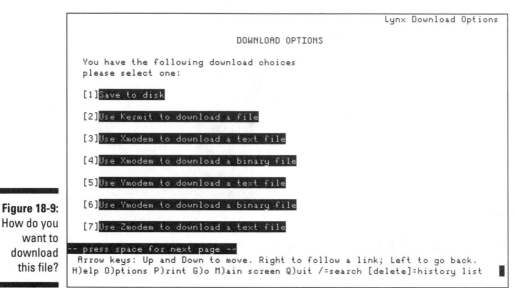

Lynx Download Options

```
                    DOWNLOAD OPTIONS

    You have the following download choices
    please select one:

    [1]Save to disk

    [2]Use Kermit to download a file

    [3]Use Xmodem to download a text file

    [4]Use Xmodem to download a binary file

    [5]Use Ymodem to download a text file

    [6]Use Ymodem to download a binary file

    [7]Use Zmodem to download a text file

-- press space for next page --
 Arrow keys: Up and Down to move. Right to follow a link; Left to go back.
 H)elp O)ptions P)rint G)o M)ain screen Q)uit /=search [delete]=history list
```

Figure 18-9:
How do you
want to
download
this file?

Here are a few tips for downloading files with Lynx:

✔ It may take some time to connect to the FTP server. Many FTP servers are overburdened and overbooked — you may not be able to connect at all in some cases.

✔ If you start at the root directory of the FTP server, you may have to press PgDn once or twice before you get to the directories you are looking for. (Many FTP servers store their publicly accessible files in a directory called /pub.)

✔ If you want to use Lynx to access an FTP site, just type **g** and then type **ftp://*ftpsite*/**, replacing ftpsite with the name of the site. To look at the files at gatekeeper.dec.com, for example, type **ftp://gatekeeper.dec.com/**.

✔ If the file transfer doesn't seem to work, try another type of transfer in Step 4. You may have to exit from Lynx and use the ls command to see whether the file has, in fact, arrived. If it still doesn't work, it's time to make a note of the FTP server name and the file you want and then fire up the regular FTP program.

Lynx can act like telnet, too

Chapter 21 explains how you can log in to other computers to get information. Some of the computers are mentioned on Web pages, and amazingly enough, you can use Lynx to telnet to them.

When you click a telnet link, Lynx automatically connects by way of telnet. You have to log in and so on, just as you would if you were using the telnet program. When you are finished, be sure to log out — you can press **q** to tell Lynx to log you out. When you see the `Connection closed by foreign host` message, you are logged out.

Remembering the good parts

The World Wide Web has tens of millions of pages in it, and thousands are added every day (well, almost). When you find one that looks really interesting and useful (or fun), it would be nice to be able to return to it easily. Otherwise, it can be impossible to find it again!

There is! You can create a *bookmark* for the page — that is, add its address (its URL) to a list of your favorite Web pages.

Before you can begin making your own bookmarks, you have to tell Lynx where to store them. Press **O** (the letter) to see the Options Menu, which is described in more detail in the next section. The third option is the name of the file in which bookmarks are stored. If you see a filename for this option, fine — just leave it alone. It may already be set to something such as `lynx_bookmarks.html`. If no filename appears, press **B,** type a filename, and then press Enter. To leave the Options Menu, press > (that is, Shift+) to save your changes and then press **r** to return to your normal Lynx screen.

Now you have a file just waiting to contain some bookmarks. To add a page to your bookmark file, press **a**. Lynx asks whether you want to make a bookmark for that page you are viewing (if so, press **d**) or to the page you would see if you chose the selected link (if so, press **l** — the letter). All that seems to happen is that Lynx displays the friendly, upbeat message `Done!`

Behind the scenes, however, Lynx has added the URL of the current page or link to your bookmark file. To see your list of bookmarks, press **v**. You see a page like the one shown in Figure 18-10. To go to a Web page on your list of bookmarks, just select its link. It's like having your own Web page full of your favorite links!

Figure 18-10:
Some of our
favorite
places.

Controlling your Lynx

Lynx has some options you can set to control some things about how it works. When you press **o**, you see the Lynx Options Menu, shown in Figure 18-11.

```
                         Options Menu

        E)ditor                  :
        D)ISPLAY variable        : ieco.com:0
        B)ookmark file           : lynx_bookmarks.html
        F)TP sort criteria       : By Filename
        P)ersonal mail address   : moreunix@dummies.com
        S)earching type          : CASE INSENSITIVE
        C)haracter set           : ISO Latin 1
        V)I keys                 : ON
        e(M)acs keys             : ON
        K)eypad as arrows
            or Numbered links    : Links are numbered
        U)ser mode               : Novice




        Select first letter of option line, '>' to save, or 'r' to return to Lynx.
        Command:
```

Figure 18-11:
Controlling
how Lynx
works.

To change an option, type the capitalized letter in the option name. For some options, you then type the setting you want (such as the name of your favorite editor for the Editor option). For other options, there are only a few possibilities, and you can press any key (except Enter) to flip among them. Then press Enter when you see the one you want.

When you finish setting your options, press > to save them. Then press **r** to return to what you were doing in Lynx.

Here are some options you might want to fool with:

- ✔ **Editor:** This option controls which editor Lynx runs when you use it for sending mail. We recommend emacs because it's our favorite, but you may prefer pico or vi. Type the full pathname of your editor. You can send e-mail to the owners of most Web pages by using the Lynx **c** command.

- ✔ **Personal mail address:** Set this option to your own, complete e-mail address. Lynx uses it when you mail Web pages to yourself or as your return address when you mail things to others.

- ✔ **Keypad as arrows or numbered links:** If you set this option to numbered links, each link in a page is numbered, and you can choose a link by typing its number. *Note:* After you change this option, exit from Lynx and start it up again.

- ✔ **User mode:** This option is usually set to Novice, so that Lynx displays two lines of helpful menu items at the bottom of the screen. If you already know all the Lynx commands you need and would rather see two more lines of Web page, set this option to Intermediate. If you want to see the URL of each Web page, set it to Advanced.

Problems

The third line from the bottom of the screen displays various messages to tell you what to do or to let you know what's going on. Here are a few messages you might see:

- ✔ Making HTTP connection to kufacts.cc.ukans.edu. This message means that Lynx is asking kufacts.cc.ukans.edu, or whatever host computer it mentions, for the Web page you want.

- ✔ http request sent: waiting for response. If the Internet is very busy, a message like this one tells you that there's a brief delay. Lynx has spoken (metaphorically) to the host on which the Web page lives and is waiting to get the actual page.

✔ `Alert! Unable to connect to remote host` or `Alert! Unable to access document.` If you see this message, the host on which the information is stored is so busy that it doesn't have time for you. Or maybe it's down for repairs. Either way, try again later.

Browsing with Pictures: Netscape

Other browsers are available for UNIX, but Netscape currently wins the prize for most ubiquitous Web browser for UNIX computers. (At this writing, Microsoft's Internet Explorer, Netscape's chief rival in PC-land, is not available for UNIX.) There are versions of Netscape for UNIX, for Windows, and for the Macintosh. They all work in more or less the same way.

The Netscape Corporation calls their browser Netscape "Navigator" to distinguish it from Netscape Mail and Netscape News, but everyone else just calls the browser "Netscape."

Browser versions never rest

As we write this, Netscape version 3.01 is the predominant version of Netscape. (Netscape version 2 is not that much different.) Just around the corner is Netscape version 4.0, which Netscape has dubbed "Netscape Communicator." This package bundles the Navigator browser with a bunch of other software that you may or may not find useful. Aside from having a completely new interface (did we say confusing?), other programs in addition to the Navigator browser, and an appetite for lots more disk space and memory, version 4 does pretty much the same stuff as version 3. The commands we mention in the following sections are for version 4.

(Don't bother) configuring Netscape

Because Netscape is an X and Motif application, it uses dozens and dozens of X resources that you can customize. But here's our advice: Forget it. The standard configuration works fine, and our sad experience is that most changes you can make only make it worse.

Starting it up

You start Netscape by typing **netscape** to your shell. (Or with luck, maybe you have a Netscape entry on your Motif Menu.)

Netscape automatically loads the Netscape home page from its headquarters. You see a window like the one in Figure 18-12.

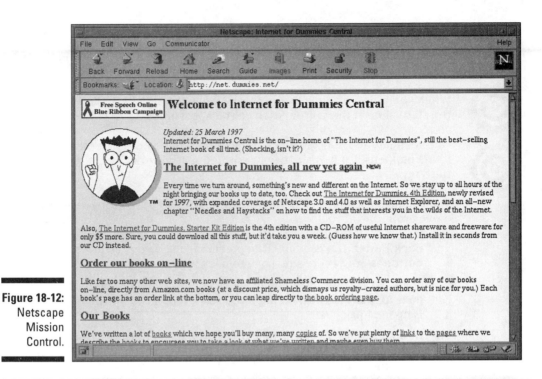

Figure 18-12:
Netscape
Mission
Control.

If you have a slow Internet connection, it may take quite a while to load the attractive nautical graphic at the top of the window. If you find yourself getting impatient, choose Options⇨Auto Load Images to tell it not to bother loading the images in pages you retrieve. In that case, it replaces the images with little graphic icons. To tell it to load an image, click the icon. Netscape is relatively smart about remembering which images it already has, so if a page uses an image it already has, it automatically displays the image.

Leaving

When you finish using Netscape, choose File⇨Exit from the menu. (You can also use the keyboard shortcut Alt+Q.)

Jumping around the Web

When you are looking at a Web page, some words and phrases are under-lined and displayed in a different color (usually, but not always, blue). These things, called *links,* refer to another, related Web page about that topic. For example, if you see *Netscape* underlined and in blue, it is a link to a Web page about (not surprisingly) Netscape.

A link may not necessarily lead to another Web page — instead, it may connect to a Gopher menu, a Usenet newsgroup, or an FTP site. In any case, the information is related to the topic you click, and Netscape can display it just fine.

When you point to a link on a Netscape page, the URL of the link appears on the status line at the bottom of the Netscape window.

Occasionally, you may get an error message when you try to retrieve a page. If this happens, try it again, because it frequently works on the second or third try.

You can also use buttons in the navigation toolbar at the top of the screen to move around:

- **Back button:** Takes you to the preceding page you retrieved. If the button is gray, there's no page to back up to.

- **Forward button:** After you have backed up by using the Back button, goes forward to the next page you retrieved. If the button is gray, there *is* no next page yet.

- **Reload button:** Reloads the current Web page. Click it if Netscape can't load a page correctly or if you think that the page may have changed since the last time Netscape loaded it and you want to try again.

- **Home button:** Returns you to your home page, which is usually a page about Netscape, unless your system manager has made it something else.

- **Search button:** Search the World Wide Web for a topic. This button takes you to a page where you can select from among several different search engines.

- **Places button:** Enables you to go to various places on the Internet that Netscape has deemed interesting.

- **Images button:** If you have loaded a page with Options⇨Auto Load Images turned off, clicking this button will turn all the graphic icons in the page to the images that they represent.

- **Print button:** Prints the current page.

- **Security button:** Options for the paranoid: This button enables you to change security settings, such as encryption of Web pages and e-mail. Unless you are really into network security issues, it's probably best to leave these unchanged.

- **Stop button:** If Netscape takes forever to retrieve something, click this to tell it to forget it.

Finding other Web pages

If you know the URL (the official technical name) of a Web page you want to see, you can tell Netscape to go directly to it:

1. **Choose File⇨Open Page from the menu (or type Alt+O).**

   Netscape asks for the URL name, using the dialog box shown in Figure 18-13.

2. **In the URL box, type the URL.**

   With luck, you have the URL in a file on your computer somewhere, so you can copy it by using copy and paste with the mouse.

3. **Click OK or press Enter.**

   Netscape retrieves the URL you requested.

The URL of the page you are looking at is displayed in the Location box at the top of the Netscape window. To go to a new URL, you can just type it into this box instead of using the File⇨Open Page menu item.

Figure 18-13:
Where to now?

Netscape: Internet for Dummies Central

File   Edit   View   Go   Communicator   Help

Back Forward Reload Home Search Guide Images Print Security Stop

Bookmarks: Location: http://net.dummies.net/

Welcome to Internet for Dummies Central
Free Speech Online
Blue Ribbon Campaign

Updated: 25 March 1997

Netscape: Open Page

Enter the World Wide Web location (URL) or specify the local file you would like to open:

[   ]   Choose File...

Open location or file in: ◇ Navigator
                            ◇ Composer

[Open]   [Clear]   [Cancel]

Also, The Internet for Dumm... ...ware and freeware
for only $5 more. Sure, you c... ...Install it in seconds
from our CD instead.

Order our books on-...

Like far too many other web sites, we now have an affiliated Shameless Commerce division. You can order any of our books on-line, directly from Amazon.com books (at a discount price, which dismays us royalty-crazed authors, but is nice for you.) Each book's page has an order link at the bottom, or you can leap directly to the book ordering page.

Our Books

We've written a lot of books which we hope you'll buy many, many copies of. So we've put plenty of links to the pages where we

Often you get e-mail or read a Usenet item that contains a URL. Rather than retype the URL, highlight the URL in the mail or news window, and then switch to Netscape, click Open, click Clear (if there's already some text in the text window), and then click the *middle* mouse button in the text window to paste in the URL you selected.

If you want to go to a URL that has the form `http://www.something.com`, Netscape offers you a shortcut: You can simply type the `something` part of the URL in the Location box, and Netscape will fill in the rest automatically.

Clicking on the shooting-star N logo in the upper-right corner takes you to Netscape's home page. This is the place to check for new releases and developments in Netscape.

Printing, saving, or copying good stuff

To print the displayed page, choose File➪Print from the menu. It suggests a print command, which you generally should leave alone, and asks whether you want to print to the printer or to a file. If you select file, a box enables you to set the filename. Then click the Print button in that window to send the page to the printer.

Remembering good places

When you find a particularly interesting page, you can add it to your list of Bookmarks of favorite Web pages. Choose Bookmarks➪Add Bookmark (or press Alt+D) to remember the current page.

To go to a page in your Bookmark list, follow these steps:

1. **Choose Bookmarks.**

2. **Scroll down to the entry you want in the bookmark list.**

3. **Release the mouse button.**

To delete a bookmark or change its name choose Bookmarks➪Edit Bookmarks (or Alt+B), as shown in Figure 18-14.

Highlight the bookmark you want to edit, and select Edit➪Bookmark Properties to change it, or Edit➪Delete to delete it.

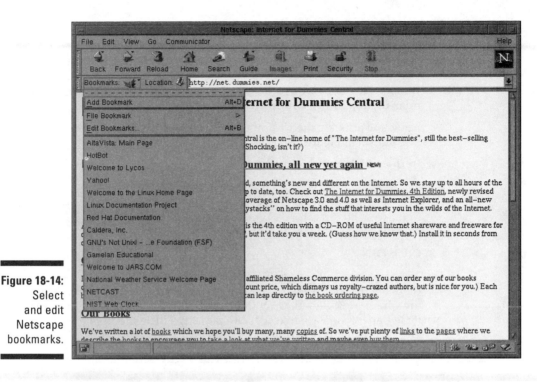

Figure 18-14:
Select
and edit
Netscape
bookmarks.

Searching for info

There are a bunch of Web directories (or "search engines," as they are known), but one of the best is AltaVista, at `http://altavista.digital.com/`. Enter keywords you want to search for, and AltaVista begins searching through millions of Web pages around the world.

Another good bet is Yahoo!, at `http://www.yahoo.com/`. The Yahoo! home page has links to categories and subcategories and, a couple of levels down, to interesting pages all over the Internet.

Several search engines are available to you by clicking on the "Search" button on the toolbar.

For a list of the search pages we find useful, check out `http://net.gurus.com/favorite.html` — you'll see a list of some of our favorite Web sites, too.

If you think that you'll use AltaVista or Yahoo! a great deal, add them to your bookmarks by choosing Bookmarks⇨Add Bookmark from the menu.

Files on the Web

You can use Netscape to download files from FTP servers. Follow these steps:

1. **Choose File⇨Open Page (or press Alt+O, or click on the Location box near the top of the window).**

   Netscape asks for the URL of the information you want, using the dialog box shown in Figure 18-12.

2. **In the URL box, enter a URL like the following:**

   ```
   ftp://hostmachine/
   ```

   In place of `hostmachine`, type the name of the FTP server. Don't forget the two slashes before it and one slash after it.

3. **Click OK.**

   Netscape connects to the FTP server, logs in as `anonymous`, and displays the root directory of the system. Items with a little folder icon are directories, and clicking them moves to that directory. Items with little paper icons are text files. Items with a little block of ones and zeroes are binary information.

Uploading Web pages

You can create Web pages stored on your own computer, and you can see them by using your own Web browser. Anyone with access to your hard disk can see the pages, but no one else can. How can you make your Web pages visible to the wide world of the Web?

Store the Web pages on a Web server, that's how. A *Web server* is a computer (usually a UNIX system) that runs a Web server program that delivers Web pages in response to requests from other people's Web browsers. Most Web servers are permanently connected to the Internet, so that your Web pages are available 24 hours a day.

To upload your Web pages to a Web server, you use FTP (see Chapter 20 for how to transfer files). Ask your Internet service provider, or whoever runs the Web server you are using, where to put your Web page files. Also ask if you need to give any special commands to tell the Web server about your files.

Here are some tips for uploading Web pages:

- ✔ Web pages are text, so upload your Web pages as ASCII (not Binary) files. Graphics files are not text, so upload them as Binary files.

- ✔ UNIX cares about capitalization in filenames. If you create Web pages on a PC or Mac and upload them to a UNIX-based Web server, check the capitalization of your filenames.

- ✔ Name your main Web page with the name `index.html`, which is the default Web page name. If you omit the filename from la URL when retrieving a Web page, your Web browser usually gets the page `index.html`. For example, if someone types the URL **http://www.greattapes.com/**, the Web browser displays the `index.html` file on that computer.

Serve those Web pages!

A *Web server* is a computer that hosts Web pages. The Web server computer runs a program that fulfills requests from other computers for Web pages stored on the Web server's disks. A UNIX machine makes a great Web server, because the Web was designed using UNIX programs. Two excellent Web server programs that run on UNIX systems are Netscape Enterprise Server and Apache.

For example, John has a computer named `net.dummies.net` on the Internet. `net.dummies.net` runs Apache (an excellent choice on John's part, because Apache is fast, reliable, and — most important — free). When you view the author team's Web site at `http://net.dummies.net`, your computer sends a request for a Web page to the Apache program on `net.dummies.net`, and Apache sends the page back to your computer so you can see it on your screen. Other popular Web servers include Netscape's and the NCSA server (Apache's grandfather).

After you've installed a Web server on your UNIX system, you tell the Web server the directory where the Web pages will be stored (the Web directory). You can store Web pages in that directory and its subdirectories. To make a Web page accessible to the world, you create the page with a Web authoring program (or with any text editor), test it on your own system to avoid embarrassing typos, and move or copy the page to your Web directory. After the page is in the Web directory, anyone can see the page if they know its URL (Web address).

If you're learning UNIX to be a Webmaster (the author and manager of a Web site), you need to know how to

✔ Install, configure, and maintain your Web server program

✔ Create and modify Web pages

If other people will be working on the Web site too, you'll need to know how to give them permissions to create and modify the files in the Web directory and its subdirectories. If you want "active" web pages with forms and other interaction, you'll also dabble in the mysteries of server-side includes and CGI scripts.

For more on Webmastering, see *Setting Up An Internet Site For Dummies,* 2nd Edition, by Jason and Ted Coombs (IDG Books Worldwide, Inc.).

4. **Move to the directory that contains the file you want.**

5. **Click the file with the right mouse button to download it.**

Using the right button pops up a menu instead of displaying the link. From the menu, select Save Link As. Netscape asks you where to put the file, and then it retrieves the file and stores it to your disk.

Telnetting with Netscape

If you are given a URL that begins with `telnet`, you can use Netscape to run a telnet program for you and look at particular information on other systems by following these steps:

1. **Choose File➪Open Page (or press Ctrl+O).**

2. **In the URL box, enter the URL that begins with** `telnet`.

   Netscape starts an `xterm` window running telnet, which connects to the Internet host computer, asks you for the username and password to use, and displays whatever the information is that the URL describes.

   This is the same telnet program you can run directly. See Chapter 21 for details.

Chapter 19

Turbocharge Your Newsreading

• •

• •

How to Read So Much Electronic Gossip That You Have No Time Left to Work

Not long after e-mail was invented, some people in North Carolina thought that it would be neat to have a distributed bulletin-board system. People could send in messages from their local machine, the messages would be distributed to a couple of other machines, and users on all the machines could see all the messages. They figured that it would be pretty popular and there could be dozens of messages per day.

Well, they were right: It's pretty popular. Most of the machines are now connected via the Internet, although there are still plenty of dial-up links, and there are now more than 100,000 machines hooked up, with sites on every continent. (We hear that there's even a machine on the Internet at one of the research stations in Antarctica.) The system handles about 100,000 messages totaling more than a gigabyte (that's a billion keystrokes) of text every day. This monster is known as *Usenet*, or sometimes *net news*.

Messages are filed in topic categories called *newsgroups*, of which there are about 20,000. Newsgroup topics range from technical discussions of computer architecture to gossip about old trains, nudism, and interminable political arguments. Reading all this stuff could take a large chunk of your workday (about 24 hours daily, or perhaps slightly more). Fortunately, the standard newsreading programs enable you to specify which groups you want to see and which ones you don't. You can identify, within groups, the topics and authors in which you are or are not interested.

Because a lot of the computers that run Usenet are UNIX systems, a lot of newsgroups discuss UNIX topics. Usenet can be a good way to find other people with questions and comments about UNIX. In Chapter 27, we list some UNIX-related newsgroups.

If you get Usenet, you can probably send out your own Usenet messages. Please resist the urge to do so until you have been reading news for a few weeks, so that you have an idea of what's appropriate to send and what isn't. Also read the newsgroup called news.announce.newusers; it contains helpful advice for new Usenet users.

The most amazing thing about Usenet is who's in charge of it: no one. It's just a big, informal, cooperative setup. The programs most commonly used to file and transfer news were written by a guy in Cambridge, Massachusetts, who probably should have been working on his regular job instead. The various news-reading programs come from educational and commercial sites all over the world. The money to pay for the network time is, by and large, hidden in corporate telephone budgets. It's the definitive example of pioneer networking.

For general information about Usenet newsgroups, see Chapter 11, "All the News that Fits and Considerably More," in *The Internet For Dummies,* 4th Edition, by John R. Levine, Carol Baroudi, and Margaret Levine Young (IDG Books Worldwide).

To use Usenet, you have to learn the following three Important News Skills:

- ✔ How to read the news that interests you
- ✔ How not to read the news that doesn't interest you, because far more news is sent every day than any single human could ever read
- ✔ How to post articles of your own (definitely optional)

Not every UNIX system gets Usenet newsgroups. Some employers have the benighted idea that spending hours every day reading alt.fan.power.rangers and rec.sports.baseball.ny-mets might not be the absolute best use of your time. If none of the newsreaders in the chapter works on your system, come up with some plausible reason to read newsgroups, and talk to your system administrator or Internet provider.

("Gee, I really need up-to-date information about widgets, so I have to be able to read the `comp.gizmos.widgets` newsgroup every day.")

How Do I Read It?

Most UNIX systems have at least one program for reading Usenet newsgroups — these programs are called *newsreaders*. The most basic is `rn`; more powerful versions are called things such as `trn` and `nn` and `tin`. This chapter describes `trn` in detail, because it's our favorite, and describes `nn` and `tin` a little, too. Many systems provide at least one of these programs for reading Usenet newsgroups.

Running `trn`

The `trn` program is a major improvement over `rn`, on which it is based, because it is *threaded* (in fact, its name stands for *t*hreaded *readn*ews). In newsgroup lingo, a *thread* is an article along with all its follow-up articles, including follow-ups to follow-ups and so on. The program can organize all the articles in a newsgroup into threads, list them, and enable you to choose the topics that look interesting. This capability makes it easy to find the wheat from among the chaff (the articles of interest amid all the surrounding dreck).

To run `trn`, just type **trn** — simple enough. If your system doesn't have it, tough luck. Skip ahead for information about `nn` or `tin`. This section describes `trn` version 3.6, by the way.

If you find that `trn` can't perform all the commands we tell you about in this chapter, you may have to tell it specifically that you plan to use all of its features. To do this, type `trn -x -X` to run it.

Editor swamp alert

If you decide to respond to articles, either by e-mail or by posting a follow-up article, your newsreader will run a text-editing program. We can't predict which one it will be, because it depends on the way the system is set up. It will probably be either `vi` or `emacs`, neither of which is particularly easy to use (see Chapter 10).

Remember your first time?

The first time you run `trn`, it checks in your home directory to see whether you have a file named `.newsrc`. (Yes, the filename begins with a period.) You may not have noticed the file because the period at the beginning of the filename makes it hidden in normal file listings. The `.newsrc` file stores information about which newsgroups you subscribe to and which messages you've already read in each one. (For the gory details about `.newsrc`, see the section, "Preventing Alzheimer's," later in this chapter.)

If you've ever run any newsreader, it created this file. If not, `trn` just makes you a brand-new one, in your home directory. It also figures that you must be a newbie, so it displays some (allegedly) helpful messages. Press the spacebar to make them go away.

This new `.newsrc` file is a list of every blessed newsgroup your system carries, and the list can be long. This first time you run `trn`, you have to go through them and unsubscribe to the groups you don't plan to read. Don't worry — you can change your mind later and subscribe again. For each newsgroup in the list, it asks whether you want to read it, to which you reply **y** or **n**. If you get tired of answering questions, press Shift+N to tell it not to subscribe to any more groups. (You can go back later and pick up ones you might have missed.)

After the first time

After you've run `trn` once, it remembers which newsgroups you are interested in and asks you about only those you subscribe to.

When new newsgroups are created, which happens every day now that Usenet is getting to be so popular, you have to decide whether to add them to your `.newsrc` file. You see a message similar to the following one, depending on the name of the new newsgroup:

```
Newsgroup alt.binaries.sounds.utilities not in .newsrc —
              subscribe? [ynYN]
```

To subscribe to the newsgroup and begin reading it now, type **y** (that's a lowercase *y*). To skip it forever, type **n** (again, a lowercase one). To add all the new newsgroups, press Shift+Y. To tell `trn` not to ask you about any of the new groups, press Shift+N.

If you choose to subscribe to a newsgroup, you see the following:

```
Put newsgroup where? [$^.Lq]
```

The various portions in the square brackets control exactly where in your `.newsrc` file you want to put this newsgroup. To put it at the end, just press the spacebar.

The `trn` program thoughtfully lets you know whether you have e-mail waiting. If so, it says `(Mail)` at the beginning of some prompts.

Choosing Newsgroups to Read

For each newsgroup in your `.newsrc` list, `trn` suggests that you read its articles. If this is your first time, the newsgroup is probably `news.announce.newusers`, the newsgroup for folks who are new to newsgroups. It's not a bad idea to peruse these articles, but we get to that topic later. The way `trn` suggests a newsgroup is with this message:

```
67 unread articles in news.announce.newusers — read now?
          [+ynq]
```

(The number of messages varies.) The [+ynq] tells you possible responses, which are as follows:

- ✔ Press + (the plus sign, which is usually Shift+=) to see the list of threads for this newsgroup, so you can select which threads to read. (If you choose this option, skip down to the section "Picking Up the Threads.")

- ✔ Type **y** (lowercase) to go ahead and look at the newsgroup article by article. (If you choose this one, skip down to the section "Reading the News.")

- ✔ Type **n** (lowercase) to not read this newsgroup, at least not now. You see the next newsgroup on its list.

- ✔ Type **q** (lowercase) to quit `trn` altogether.

You can also type **u** (lowercase) to unsubscribe from the newsgroup so that you will never be bothered by it again.

If you always like to look at the thread selector for a newsgroup, you can make pressing + (go to the thread selector first) the default for the newsgroup rather than **y** (go directly to reading articles). When `trn` asks whether you want to read the newsgroup, type **t** (lowercase). This choice turns thread selection on for this newsgroup, assuming that it was off. (If it was already on, it turns it off.) For each newsgroup, `trn` remembers whether you like to select threads first and presents the appropriate default so that, if you press the spacebar, you get what you want. We invariably prefer to see the thread selector unless the group has so few messages that it's easier to look at all of them.

Commanding trn

When trn gives you a list of possible commands in square brackets (such as [+ynq]), you generally can press any of the options that are listed. Don't press Enter — trn moves along right away as soon as you press a key. Also, you can press the spacebar to choose the first option in the square brackets (this one is the default option).

Occasionally, commands are more than one letter long, usually because they enable you to specify extra information, such as a filename in which to save a message. Commands that are longer than one letter must be followed by pressing Enter so that trn knows when you are finished typing.

The trn program cares about uppercase versus lowercase letters — it has so many commands that an uppercase letter frequently does something different from its lowercase counterpart. Be careful to capitalize commands the same way we do. We'll remind you which commands require capital letters.

While reading the news, trn is always doing one of four things:

✔ Offering a newsgroup to read

✔ Displaying a list of threads to choose among

✔ Offering an article to display

✔ Pausing while it displays an article that is too long to find on the screen

Confusingly, different commands work in these four situations. Luckily, you don't have to use many commands very often, and trn suggests the most likely options.

You can type **h** (lowercase) at any time to see trn's on-line help. It's rather concise but can certainly be helpful, especially as a reminder.

Picking Up the Threads

It's about time to read some news! When trn asks whether you want to read a newsgroup and offers the options [+ynq], press + (the plus sign) to see the list of threads for the newsgroup. You see a list of threads (topics) like the one shown in Figure 19-1.

The top line of the screen shows the name of the newsgroup (in this example, it's news.announce.newusers), along with the number of articles waiting to be read and whether it is moderated. (*Moderated* newsgroups have editors who control which messages get posted.)

```
┌────────────────────────────────────────────────────────────┐
│ ─                    Telnet - iecc.com                  ▼ ▲ │
│  File   Edit   Disconnect   Settings   Network   Help       │
│ news.announce.newusers          40 articles (moderated)   ↑ │
│ a David C Lawrence    1  List of Active Newsgroups, Part I   │
│   David C Lawrence    1  >List of Active Newsgroups, Part II │
│ b David C Lawrence    1  Alternative Newsgroup Hierarchies, Part I │
│   David C Lawrence    1  >Alternative Newsgroup Hierarchies, Part II │
│ d David C Lawrence    1  Mailing Lists Available in Usenet   │
│ e David C Lawrence    1  List of Moderators for Usenet       │
│ f David C Lawrence    1  How to Create a New Usenet Newsgroup │
│ g Stephanie Silva     1  Publicly Accessible Mailing Lists, Part 1/8 │
│   Stephanie Silva     1  >Publicly Accessible Mailing Lists, Part 2/8 │
│   Stephanie Silva     1  >Publicly Accessible Mailing Lists, Part 3/8 │
│   Stephanie Silva     1  >Publicly Accessible Mailing Lists, Part 4/8 │
│   Stephanie Silva     1  >Publicly Accessible Mailing Lists, Part 5/8 │
│   Stephanie Silva     1  >Publicly Accessible Mailing Lists, Part 6/8 │
│   Stephanie Silva     1  >Publicly Accessible Mailing Lists, Part 7/8 │
│   Stephanie Silva     1  >Publicly Accessible Mailing Lists, Part 8/8 │
│ i Ron Dippold         1  Usenet Newsgroup Creation Companion │
│ j Mark Moraes         1  Changes to "USENET Software: History and Sources" │
│ l Mark Moraes         1  Changes to "What is Usenet?"        │
│ ── Select threads (date order) ── Top 45% [>Z] ──           │
│ ←│                                                        → │
│ iecc.com                              VT100          1, 3    │
└────────────────────────────────────────────────────────────┘
```

Figure 19-1:
What topics
are we
talking
about?

Underneath that is a list of articles, organized into threads. Each thread is assigned a letter, down the left edge of the screen. (The list skips some letters, which are used for commands.) For each article, you see the author and the subject line.

The bottom line of the display tells you to choose some threads and tells you whether there are more articles than will fit on the screen (there usually are). For example, Figure 19-1 contains the top 45 percent of the articles in the newsgroup.

If you want to read the articles in a thread, press the letter assigned to the thread. A plus sign appears next to the thread letter, showing that this thread has been chosen. (If you change your mind, press the thread's letter again to deselect it.)

To see more threads, press > (which is usually Shift+. [period]). You can tell when you get to the end of the list of threads when you see Bot on the bottom line of text.

To back up and see previous pages of threads, press < (which is usually Shift+, [comma]). To begin at the beginning again, press ^ (Shift+6), or to go to the end, type $ (Shift+4).

When you've chosen the threads you want, use one of the following commands:

✔ Press Shift+X to mark all the articles in all the threads you *didn't* choose as having been read already so that trn doesn't ask you about them again. Then begin reading the articles in the threads you *did* pick.

> ✔ Press Shift+N to forget all about this newsgroup and look at the next one on your `.newsrc` list. Or press Shift+P to move to the preceding newsgroup.

Reading the News

If you pressed Shift+X after choosing the threads you wanted, or if you typed **y** when `trn` first asked about the newsgroup, `trn` begins showing you the articles one at a time. First, it shows you the article's headers, as shown in Figure 19-2.

Figure 19-2: Cryptic headers at the beginning of an article.

You have several options:

> ✔ To see the rest of the article (or at least the next screenful), press the spacebar. You see the next page of text. If the article is several pages long, you see a MORE prompt at the end of each page, until you get to the end of the article.
>
> You can get a sense of how long the article is by looking at how much has been read. The MORE prompt tells you what percentage of the article you've seen so that you can tell how far you have to go.
>
> ✔ If the article doesn't interest you, type **j** (a lowercase *j*) to "junk" the article. This choice marks the article as read (so that it doesn't offer it to you again later) and goes to the end of the article.

✔ If the entire topic is boring and you don't want to see any more articles that have the same subject line, type **k** (a lowercase *k*) to kill the topic. You skip any articles in this thread (or any other thread) that have the same text in the subject line.

✔ To bag the entire thread, including articles with a different subject line, press Shift+J. You skip any response to this article or responses to those responses or responses to the article that this one is a response to (you get the idea), regardless of whether they have the same subject line as this article. That is, they are marked as read.

✔ To quit looking at this newsgroup (for now, anyway), type **q**. The program asks you about the next newsgroup in your list.

At the end of the article, `trn` asks the following:

```
End of article 757 (of 818) — what next? [npq]
```

Again, you have lots of options:

✔ To see the next article that you haven't read yet, type **n** (lowercase) or press the spacebar.

✔ To see the preceding unread article, type **p** (lowercase). (If you've already read all the previous articles, nothing happens.)

✔ To see the last article `trn` displayed before the current one, press Shift+P. This choice displays the preceding article even though you read it already.

✔ To see the same article again, press Ctrl+R.

✔ To move the first article in the next selected thread, press > (Shift+. [period]).

✔ To quit reading this newsgroup, type **q** (lowercase). The program asks whether you want to read the next newsgroup in your list.

✔ To kill (mark as read) all articles that have this subject line, type **k** (a lowercase *k*).

✔ To kill the entire thread, including articles with a different subject line, press Shift+J.

✔ If you are way behind on reading this newsgroup and you want to give up the idea of ever catching up, type **c** (that's a lowercase *c*). The program marks all the unread articles in the newsgroup as read. The next time you read this group, you see only the new articles.

✔ If you have totally lost interest in this newsgroup, type **u** (a lowercase *u*) to unsubscribe from it.

Rot what?

Usenet has a system for protecting you from gross, disgusting, obscene, or otherwise offensive articles. Offensive articles can be posted by using a simple code called *Rot 13*. If you try to read an article and it appears as gibberish, you can press Ctrl+X to start the article over and decode it as it goes. But don't complain to us (or anyone else) if it offends you! Incidentally, if you press Ctrl+X by mistake and want to read the article *au naturel,* press Ctrl+R to redraw it normally.

Searching for something

You can use `trn`'s search command to find articles that contain a particular word or set of characters in the subject line, anywhere in the header, or anywhere in the article. To search for articles that contain *text* in the subject line, type the following command:

`/text`

If you want to look for articles that contain *text* anywhere in the header, type this command:

`/text/h`

For articles that contain *text* anywhere in the text of the articles themselves, as well as in the headers, type this command:

`/text/a`

To search backward through previous articles, type ? rather than / in any of these commands.

File It, Please

You can save the text of an article in a file if you want to transfer it to another machine, include it in a word-processing document, or just plain keep it. Follow these steps:

1. When you are at the end of an article you want to save, type the following command:

   `s filename`

   Type a lowercase **s**, and replace `filename` with the name you want to give to the file that contains the article.

If the file already exists, `trn` sticks the article at the end of it. (This is nice if you want to save an entire series of articles together in a file — as you save each article, `trn` adds it to the end of the file.)

If the file doesn't exist, `trn` asks what kind of file to make, as follows:

```
File /usr/margy/News/save.it doesn't exist—
    use mailbox format? [ynq]
```

2. To save it in a regular text file, type **n** (lowercase). To save it in the kind of file in which mail programs store e-mail messages, type **y** (lowercase).

If you don't tell `trn` otherwise, it saves files in a directory named `News` in your home directory. You can enter a pathname if you want to put the file elsewhere. Use a tilde (~) to tell `trn` to put a file in your home directory, as follows:

```
s ~/article.about.chickens
```

We find it most convenient to save messages in mailbox format, because then we can use a mail program such as Pine or `elm` to handle files of saved articles. (The only difference between a mailbox file and a nonmailbox file is that a mailbox has a separator line before each message.)

When Is an Article Not Really an Article?

Sometimes a news article contains not plain text, but rather a coded version of a binary file or group of files. There are two common ways to sneak files into articles: uuencoding and shar files.

In a *uuencoded* message, a single binary file is turned into a lot of ugly-looking text, like the following:

```
begin 644 sample
M5V]W(2!)9B!Y;W4@86-
            T=6%L;;'D@='E='E"EP960@:6X@=&AI<R!W:&]L92!F:69E
M(&%%%N9"!IU==61E8V]D960@:70@@<W5C8V5S<V9U;&QY+&QY+'!T*'T^6]U)W)E(&8$$@@<F5A
M;&QQ(&EE9&EEC9871E9"!R96X7@D<C97%D<0((<"!D<$@;'F]T*'1T)T92!A="%I;;;;
M=6YI0I>$!@I=96I><$+;F]W+VC!;F.;"%`;F9T*"T92!A="%I;;;;,
            09&4@=&36$)$$S+@T*
"#OH*
'
end
```

Usually, uuencoded files are much longer than this one, but they're all equally ugly. Really long ones are often split across several news messages to keep each individual article to a reasonable size. Uuencoded files are most often found in groups such as `comp.binaries.ms-windows`, in which case they're runnable programs, or in groups such as `alt.binaries.pictures.erotica`, in which case they're digitized pictures of, er, various stuff.

A *shar file* (short for *sh*ell *ar*chive) contains a group of files. Most often they contain program source code, but they can contain any text files. Here's a short example:

```
#!/bin/sh
# This is a shell archive (produced by shar 3.49)
# To extract the files from this archive, save it to a
          file, remove
# everything above the "!/bin/sh" line above, and type "sh
          file_name".
#
# made 05/25/1997 01:43 UTC by johnl@iecc
# Source directory /usr/johnl
#
# existing files will NOT be overwritten unless -c is
          specified
#
# This shar contains:
# length  mode       name
# ----------------------------------
#    112 -rw-rw-r— poem
#
# ============= poem =============
if test -f 'poem' -a X"$1" != X"-c"; then
   echo 'x - skipping poem (File already exists)'
else
echo 'x - extracting poem (Text)'
sed 's/^X//' << 'SHAR_EOF' > 'poem' &&
I eat my peas with honey
I've done it all my life
It makes them taste real funny
But it keeps them on my knife.
SHAR_EOF
chmod 0664 poem ||
echo 'restore of poem failed'
Wc_c="`wc -c < 'poem'`"
test 112 -eq "$Wc_c" ||
   echo 'poem: original size 112, current size' "$Wc_c"
fi
exit 0
```

The trn program makes it easy to extract the useful bits from uuencoded or shar files. When you see this type of message, you can extract its contents by typing **e** (lowercase) followed by the name of the directory in which to extract it. (If you just type **e** and then press Enter, trn uses your News directory.) Multipart uuencoded files are also handled more or less automatically. After you extract the contents of the first part of a uuencoded message, trn says (continued), and it's up to you to find the next part and type **e** again. After the last part, it says Done. Shar files are extracted in the same way as uuencoded files, except that there's no such thing as a multipart shar file. (Large programs may be multipart messages, but each one is a separate shar file.)

Shar and uuencode files present some enormous potential security holes. Shar files are really no more than lists of commands for the UNIX shell that create the files to be extracted. This setup offers considerable flexibility, but it also means that a prankster can stick in some commands you would just as soon not execute, such as ones that delete all your files. Shar files from moderated groups (that is, groups in which all the messages are examined and approved by a third party before being sent out) are generally okay, but the files in other groups are only as reliable as the people sending them. Shar scanning programs are available that scan shar files for untoward commands. Check with your system manager to see whether any of these programs is available on your system.

Uuencoded files of pictures are unlikely to cause any trouble, other than the hair on your palms you may get from looking at some of them. Uuencoded binary programs should be treated as skeptically as any other binary programs. Again, the ones that come from moderated groups are pretty safe; others are less so. A scan with a virus checker is always appropriate.

Dealing with Articles That Demand a Response

If you read an article that demands a response, you have two options: You can respond privately by sending e-mail to the person who wrote it, or you can post a follow-up article to the newsgroup. The following list shows you how to decide which way to go:

- ✔ If your response will be of interest to only the person who wrote the article, send e-mail.

- ✔ If you are really mad, take a walk before doing anything. If you're still mad and you just *have* to reply, send e-mail.

✔ If the original article contains errors that everyone reading it should know about, post a follow-up article, but only after checking that 12 other people haven't already done the same thing.

✔ If you have additional information about the subject that will be of universal interest to those reading the original article, post a follow-up article.

Responding privately by e-mail

When you are at the end of an article to which you want to respond privately, these steps show you what to do:

1. Decide whether you want to quote parts of the article in your e-mail.

   If you do, press Shift+R. Otherwise, type **r** (lowercase).

   You see a bunch of confusing messages, followed by a question about including a prepared file.

2. Assuming that you have not prepared a text file in advance that you now want to include in your e-mail, press Enter to tell `trn` not to include any file.

   The program now asks which editor you want to use.

3. If you don't like the editor it suggests, type the command you use to start your editor. Otherwise, just press Enter.

   The `trn` program runs the editor. If you chose to include the text of the original article, it is already sitting on-screen, indented to show that you are quoting it. The headers for the e-mail are at the top of the screen too.

4. Delete unnecessary text.

   Be sure to delete the boring header lines from the original article (not the ones that address your e-mail message, at the top of the screen — the ones that are quoted from the original article). Also delete parts of the article that you don't plan to discuss in your e-mail message. Pare the quoted text down to the bare minimum, just enough to remind the person what article it is that you just read and are responding to.

5. Type your reply. Be clear, polite, and reasonable.

6. Save your message and exit from the editor, using whatever commands work in your editor.

   The program asks the following:

```
Check spelling, Send, Abort, Edit, or List?
```

7. To run a spelling checker, type **c** (lowercase). To forget all about sending this e-mail, type **a** (lowercase). To return to the editor to make one more little change, type **e** (lowercase). And to send the message, type **s** (lowercase). Then press Enter.

The program asks whether you want it to stick your signature file at the end of the message. (A signature file is a file called .signature in your home directory, and contains your name, return address, and other info.)

8. Type **y** or **n** (both lowercase) and press Enter.

You return to you where you left off — right at the end of the article you just responded to.

Actually, you can type **r** (lowercase) to send an e-mail message to anyone, not just to the person who wrote the article you just read. If you suddenly get the urge to write a note to your mom, type **r** and follow the steps to enter the editor. After you are editing your response, you can change the To line to any address you want, instead of the article's author, and the Subject line to any subject.

Possibly making a fool of yourself

Okay, you've decided to take the plunge. You have something so interesting to say that you want to post it publicly, where it can be read, appreciated, savored, misconstrued, or laughed at. Here's how to do it:

1. Press Shift+F to tell trn that you want to post a follow-up article, and include some or all of the original article.

The program gives you a sage warning, such as the following:

```
This program posts news to thousands of machines
        throughout the entire civilized world. Your
        message will cost the net hundreds if not thou-
        sands of dollars to send everywhere. Please be
        sure you know what you are doing.

Are you absolutely sure that you want to do this? [ny]
```

2. If you have thought better of it, type **n** and press Enter. You can always send an e-mail message to the article's author, and then decide to go public later. If you still want to post an article, type **y**. Then press Enter.

The program asks whether you want to include a prepared file that is, a text file you've already written.

3. Assuming that you have not prepared a text file in advance that you now want to include in your article, press Enter to tell `trn` not to include any file.

The program may ask which editor you want to use. Or it may just dump you into an editor, probably `vi`.

4. If you don't like the editor it suggests, type the command you use to start your editor. Otherwise, just press Enter.

The `trn` program runs the editor. If you chose to include the text of the original article, it is already sitting on the screen, indented to show that you are quoting it. The headers for your follow-up article are at the top of the screen, too.

Take a look at the `Newsgroups:` line at the top of the message. It lists the newsgroups to which this article will be posted.

5. Delete any newsgroups that wouldn't be interested in your article.

6. Move down to the beginning of the text of the article you are replying to, and delete unnecessary text.

Be sure to delete the boring header lines along with any parts of the article that you don't plan to refer to. Pare the quoted text down to the bare minimum, just enough to remind newsgroup readers what exactly you are responding to.

7. Type your reply. Be clear, polite, and reasonable.

8. Save your message and exit from the editor, using whatever commands work in your editor.

. Lines in Usenet articles are usually limited to 70 characters. If any of the lines in your article are longer than that, `trn` warns you about it, so you can go back and fix it. Then it gives you the following choice:

```
Check spelling, Send, Abort, Edit, or List?
```

9. To run a spelling checker, type **c**. To forget all about posting this article, type **a**. To return to the editor to make one more little change, type **e**. And to send the message, type **s**. Then press Enter.

Your article wings out across the universe, and `trn` displays a message confirming this. Then you are back at the end of the article you responded to.

When you post an article to an unmoderated newsgroup, the article is distributed directly all over the Internet. When you post to a moderated newsgroup, the article is e-mailed to the person (or group) who moderates the newsgroup. The moderator decides whether the article is appropriate to post. You generally get an automated response from the moderator's computer, and sometimes follow-up mail from the moderator.

Before sending a real posting to a real newsgroup, experiment in the `misc.test` newsgroup, which exists exactly for this purpose. You won't annoy anyone by posting to `misc.test` — no one reads the message there anyway.

Being Original

You can post an article that isn't a follow-up to any other message. That is, you can launch a brand-new thread on a brand-new topic, if you like.

To do so, type **f** when you are reading the newsgroup to which you want to post the article. The program asks whether you want to respond to the article you just read or start a new topic. Type **y** to start a new topic, and type the subject of the article when `trn` asks.

Fiddling with Your Newsgroups

When `trn` offers a newsgroup for you to read, you can give dozens of commands. In addition to the four commands listed earlier in the chapter (+, y, n, and q), you can use the following commands to add or delete newsgroups from your list:

✔ To delete a newsgroup from your list (that is, to unsubscribe to it), type **u** (that's a lowercase *U*).

✔ To add a newsgroup that's not on your `.newsrc` list, type the following command:

```
g newsgroupname
```

Replace `newsgroupname` with the exact name of the newsgroup. For example, if you are interested in naturist activities, type this command:

```
g rec.nude
```

✔ If you are not sure of the exact name of the newsgroup you are looking for, type the following:

```
a text
```

Replace `text` with a word or part of a word. For example, if you are interested in gardening, type this:

```
a garden
```

If `trn` finds any newsgroups with names that contain those characters, it asks whether you want to subscribe to each one. Type **y** or **n** to subscribe or not. When `trn` asks where to put the newsgroup, just press the spacebar.

Preventing Alzheimer's

All newsreading programs store information about your particular preferences and situation, including what newsgroups you subscribe to, and which messages you've already read. (Messages in each newsgroup are numbered, so it can just remember the range of message numbers that you've seen.) The information is stored in a file named `.newsrc`. Whether you use `rn`, `trn`, or `nn` to read the news, they all share the information in the `.newsrc` file. This file is the way that most newsreading programs don't forget all about what you've subscribed to and what you've already read.

To look at your `.newsrc` file, when `trn` asks whether you want to look at a newsgroup, press Shift+L. You see a listing like the following:

```
#  Status   Newsgroup
  0 (READ)   local.risks! 1-5548,5551-5556
  1 (UNSUB)  local.pcdigest! 1-7197
  2 (UNSUB)  comp.binaries.ibm.pc.d! 1-17823
  3 (UNSUB)  comp.sys.ibm.pc.digest! 1-580
  4 (UNSUB)  comp.text.desktop! 1-2558
  5 (UNSUB)  rec.food.veg! 1-36863,37791,37958
  6     37   rec.humor.funny! 1-3424
  7 (UNSUB)  rec.humor! 1-105750,106727,107119
  8    152   rec.arts.startrek.info! 1-1942
  9 (UNSUB)  news.lists.ps-maps! 1-1111
 10 (UNSUB)  comp.sys.ibm.pc.programmer! 1-5748
 11 (UNSUB)  comp.specification! 1-1337
 12 (UNSUB)  comp.text.tex! 1-35685
```

The first column of the listing just numbers the groups for your reference. The second column says:

- a number, meaning that you subscribe to the group and that's how many unread articles are waiting for you

- READ, meaning that you subscribe to the group and have read all its articles

- UNSUB, meaning that you once subscribed to it but unsubscribed in disgust

- BOGUS, meaning that it's not in the official list of real newsgroups

- JUNK, meaning nothing (`trn` ignores lines that say *JUNK* here)

A colon after a newsgroup name means you're subscribed to the group; an exclamation point means you're not. The number ranges are the article numbers of the articles that are marked as having been read.

Reading the best ones first

The `trn` program goes down the list of newsgroups in your `.newsrc` file, asking you about each one in order. If your `.newsrc` file has many newsgroups in it, it's a good idea to put the ones you read most often first. This avoids having to skip over the less interesting ones each time.

When `trn` asks whether you want to read a newsgroup, and you want to move this newsgroup, type **m** and Enter. Now press one of the following:

- ✔ Type ^ to put it first.
- ✔ Type $ to put it last.
- ✔ Type a number to tell `trn` what line number to put in on in your `.newsrc` file.
- ✔ Press + and the name of another newsgroup to put it after that newsgroup.
- ✔ Type **q** (lowercase) to forget the whole thing.

Killing Articles That Displease You

We abhor violence as much as you do, but sometimes you gotta do what you gotta do. An ugly fact of Usenet life is that a lot of garbage appears in newsgroups, mixed in with the good stuff. One powerful method of avoiding it is to use `trn`'s thread selector, described earlier in this chapter. A more permanent method is the *kill file*.

What's a kill file?

The `trn` program has two kinds of kill files: your global kill file, which applies to all your newsgroups, and kill files for each newsgroup. Both types of kill files contain information about which types of Usenet messages you never, never want to see. Messages described in your kills files are simply skipped over by `trn`, so they never bother you.

For example, what if some idiot decides that it is very funny to send gross and useless messages to a newsgroup that you like to read. You can skip over them, true, but wouldn't it be nice to just tell `trn`, "Look, if you get any message from that idiot, ignore them! I don't want to see them!" With kill files, you can.

Alternatively, if you are interested only in a small subject of the articles in a newsgroup, you can tell `trn`, "In this newsgroup, I only want to see articles that contain thus-and-such in the subject." Rather than killing a group of articles, you can kill all but a group of articles. You can use kill files to select articles, too.

The global kill file contains a list of commands that `trn` executes every time you begin reading a newsgroup. Newsgroup kill files contain the commands that `trn` executes when you enter that particular newsgroup. The commands usually tell `trn` which articles to kill (that is, ignore and never show you) or select (that is, ignore all the *other* articles). Your global kill file is stored in your `News` directory, and is named `KILL`.

The kill files for each newsgroup are stored in subdirectories of your `News` directory. For example, your kill file for the `rec.humor.funny` newsgroup is stored in `News/rec/humor/funny/KILL`.

It's usually better to use newsgroup kill files rather than the global kill files, because the types of articles you want to kill or to select tend to differ widely from newsgroup to newsgroup. It can slow down your newsreading if `trn` has to execute a bunch of unnecessary commands at the beginning of each newsgroup. On the other hand, there has been an unfortunate spate of advertisements posted to every newsgroup in the known universe (a practice known as *spamming*, which is an insult to Spam Brand Meat-Type Product) for which a global kill file is the best response.

License to kill

You can add commands to your newsgroup kill file when you are choosing the threads to read, but the best time is when you are reading articles. When you are looking at a particularly obnoxious article, here's how to draw some blood:

1. Press Shift+A.

    This adds a command to the newsgroup kill file, telling `trn` what to do with all articles that have the same subject as this article, both now and in the future, forever.

    The program then asks `[+j.,]` (surely one of the most inspired prompts of all time) — this is its way of asking what exactly you want to do with these articles.

2. To kill (skip) all the articles, type **j** (lowercase). To kill all the articles as well as any replies to them, press , (a comma).

A faster way of killing articles on the same subject as the current article is pressing Shift+K. This is the same as typing **Aj**.

Narrowing your view

Alternatively, you may want to tell `trn` that you are *only* interested in articles on a certain subject, now and forever. When you are looking at an article on that subject, press Shift+A (uppercase). Then press + to look at only articles on that subject. Or press . (period) to look at only those articles and replies to them.

Editing the kill file

You can use a text editor to look at what's in your kill file and make some changes. To edit your global kill file, wait until `trn` is asking you whether you want to read a newsgroup. Instead of answering, press Ctrl+K. To edit a newsgroup kill file, when you are reading that newsgroup, press Ctrl+K. Either way, `trn` runs a text editor and loads up the appropriate kill file.

Each line in a kill file contains one command, telling `trn` to either skip all articles that fit a certain description, or to look only at articles that fit a description. The first line in a kill file tells `trn` the message number of the latest message that `trn` has looked at, as in the following:

```
THRU 13567
```

Commands look like this:

```
/Buzz off, buddy!/:j
```

The text between the slashes tells `trn` what text to look for in the subjects of articles. The character after the colon (a *j* in this example) tells `trn` what do with the articles: *j* to junk them, a comma to junk them and their replies, a + to select only them, and a period to select only them and their replies. Not exactly easy to remember!

Here's another example: Let's say that you read the newsgroup `news.groups`, which is where discussions about new newsgroups take place. However, there can be several hundred messages a day. You are only interested in articles that have anything to do with cats. To see only those articles, you can add the following line to the kill file for the `news.groups` kill file:

```
/cat/:+
```

This command selects all articles with a subject line that contains the word *cat*.

New hope for the dead

If you add a command to a kill file and then you change your mind, the only way to get rid of it is to edit the kill file. When you are in the newsgroups, press Ctrl+K to edit the file. Look for the command (if it's the last one you created, it's at the end of the file). Using your editor's commands, delete the whole like, or modify it until it does what you want.

Using tin

The last newsreader we'll look at, briefly again, is tin, written by Iain Lea at Siemens in Germany. This program makes better use of a terminal screen than do the other newsreaders, so many users prefer it to the other leading brands.

Start tin by typing **tin** (tricky, eh?) You'll see a screen like the one in Figure 19-3.

Figure 19-3:
tin shows you some newsgroups.

```
  File  Edit  Disconnect  Settings  Script  Network  Help
                         Group Selection (125)              Type 'h' for help

->    21   news.groups                      13
      22   news.groups.reviews              1
      23   news.lists
      24   news.lists.ps-maps
      25   comp.arch
      26   comp.archives                    148
      27   comp.compilers
      28   comp.compression
      29   comp.compression.research
      30   comp.dcom.lans.ethernet
      31   comp.dcom.telecom                19
      32   comp.dcom.telecom.tech           2
      33   local.telecom
      34   alt.dcom.telecom                 1
      35   alt.snail-mail
      36   local.teletech                   2
      37   comp.society.privacy             1
      38   comp.doc
      39   comp.doc.techreports
      40   comp.internet.library

  Ready                                            VT100          24, 1
```

Choosing newsgroups

Your subscribed groups are listed with a line number at the left, and the number of unread articles at the right. You can move up and down using cursor keys and PgUp and PgDn, or by typing the line number. To look at the articles in a group, move the cursor to that group's line and press Enter.

The `tin` program updates the index files it keeps for the group (which can take a while for a busy group), and then displays a list of articles.

Choosing and reading articles

For each topic, there's a line number, a plus sign if there are unread articles with that topic, the number of follow-ups to the article, the title, and the author.

To read a particular article, move to the article with cursor keys or by typing the line number, and then press Enter. It's usually more convenient to press Tab to go to the next unread article.

In an article, you can use the following keys:

- ✔ Pressing Tab goes to the next page of the article, or on the last page, to the next unread article. On the last page of the last unread article, it goes to the next group with unread news. (Perhaps we should offer a "`tin` convenience keyboard" that has only a giant tab key.)

- ✔ If you want to skip to the next article without reading the rest of the current one, type **n** to move to the next article or press Shift+N to move to the next unread article.

- ✔ Type **i** to go back to the article index (the list of article names) and type **i** again to return to the index of newsgroups.

- ✔ Most other commands are similar to `trn` and `nn`: type **r** or Shift+R to reply to the author of an article, **f** or Shift+F to post a follow-up, **c** to catch up a group (pretend that you've read it all), and so forth.

- ✔ Type **h** at any point for a surprisingly readable help screen

Getting uuencoded and shar files out of articles

One thing that `tin` does quite differently is extracting uuencoded or shar files. It's not hard, but it's not obvious. Follow these steps:

1. Display the article index for the group with the articles you want to extract.

2. Move to each article to be extracted (just one for a shar file, one or more for a multi-part uuencoded file) and tag each one by pressing Shift+T.

   The program displays sequential numbers for each article tagged.

3. Tell tin to save the tagged articles in a temporary file by typing **s**.

4. When tin asks for a file name, give it one.

   A traditional temporary file name is foo.

   After tin saves the articles, it asks what to do with them.

5. Type **s** to extract a shar file, or **u** to extract a uuencoded file.

   The program thoughtfully deletes the temporary file if the extract worked.

6. Press Shift+U to untag the articles you just saved and extracted.

Leaving tin

Type **q** for quit. (You probably guessed that.) The program asks whether it should catch up all the groups you looked at (that is, mark all unread articles as read). Type **n**, and you're finished.

Using Graphical Newsreaders

Several graphical newsreaders are available for UNIX. They don't necessarily do the job of reading newsgroups any better than their text-based counterparts, but they're certainly prettier and arguably easier to learn. If you prefer clicking buttons with the mouse to typing obscure commands, see whether any of these are available on your system. The most commonly encountered graphical newsreaders that run under X Windows are knews, nn-tk (which, as its name suggests, is based on nn), and Qnews. And, of course, there is Netscape, whose Collabra newsreader comes bundled with the Netscape Communicator package.

Chapter 20

Grabbing Files from the Net

● ●

● ●

Hey, Man, Wanna File?

In Chapter 18, we explained how to use your Web browser to grab files that are stored on the Internet. Web browsers are definitely the easiest way to download files to your computer; just find a Web page with a link to the file and click the link.

If you want to copy to or from a non-UNIX machine, however, or if you want to retrieve files from a public file archive on a machine on which you don't have a personal account, you need a real industrial-strength file copying program. Your Web browser just can't cut the mustard (whatever that means). Instead, you can use the File Transfer Protocol system (FTP), which is widely used on computers all over the Internet.

You can use FTP to transfer files to or from computers on which you have accounts. You can also use FTP to *download* (transfer to your computer) files from any of a bunch of publicly available FTP servers out there on the Internet. Thousands of public FTP servers are on the Internet, each with hundreds of files that might be of use, including text, pictures, and programs. It's just a matter of locating them and downloading them!

After we tell you about how to use FTP, we list some of the big FTP servers you might want to use.

You're a Copying Machine

It's pretty simple to copy a file from one place to another (but don't forget — computers are involved). Here's how it works: Log in to the other computer for FTP and tell it what you want to copy and where you want it copied.

Getting connected

To run the `ftp` program, you type **ftp** and the name of the host computer where the FTP server you want is, as follows:

```
ftp iecc.com
```

(That's John's computer. It has files, but perhaps not all that many in which you're interested, unless you care deeply about techniques for translating one programming language to another.) Substitute the FTP server's name for `iecc.com`.

Assuming that it's not too busy to let you connect, the FTP server greets you with a message like the following:

```
Connected to iecc.com.
220 iecc FTP server (Version 4.1 8/1/91) ready.
```

The computer asks for your username and password on the host computer. If you don't have an account on the computer, don't panic. See the section "No Names Please," later in this chapter. (On this particular computer, unless you happen to be one of the authors of this book, it's extremely unlikely that you have an account. We're using it as an example.)

If the FTP server likes you, it says something like this:

```
230 User johnl logged in.
ftp>
```

The `ftp>` is FTP's prompt, telling you that it's ready for you to type a command.

Getting your file

To copy a file from the FTP server (the host computer) to your own computer, use the `get` command, as follows:

```
get README
```

Substitute the name of the file in place of README in this command. FTP says something like the following:

```
150 Opening ASCII mode data connection for README (12686
          bytes).
226 Transfer complete.
local: README remote: README
12979 bytes received in 28 seconds (0.44 Kbytes/s)
```

FTP always tells you far more than you want to know about the transfer. When it says that the transfer is complete, you've got the file.

You have to type the filename by using the syntax the server uses. In particular, if the server is a UNIX system (as most are), upper- and lowercase are different, so *README, Readme,* and *readme* are different filenames.

Getting out

When you finish transferring files, type the command **quit**. FTP responds with this heart-felt message:

```
221 Goodbye.
```

Files with Finesse

That's basically how FTP works, but, of course, you need to know about 400 other odds and ends to use FTP effectively.

When is a file not a file?

When it's a text file. The FTP definition specifies six different kinds of files, of which only two types are useful: ASCII and binary. An *ASCII file* is a text file. A *binary file* is anything else. FTP has two modes, ASCII and binary (also called *image* mode), to transfer the two kinds of files. When you transfer an ASCII file between different kinds of computers that store files differently, ASCII mode automatically adjusts the file during the transfer so that the file is a valid text file when it is stored on the receiving end. A binary file is left alone and transferred verbatim.

You tell FTP which mode to use with the binary and ascii commands, as follows:

```
ftp> binary
200 Type set to I.
ftp> ascii
200 Type set to A.
```

In the preceding example, the *I* is for binary or image mode (after 25 years, the Internet protocol czars still can't make up their minds what to call it), and the *A* is for ASCII mode. Like most FTP commands, `binary` and `ascii` can be abbreviated by lazy typists to the first three letters — so `bin` and `asc` will suffice.

How to foul up your files in FTP

The most common FTP error made by inexperienced Internet users (and by experienced users, for that matter) is transferring a file in the wrong mode. If you transfer a text file in binary mode from a UNIX system to a DOS, Windows, or Macintosh system, the file looks something like this (on a DOS or Windows machine):

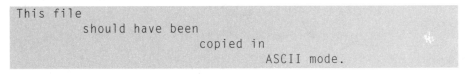
```
This file
         should have been
                          copied in
                                    ASCII mode.
```

On a Mac, the entire file looks like it's on one line. When you look at the file with a text editor on a UNIX system, you see strange ^M symbols at the end of each line. You don't necessarily have to retransfer the file. Many networking packages come with programs that do ex-post-facto conversion from one format to the other.

If, on the other hand, you copy something that isn't a text file in ASCII mode, it gets scrambled. Compressed files don't decompress; executable files don't execute (or they crash or hang the machine); images look unimaginably bad. When a file is corrupted, the first thing you should suspect is the wrong mode in FTP.

If you are FTP-ing (Is that a verb? It is now.) files between two computers of the same type, such as from one UNIX system to another, you can and should do all your transfers in binary mode. Whether you're transferring a text file or a nontext file, it doesn't require any conversion, so binary mode does the right thing.

It's often comforting to get a directory listing before issuing a `get` or `put` command, so that you can have an idea of how long the copy will take.

WARNING!

Patience is a virtue

The Internet is pretty fast, but not infinitely so. When you are copying stuff between two computers on the same local network, information can move at about 200,000 characters per second. When the two machines are separated by a great deal of intervening Internet, the speed drops — often to 1,000 characters per second or fewer. So if you're copying a file that's 500,000 characters long, it takes only a few seconds over a local network, but it can take several minutes over a long-haul connection.

The directory thicket

Every machine you can contact for FTP stores its files in many different directories, which means that to find what you want, you have to learn the rudiments of directory navigation. Fortunately, you wander around directories in FTP in pretty much the same way as you do on your own system. The command you use to list the files in the current directory is dir, and to change to another directory, you use the command cd, as in the following example:

```
ftp> dir
200 PORT command successful.
150 Opening ASCII mode data connection for /bin/ls.
total 23
drwxrwxr-x   19 root      archive       512 Jun 24 12:09 doc
drwxrwxr-x    5 root      archive       512 May 18 08:14 edu
drwxr-xr-x   31 root      wheel         512 Jul 12 10:37
             systems
drwxr-xr-x    3 root      archive       512 Jun 25  1992
             vendorware
   ... lots of other stuff ...
226 Transfer complete.
1341 bytes received in 0.77 seconds (1.7 Kbytes/s)
ftp> cd edu
250 CWD command successful.
ftp> dir
200 PORT command successful.
150 Opening ASCII mode data connection for /bin/ls.
total 3
 -rw-rw-r-    1 root      archive     87019 Dec 13  1996 R
```

```
-rw-rw-r—   1 root      archive     41062 Dec 13  1996 RS
-rw-rw-r—   1 root      archive    554833 Dec 13  1996 Rings
drwxr-xr-x  2 root      archive       512 May 18 09:31 ad-
            ministrative
drwxr-xr-x  3 root      archive       512 May 11 06:44 ee
drwxrwxr-x  8 root      234           512 Jun 28 06:00 math
226 Transfer complete.
200 bytes received in 63 seconds (0.0031 Kbytes/s)
ftp> quit
221 Goodbye.
```

In a standard UNIX directory listing, the first letter on the line tells you whether something is a file or a directory. d means that it's a directory — anything else is a file. In the directory edu in the preceding example, the first three entries are files, and the last three are other directories. Generally, you FTP to a host, get a directory listing, change to another directory, get a listing there, and so on until you find the files you want. Then you use the get command to retrieve them.

You often find that the directory on your machine in which you start the FTP program is not the one in which you want to store the files you retrieve. In that case, use the lcd command to change the directory on the local machine.

To review: cd changes directories on the other host; lcd changes directories on your own machine. (You might expect cd to change directories correspondingly on both machines, but it doesn't.)

What's that name again?

Sometimes on your machine, you have to give a file a name that's different from the name it has on a remote machine. (This is particularly true on DOS machines, on which many UNIX names are just plain illegal, as well as when you're retrieving Macintosh, Windows 95, or Windows NT files, which can contain spaces and special characters.) Also, if you need to get a bunch of files, it can be tedious to type all the get commands. Fortunately, FTP has workarounds for both those problems. Suppose that you've found a file named rose and you want to download it as rose.gif because it contains a GIF-format image. First, make sure that you're in binary mode, and then retrieve the file with the get command. This time, however, you give two names to get — the name of the file on the remote host and the local name — so that it renames the file as the file arrives. Do this as shown in the following interaction:

```
ftp> bin
200 Type set to I.
ftp> get rose2 rose2.gif
200 PORT command successful.
150 Opening BINARY mode data connection for rose2 (47935
        bytes).
226 Transfer complete.
local: rose2.gif remote: rose2
47935 bytes received in 39 seconds (1.2 Kbytes/s)
```

Next, suppose that you want to get a bunch of the files that begin with ru. In that case, you use the mget (which stands for *m*ultiple *GET*) command to retrieve them. The names you type after mget can be either plain filenames or wildcard patterns that match a bunch of filenames. For each matching name, FTP asks whether you want to retrieve that file, as in the following example:

```
ftp> mget ru*
mget ruby? n
mget ruby2? n
mget ruger_pistol? n
mget rugfur01? n
mget rush? y
200 PORT command successful.
150 Opening BINARY mode data connection for rush (18257
        bytes).
226 Transfer complete.
local: rush remote: rush
18257 bytes received in 16 seconds (1.1 Kbytes/s)
mget rush01? y
200 PORT command successful.
150 Opening BINARY mode data connection for rush01 (205738
        bytes).
local: rush01 remote: rush01
205738 bytes received in 200.7 seconds (1.2 Kbytes/s)
mget rush02?
```

If you find that mget matches more files than you expected, you can stop it with the usual interrupt character for your system — typically Ctrl+C or Delete, as the following shows:

```
^C
Continue with mget? n
ftp> quit
221 Goodbye.
```

You can even interrupt in the middle of a transfer if a file takes longer to transfer than you want to wait.

You also can do an *express* mget, which doesn't ask any questions and enables you to find exactly the files you want. To tell FTP not to ask you about each file, use the prompt command before you give the mget command, as this example shows:

```
ftp> prompt
Interactive mode off.
ftp> mget 92-1*
200 PORT command successful.
150 Opening BINARY mode data connection for 92-10.gz
          (123728 bytes).
226 Transfer complete.
local: 92-10.gz remote: 92-10.gz 123728 bytes received in
          2.8 seconds (43 Kbytes/s)
200 PORT command successful.
150 Opening BINARY mode data connection for 92-11.gz
          (113523 bytes).
226 Transfer complete.
local: 92-11.gz remote: 92-11.gz 113523 bytes received in
          3.3 seconds (34 Kbytes/s)
200 PORT command successful.
150 Opening BINARY mode data connection for 92-12.gz
          (106290 bytes).
226 Transfer complete.
local: 92-12.gz remote: 92-12.gz 106290 bytes received in
          2.2 seconds (47 Kbytes/s)
```

Here's a file in your eye

Okay, now you know how to retrieve files from other computers. How about copying the other way? It's just about the same procedure, except that you use put rather than get. The following example shows how to copy a local file called rnr to a remote file called rnr.new:

```
ftp> put rnr rnr.new
200 PORT command successful.
150 Opening ASCII mode data connection for rnr.new.
226 Transfer complete.
local: rnr remote: rnr.new
168 bytes sent in 0.014 seconds (12 Kbytes/s)
```

(As with get, if you want to use the same name when you make the copy, leave out the second name.)

The mput command works just like the mget command does, only in the other direction. If you have a bunch of files whose names begin with uu and you want to copy most of them, issue the mput command, as in the following example (the bold is the user's input):

```
ftp> mput uu*
mput uupick? y
200 PORT command successful.
150 Opening ASCII mode data connection for uupick.
226 Transfer complete.
local: uupick remote: uupick
156 bytes sent in 0.023 seconds (6.6 Kbytes/s)
mput uupoll? y
200 PORT command successful.
150 Opening ASCII mode data connection for uupoll.
226 Transfer complete.
local: uupoll remote: uupoll
200 bytes sent in 0.013 seconds (15 Kbytes/s)
mput uurn? n
```

(As with mget, you can use the prompt command to tell it to go ahead and not to ask any questions.)

Most systems have protections on their files and directories that limit where you can copy files. Generally, you can use FTP only to put a file anywhere that you could create a file if you were logged in directly. If you're using anonymous FTP (see the section "No Names, Please," later in this chapter), you usually can't put any files to the other host.

A bunch of other file-manipulation commands are sometimes useful, as in the following example of the delete command:

```
delete somefile
```

(Replace *somefile* with the name of the file you want to delete.) This command deletes the file on the remote computer, assuming that the file permissions enable you to do so. The mdelete command deletes multiple files and works like mget and mput do. The mkdir command makes a new directory on the remote system (again assuming that you have permissions to do so), as in the following:

```
mkdir newdir
```

What's with all these three-digit numbers?

You may notice that whenever you give a command to FTP, the response from the remote host begins with a three-digit number. (Or you may not notice; in which case, never mind.)

The three-digit number is there so that the FTP program, which doesn't know any English, can figure out what's going on. Each digit means something to the program.

Here's what the first digit means:

1 means that it has begun to process your request but hasn't finished it.

2 means that it has finished.

3 means that it needs more input from you, such as when it needs a password after you enter your username.

4 means that it didn't work but may if you try again.

5 means you lose.

Here's what the second digit means: The second digit is a *message subtype*.

The third digit distinguishes messages that would otherwise have the same number (something that in the computer world would be unspeakably awful).

If a message goes on for multiple lines, all the lines except the last one have a dash rather than a space after the number.

Note: Most FTP users have no idea what the numbers mean, by the way, so now that you're one of the few who does know, you're an expert.

(Replace *newdir* with the name of the directory you want to make.) After you create a directory, you still have to use cd to change to that directory before you use put or mput to store files in it.

If you plan to do much file deleting, directory creation, and the like, it's usually much quicker to log in to the other system by using telnet to do your work and using the usual local commands.

No Names, Please

So far, you have seen how to FTP to systems where you already have an account. What about the other 99.9 percent of the hosts on the Internet, where no one has ever heard of you?

You're in luck. On thousands of systems, you can log in with the username anonymous. For the password, enter your e-mail address. (This is strictly on the honor system — if you lie, they still let you log in.) When you log in for *anonymous FTP*, most hosts restrict your access to only certain directories that are allowed to anonymous users. You can hardly complain, though, because anonymous FTP is provided free out of sheer generosity.

Hello, anonymous!

When you log in, you frequently get a friendly message, like this one:

```
230-   If your FTP client crashes or hangs shortly after
            login please try
230-   using a dash (-) as the first character of your pass-
            word. This will
230-   turn off the informational messages that may be con-
            fusing your FTP
230-   client.
230-
230-   This system may be used 24 hours a day, 7 days a
            week. The local
230-   time is Tue Aug 12 12:15:10 1997.
230-
230-   You are user number 204 out of a possible total of
            250.
230-
230-   All transfers to and from wuarchive are logged. If
            you don't like
230-   this then disconnect now!
230-
230-   Wuarchive is currently a DEC Alpha AXP 3000, Model
            400. Thanks to
230-   Digital Equipment Corporation for their generous
            support of wuarchive.
230-
230-Please read the file README
230    it was last modified on Sat May 17 15.02.13 1997 - 87
            days ago
230 Guest login ok, access restrictions apply.
```

When you're logged in, you use the same commands to move around and retrieve files as you always do.

A few anonymous FTP tips

Here are a few items to remember when FTPing:

  ✔ Some hosts limit the number of anonymous users or the times of day that anonymous FTP is allowed. Please respect these limits, because no law says that the owner of the system can't turn off anonymous access.

  ✔ Don't store files in the other computer unless the owner invites you to do so. Usually a directory called `incoming` or something similar is available where you can put stuff.

An FTP Cheat Sheet

Command	Description
get *old new*	Copies remote file *old* to local file *new*; can omit *new* if same name as *old*
put *old new*	Copies local file *old* to remote file *new*; can omit *new* if same name as *old*
del *xxx*	Deletes file *xxx* on remote system
cd *newdir*	Changes to directory *newdir* on the remote machine
cdup	Changes to next higher directory
lcd *newdir*	Changes to directory *newdir* on the local machine
asc	Transfers files in ASCII mode (use for text files)
bin	Transfers files in binary or image mode (all other files)
quit	Leaves FTP
dir *pat*	Lists files whose names match pattern *pat;* if no *pat,* lists all files
mget *pat*	Gets files whose names match pattern *pat*
mput *pat*	Puts files whose names match pattern *pat*
mdel *pat*	Deletes remote files whose names match pattern *pat*
prompt	Turn name prompting on or off in mget and mput

✔ Some hosts allow anonymous FTP only from hosts that have names. That is, if you try to FTP anonymously from a host that has a number but no name, these hosts don't let you in. This problem occurs most often with personal computers, which, because they generally offer no services that are useful to other people, don't always have names assigned. If you have that problem, check with your local administrator to see whether it's possible to assign a name to your PC and to set up the reverse lookup database the remote host uses to figure out what your name is.

NETWORK

URLs for FTPing

URLs? Yikes! There's that three-letter acronym from Chapter 18. More than just a way to denote hypertext Web pages, URLs are ways of naming general Internet resources, including FTP sites. The way you describe a file you can get over the Internet using the `ftp` program is as follows:

```
ftp://hostname/pathname
```

Suppose that you see the following URL:

```
ftp://rtfm.mit.edu/pub/net/
internet.txt
```

That means to FTP to `rtfm.mit.edu`, move to the `/pub/net` directory, and get the `internet.txt` file.

Mouse-centric Approaches to FTP

If all these commands look like way more trouble than they're worth, there are alternatives. A handful of graphical FTP programs are available if you're running X Windows. Probably the most common of these are a couple from the Lawrence Livermore National Lab in California: a simple X-based program called, surprisingly enough, `xftp`, and its big brother, `xdir`. To see whether these are on your system, try typing **xftp** or **xdir**. If they're not there, you'll need to bug your system administrator about installing one of them.

The most popular FTP program these days, though, is undoubtedly our old, Web-browsing friend, Netscape. By entering the FTP site as a URL to Netscape (see sidebar), you can download files with the simple click of a mouse. (You can't download multiple files at once, as you can with `xftp` or `xdir`, or even with the `mget` command from plain FTP, but everything has its drawbacks.)

Great Stuff on FTP

Hundreds of gigabytes of stuff are available for FTP, if you know where to find them. But before you start cruising FTP sites, a few words about strategy.

A word from those etiquette ladies again

Please recall that all *anonymous FTP* servers (hosts that enable you to log in for FTP without requiring that you have an account there) exist purely because someone feels generous. Any or all can go away if the provider feels taken advantage of, so remember these rules:

✔ Pay attention to restrictions on access times noted in the welcome message. Remember that servers are in time zones all over the world. If the server says to use it only between 6 p.m. and 8 a.m., but it's in Germany and you're in Seattle, you can use it between 9 a.m. and 11 p.m. your time.

✔ Do not upload material unless you're invited to. (And don't upload material inappropriate to a particular archive — we hope that this advice would be obvious, but experience suggests otherwise.)

Mirror, mirror, on the Net, where's the file I want to get?

Many archives are *mirrored*, which means that the contents of an archive are copied mechanically from the home server to other servers. Usually, the mirroring systems are larger and faster than the home server, so it's easier to get material from the mirror than from the home system. Mirrors are usually updated daily, so everything on the home system is also at the mirrors.

A few words about navigation

All the FTP servers discussed in this chapter require you to log in by using the username anonymous. For the password, use your e-mail address.

Many servers have a small file called readme that you should retrieve the first time you use the server. This file usually contains a description of the material that's available and the rules for using the server.

If you log in to an FTP server and don't see any interesting files, look for a directory called pub (for public). For reasons lost in the mists of history, it's a tradition on UNIX systems to put all the good stuff there.

When you have a choice of mirrors, use the one that's closest to you. You want the one that's closest in terms of the number of network links between you and it. But because the number of hops is practically impossible to figure out, use the mirror that's physically closest. In particular, use one in your own country if at all possible, because international network links are relatively slow and congested.

The FTP Hit Parade

This section lists some available FTP systems, including the following information:

- ✔ Name and location of the system
- ✔ Particular rules for use
- ✔ What's there

UUNET

ftp.uu.net
UUNET Communications, Virginia
Accepts FTP only from hosts with registered names

UUNET is probably the largest archive available on the Internet. It has masses of software (mostly for UNIX in source form), archives of material posted on Usenet, files and documents from many publishers and vendors, and mirrors of many other archives around the Internet.

SIMTEL

Mirrored at wuarchive.wustl.edu, oak.oakland.edu, ftp.uu.net,
nic.funet.fi, src.doc.ic.ac.uk, archie.au, and nic.switch.ch

SIMTEL, the premier archive for MS-DOS material, also has a great deal of stuff for Macs, CP/M (remember that?), and UNIX. SIMTEL itself was an ancient DEC-20 computer at an Army base in New Mexico. It has long since shut down, but the mirror systems are still available, and someone is still updating and maintaining the archive.

RTFM

rtfm.mit.edu
Massachusetts Institute of Technology, Massachusetts

RTFM is the definitive archive of all the *FAQ (frequently asked questions)* messages on Usenet. Hence, RTFM is a treasure trove of information for everything from the state of the art in data compression to how to apply for a mortgage to sources of patterns for Civil War uniforms. Look in the directories pub/usenet-by-group and pub/usenet-by-hierarchy. RTFM also has an experimental Usenet address database, containing the e-mail address of every person who has posted a message to Usenet in the past several years. That database is in pub/usenet-addresses.

Because RTFM is an extremely popular site and limits itself to 50 simultaneous non-MIT connections, it can be extremely difficult to get into. Sometimes it has taken us several days.

INTERNIC

ftp.internic.net
Internet Network Information Center, California

This central repository for information about the Internet includes copies of all the standards and RFC documents that define the network. Also, INTERNIC has information about other FTP archives on the Internet.

NSFNET

nic.nsf.net
National Science Foundation c/o MERIT, Michigan

The NSFNET is (or at least used to be) the largest backbone network on the Internet. It has a great deal of boring administrative stuff and some interesting statistics on how big the Internet is and how fast it's growing. Look in statistics/nsfnet. NSF publications not related to the NSFNET can be found at stis.nsf.gov, **mail server** stisserv@nsf.gov.

The list of lists

sri.com
SRI International, California

Look in the directory netinfo for the file interest-groups. This is one of the largest available lists of public mailing lists on various topics. The contents of this list are published in book form and sold for about $25, but you can get it via FTP or e-mail for free!

Chapter 21

Stealing Computer Time and Files — Network Bandits

. . . .

In This Chapter

▶ How to log in to other computers

▶ How to copy files to and from other computers

▶ Computers to check out on the network

▶ How to tell if your files are on a different computer

. . . .

*I*f your computer is on a network, sooner or later you have to use computers other than your own. You can do lots and lots of things over a network, but the two most widespread activities are remote login and file transfer. If your computer is on a LAN (local area network), you can probably use files directly that are located on other computers.

How You Can Be in Two Places at Once When You're Not Anywhere at All?

Many UNIX systems are attached to the Big Mazooma of networks, the Internet, which hooks together several million computers around the world. Most of the UNIX network software was originally written at Berkeley specifically for use on the Internet, so all of these commands work just fine on the Internet. The only difference you may notice is that although you can refer to computers on your own network with simple names, such as pumpkin, to talk to computers on the Internet, you have to give their true names, which can be long and tedious, such as iecc.cambridge.ma.us (the name our computer used to have).

Remote login is no more than logging in to some other computer from your own. While you're logged in to the other computer, whatever you type is passed to the other computer; whatever responses the other computer makes are passed back to you. In the great UNIX tradition of never leaving well enough alone, there are two slightly different remote-login programs: `telnet` and `rlogin`. A variant of `rlogin` called `rsh` enables you to do commands one at a time on other computers.

A *file transfer* copies files from one system to another. You can copy files from other systems to your system, and from your system to others. There are two different file-transfer programs (how did you know that?): `ftp` and `rcp`. We talk about `ftp` in Chapter 20.

Logging In, Logging Out

Telnetting (in English, you can verb any word you want) involves no more than typing **telnet** and the name of the computer you want to log in to, as follows:

```
telnet pumpkin
```

UNIX tells you that it is making the connection and then gives the usual login prompt, namely:

```
Trying...

Connected to pumpkin.bigcorp.com.

Escape character is '^]'. SunOS UNIX
(pumpkin.bigcorp.com)

login:
```

At the login prompt, you type your user name and then your password. After the other computer connects, you log in exactly as though you were sitting at the other computer. In the following example, we typed **john1** as our user name and then gave our secret password:

```
login: john1
```

```
Password:

Last login: Thu Jan 7 23:03:58 from squash
```

```
SunOS Release 4.1.2 (PUMPKIN) #3: Fri Oct 16
     00:20:44 EDT

1992 Please confirm (or change) your terminal
     type.

TERM = (ansi)
```

If the other computer asks you what type of terminal you're using, give the answer appropriate to the terminal you're using. (If you're using an X terminal window, it's xterm. Try VT-100, ANSI, or TTY if you're using a dumb terminal or PC.)

The normal way to leave telnet is to log out from the other computer, as follows:

```
logout
```

UNIX gives you the following message to tell you that the other computer has hung up the phone, so to speak:

```
Bye Bye

Connection closed by foreign host.
```

Sometimes the other computer is recalcitrant and doesn't want to let you go. Remember that you're in control. To force your way out, you first must get the attention of the telnet program by pressing Ctrl+] (that's a right square bracket). A few versions of telnet use a different escape character to get telnet's attention. (It tells you which character when you first connect to the other system.) After you get telnet's attention, type **quit** to tell telnet to wrap things up and return to the shell, as follows:

```
Ctrl-]
telnet> quit
```

What telnet is really useful for

We mostly use telnet to check our mail while we're out of town. If you have access to a computer at a friend's home or office or you wander by a cybercafé, you can telnet back to your home computer to check your mail and otherwise put your digital life in order. It's the next best thing to being there.

Terminal type tedium

If you use a full-screen program, such as the UNIX text editors `emacs` and `vi` or the mail programs `elm` and Pine, you have to set your *terminal type.* This problem shouldn't exist in the first place, but it does, so you have to deal with it.

The problem is that about a dozen different conventions exist for screen controls such as *clear screen* and *move to position (x,y).* The program you're using on the remote host has to use the same convention your terminal does (if you're using a terminal) or that your local terminal program does (if you're on a PC or a workstation).

If the conventions are not the same, you get *garbage* (funky-looking characters) on-screen when you try to use a full-screen program. In most cases, the remote system asks you what terminal type to use. The trick is knowing the right answer.

✔ If you're using the X Window system, with or without Motif, the answer is more likely to be *VT-100,* a popular terminal from the

1970s that became a de facto standard. You might also try *xterm,* the name of the standard X program that does terminal emulation.

✔ If you're using a PC and an emulation program, the best answer is usually *ANSI,* because most PC terminal programs use ANSI terminal conventions. (*ANSI* stands for the *American National Standards Institute.* One of its several thousand standards defines a set of terminal control conventions that MS-DOS PCs — which otherwise wouldn't know an ANSI standard if they tripped over one — use.)

✔ In places where a great deal of IBM equipment is used, the terminal type may be *3101,* an early IBM terminal that was also popular.

The ANSI and VT-100 conventions are not much different from each other, so if you use one and your screen is only somewhat screwed up, try the other.

The Attack of the IBM Terminals

All the terminals discussed earlier that are handled by telnet are basically souped-up Teletypes, with data passed character by character between the terminal and the host. This kind of terminal interaction can be called *Teletype-ish.*

IBM developed an entirely different model for its 3270-series display terminals. The principle is that the computer's in charge. The model works more like filling in paper forms. The computer draws what it wants on the screen, marks which parts of the screen users can type on, and then unlocks the keyboard so that users can fill in whichever blanks they want. When a user presses Enter, the terminal locks the keyboard, transmits the changed parts of the screen to the computer, and awaits additional instructions from headquarters.

To be fair, this is a perfectly reasonable way to build terminals intended for dedicated data-entry and data-retrieval applications. The terminal on the desks at your bank or the electric company are probably 3270s — or, more likely these days, cheap PCs *emulating* 3270s. The 3270 terminal protocol squeezes a great deal more on a phone line than Teletype-ish, so it's quite common to have all the 3270s in an office sharing the same single phone line, with reasonable performance.

The Internet is a big place, and plenty of IBM mainframes run applications on the Internet. Some of them are quite useful. Most large library catalogs, for example, speak 3270-ish. Usually, if you telnet to a system that wants a 3270, it converts from the Teletype-ish that telnet speaks to 3270-ish so that you can use it anyway. But some 3270 systems speak only 3270-ish, and if you telnet to them, they connect and disconnect without saying anything in between.

A variant of telnet that speaks 3270-ish is called *tn3270*. If you find that a system keeps disconnecting, try typing the command **tn3270** instead. (Large amounts of UPPERCASE LETTERS and references to the IBM operating systems VM or MVS are also tipoffs that you're talking to a 3270.) Even if a 3270 system allows regular telnet, you get a snappier response if you use tn3270 instead.

The Lazy Man's Remote Login

The `telnet` command is general. You can use it to log in to all sorts of machines — whether or not they're running UNIX. If you want to log in to another UNIX system, the `rlogin` command is usually more convenient because it automates more of the process. You use `rlogin` in much the same way you use `telnet`. Following is the syntax for `rlogin`:

```
rlogin pumpkin
```

UNIX responds with the following:

```
Last login: Fri Jan 8 14:30:28 from squash

SunOS Release 4.1.2 (PUMPKIN) #3: Fri Oct 16 00:20:44 EDT

Please confirm (or change) your terminal type.

TERM = (ansi)
```

Hey! It didn't ask for the user name or password. What happened? You frequently have a setup in which a bunch of machines use the same set of user names. There's even a database called NIS that helps keep all the names consistent across all the machines. In that case, after you log in to one machine, all the others can safely assume that, if you log in to one of them, you will use the same user name to log in to others.

The `rlogin` command also passes along the type of terminal you're using, so that, even if the other system asks you to enter your terminal type, it always guesses correctly if you don't tell it explicitly.

If the remote system doesn't recognize your user name, it asks you to type a user name and password, just as `telnet` does.

Escaping from `rlogin`

One place where `rlogin` is quite different from `telnet` is in how you escape from a recalcitrant remote system: You type ~. (a tilde followed by a period) on a line by itself. What you have to press is Enter, tilde, period, Enter.

User-name matching for `rlogin`

This section is pretty nerdy. If you work in an office with a bunch of workstations, you can assume that they generally all share user names, and skip this section.

Two files control `rlogin`'s assumption that you want to use the same user name when you are logging in to other machines. The first is called `/etc/hosts.equiv`. On every machine, this file lists all the other machines it can "trust" to have matching user names. If you look at the file and find lines with + and @ signs, they mean that NIS is providing its own list of trustworthy machines (generally, all the machines in the department or in the entire company).

Individual users may have accounts on machines outside the local group or department. If you are in this situation, you can have your own file called `.rhosts`, which is sort of a private trusted-machine list. `.rhosts` has a list of machine names, one per line. If you use `rlogin` from any of those machines, `rlogin` forgoes asking for your name and password. If you have different user names on different machines, edit the file and put the appropriate user name after the machine name, as shown in the following example:

```
pumpkin

squash

gerbil steph
```

Translation: You have accounts on pumpkin and squash with the same user name as on the machine you're using now. You also have an account on gerbil, but your user name there is steph.

When you have a different user name on the system you're logging in to, you have to use -1 to tell rlogin the name to use. Suppose that you want to log into prune, where your login name is sdl:

```
rlogin prune -l sdl
```

Note that the system name comes first. If you have an .rhosts file on prune that lists both the machine from which you are logging in and your user name on that machine, it won't ask you for a password.

One Command at a Time

Sometimes rlogin is overkill for what you want to do — you just want to run one command at a time. In this type of situation, the rsh command (for *remote sh*ell) does the trick, as follows:

```
rsh pumpkin lpq
```

You give rsh the name of the system you want to use and the command you want to run on that system. This example runs the command lpq on system pumpkin. (Remember that lpq asks what's waiting for the printer on pumpkin.)

Dialing out

Another command that acts sort of like telnet is cu (for *call U*NIX). It activates a simple "terminal emulator" program that calls out over the phone. Despite its name, cu can call *any* system that has a modem compatible with the one on your computer. The program is useful for calling on-line services such as MCI Mail and CompuServe.

Your system administrator has to set up the list of system names and phone numbers that cu uses. After they are set up, you call out by simply typing the following line:

```
cu systemname
```

You escape from cu and hang up the phone in the same way you escape from rlogin: by typing ~. (a tilde followed by a period on a line by themselves).

The `rsh` command uses the same user-name strategy `rlogin` does, so if you can use `rlogin` to access a system and not give a user name or a password, you can use `rsh` also. But because `rsh` doesn't handle the terminal very cleverly, you can't use full-screen commands, such as `vi` and `emacs`. You can use `ed`, however. Wow.

An old program, also called `rsh`, sometimes conflicts with the `rsh` we're talking about here. The old `rsh` is the *r*estricted *sh*ell: a version of the Bourne shell that is of no use to you. If you type `rsh pumpkin` and UNIX responds by displaying `pumpkin: pumpkin: cannot open` or displays a $ and sits there, you have the old `rsh`. If UNIX displayed the $, type **exit** to make it go away. If you have the old `rsh`, what we're calling `rsh` is probably called `remsh` or `rshell`, so try those names instead.

Blatting Files across the Network

Although `telnet` and `rlogin` may be the next best thing to being there, sometimes there's no place like your home machine. If you want to use files that are on another machine, `rcp` is often the easiest thing to do. We talk about `ftp` in Chapter 20.

The idea behind `rcp` is that it works just like `cp` (the standard copy command) — except that it also works on remote files that you own or that you at least have access to. To refer to a file on another machine, type the machine name and a colon before the filename. To copy a file named `mydata` from the machine named `pumpkin` and call it `pumpkindata`, you type the following:

```
rcp pumpkin:mydata pumpkindata
```

To copy it the other way (from a file called `pumpkindata` on your machine to a file called `mydata` on a machine called `pumpkin`), you type this line:

```
rcp pumpkindata pumpkin:mydata
```

The `rcp` program uses the same user-name rules as do `rlogin` and `rsh`. If your user name on the other system is different from that on your own system, type the user name and an @ sign before the machine name, as follows:

```
rcp steph@pumpkin:mydata pumpkindata
```

If you want to copy files in another user's directory (`tracy`, for example) on the other system, place the user's name *after* a ~ (a tilde) *before* the filename. Suppose that you need one of Tracy's files. You type the following command:

```
rcp pumpkin:~tracy/somefile tracyfile
```

To copy an entire directory at a time, you can use the -r (for *recursive*) flag to tell rcp to copy the entire contents of a directory, as follows:

```
rcp -r pumpkin:projectdir .
```

This command says to copy the directory projectdir on machine pumpkin into the current directory (the period is the nickname for the current directory) on the local machine.

You can combine all this notation in an illegible festival of punctuation, as shown in the following example:

```
rcp -r steph@pumpkin:~tracy/projectdir tracy-project
```

Translation: Go to machine pumpkin, where my user name is steph, and get from user tracy a directory called projectdir and copy it to a directory on this machine called tracy-project. Whew!

In the finest UNIX tradition, rcp is extremely taciturn: It says nothing unless something goes wrong. If you are copying a lot of files over a network, it can take a while (a couple of minutes), so you may have to be more patient than usual while waiting for it to do its work. It is finished when you see the UNIX prompt.

If you copied stuff *to* another machine and want to see whether it worked, use rsh to give an ls command afterward to see which files are on the other machine, as follows:

```
rcp -r projectdir pumpkin:squashproject
rsh pumpkin ls -l squashproject
```

Although rcp is pretty reliable (if it didn't complain, the copy almost certainly worked), it never hurts to be sure.

You'll Never Find Your Stuff

If your computer is on a LAN, it's probably set up to share files with other computers. Quite a few different schemes enable computers to use files on other machines. They are named mostly with TLAs (*three-letter acronyms*) such as AFS, RFS, and NFS. This chapter talks mostly about NFS, because that's the most commonly used scheme, even though, in many ways, it works the worst. If you didn't like the C shell or the vi editor, you won't like NFS either; it also was written by Bill, the big guy with the strong opinions.

What's NFS?

The NFS (*Network File System*) program enables you to treat files on another computer in more or less the same way you treat files on your own computer.

You might want to use NFS for several reasons:

✔ Often you have a bunch of similar computers scattered around, all running more or less the same programs. Rather than load every program on every computer, the system administrator loads one copy of everything on one computer (the server) so that all the other computers (the clients) can share the programs.

✔ Centralizing the files on a server makes backup and administration easier. It's much easier to administer one disk of 4,000 megabytes than to administer 10 disks of 400 megabytes apiece. It's also easier to back up everything, because everything is all in one place rather than spread around on a dozen machines.

✔ Another use of NFS is to make a bunch of workstations function as a shared time-sharing system. It is reasonably straightforward to set up a bunch of workstations so that you can sit down at any one of them, log in, and use the same set of files regardless of where on the network they physically reside. This capability is a great convenience. Also, by using programs such as telnet (discussed later in this chapter), you can log in to another machine on the network and work from that machine (which is handy if the other machine is faster than yours or has some special feature you want to use).

✔ A final use of NFS is in heterogeneous networks, a fancy term for networks with different kinds of computers. NFS is available for all sorts of computers, from PCs to mainframes. It's common to run a version of NFS on PCs to enable PC users to use files physically located on UNIX or other systems.

Ignoring NFS

Except when NFS screws up, you don't have to worry about using it. Your system administrator did all the hard work when installing it.

Files passed over the network act almost exactly like those on the local machine; in most cases, you can treat them the same. The primary difference is that access to files through NFS is about twice as slow as access to files on the local machine. This problem usually isn't a big one because, for most of the stuff you do, the machine doesn't spend much time waiting for the disk anyway.

When you do something *really* big and slow (such as repaginating a 500-page document), it might be worth it to see whether you can log in to the machine on which the files reside and run the program there.

Where are those files, anyway?

NFS works by mounting remote directories. *Mounting* means pretending that a directory on another disk or even on another computer is actually part of the directory system on your disk. This means that files that are stored in lots of different places can appear to be nicely organized into one tree-structure directory.

Whenever UNIX sees the name of a directory — /stars/elvis, for example — it checks to see whether any names in the directory are *mount points*, which are directories where one disk is logically attached to another.

Your system may have the directory /stars mounted from some other machine, for example, and then the directory elvis and all the files in it reside on the other machine.

The easiest way to tell which files are where is with the df (Disk Free space) command. It prints the amount of free space on every disk and tells you where the disks are. Here's a typical piece of df output:

```
Filesystem       kbytes      used    avail capacity   Mounted on
/dev/sd0a         30383       6587    20758    24%     /
/dev/sd0g        157658     124254    17639    88%     /usr
/dev/sd0h        364378     261795    66146    80%     /home
/dev/sd3a         15671       1030    13074     7%     /tmp
/dev/sd3g       1175742     758508   299660    72%     /mnt
server-sys:/usr/spool/mail
                 300481     190865    79567    71%     /var/
                 spool/mail
server-sys:/usr/lib/news
                 300481     190865    79567    71%     /usr/lib/
                 news
server-sys:/usr/spool/news
                 298068     243877    24384    91%     /var/
                 spool/news
```

In this example, the directory / resides on a local disk (a disk on your own computer) named /dev/sd0a; /usr resides on /dev/sd0g; /home resides on /dev/sd0h; and so forth. (We won't go into disk names other than to say that anything in /dev is on the local machine.) The directory /var/

`spool/mail` is really the directory `/usr/spool/mail` on machine `server-sys`, `/usr/lib/news` is really `/usr/lib/news` on machine `server-sys`, and so forth.

Some of the local directory names are the same as the remote machine's directory names — and some aren't. This can and often does cause considerable confusion; unfortunately, it's usually unavoidable. A system administrator with any sense will at least mount each directory with a consistent name wherever it's mounted so that `/var/documents/bigproject` is the same no matter which computer you're working on.

A database known as NIS (Network Information System) makes it easier to keep the naming process straight. Don't worry about it unless your system administrator messes up.

NFS and system crashes

What happens if you're working with NFS, your files are stored on a server, and the server crashes? The answer is, you wait. Eventually, when the server comes back, you continue from where you left off. If it's a severe crash, you may wait a long time. In one extreme case (so we have heard), a program on an NFS client system waited more than six months while the server crashed, was dismantled and shipped back to the manufacturer and then was refurbished, shipped back, reloaded from tape, and rebooted — at which point the client program continued. You probably won't be so patient.

The worst practical problem is that, if a program stalls while it is waiting for a dead NFS server, there is no way to stop or kill the program, short of rebooting your UNIX computer.

Recent versions of NFS have features called soft and hard mounts (not as indecent as they sound, but close) that make it possible to stop a program that has stalled while waiting for a dead server. The problem is that, if a server is merely slow and not dead (and believe us, a server loaded with hundreds of clients can be impressively slow), a client may assume that the server is dead and stop a program. Had the client been a little more patient, the server would have responded, and the program could have completed its task.

Part V
Help!

In this part . . .

The point of this book is to help you when things go wrong. That's what makes it different from "good news" books that talk only about how everything *should* work in a perfect world. This part of the book lists things that go wrong, error messages you may see, and what you can do about them.

Chapter 22

Disaster Relief

• •

• •

*T*here is always the tiny, infinitesimal chance that you may run into some kind of problem with your computer. It can be something major (such as losing the funniest interoffice memo you have seen in years) or minor (perhaps accidentally deleting the analysis you have spent two months creating).

Some computer problems you can fix — some you can't. It's similar to cars: You can pump gas yourself and maybe change the oil, but when it's time to rebuild the engine, call for help. (We do, anyway.)

This chapter describes some problems you may run into, with suggestions for what to do.

My Computer Won't Turn On

You come in to the office one morning, flip the switch on your computer, and nothing happens. No friendly whir, nothing on-screen. Uh-oh. Lots of things could have happened, so check these possibilities:

> ✔ **Is the computer plugged in?** It sounds stupid, but we have had computer problems when the people who clean the office bumped their vacuum cleaners into the outlet that all our equipment was plugged in to. If you're using a terminal or X terminal, this check applies to both the terminal and the computer.

- **Check the power strip switch.** If the computer is plugged into a power strip that has its own on-off switch, check that switch's position. People have been known to turn off the switch inadvertently with their toes.

- **Is the computer still attached?** Are the cables that connect the computer, keyboard, screen, and whatever else still connected? If your terminal is connected to a network, is the network cable firmly attached to the computer? Try wiggling it a little, even if it looks okay.

- **Is there power in the rest of the office?** Plug a lamp into the same outlet as the computer and make sure that it turns on. (True story: "Hello, help desk? My computer won't turn on." "Is it plugged in correctly?" "I can't tell. The power failed and none of the lights work.")

- **Is the picture on the screen turned off?** The computer can be on, and the screen can even be on, but the picture on the screen can be dimmed. Fool with the brightness knob. (Remember where the knob was positioned when you started fiddling with it.)

- **Does your computer have a screen-blanker program?** Press a key to make sure that a screen-blanker program didn't black out your screen as a favor to you. (We like to press the Shift key, because it has no other effect on the computer.) Moving the mouse a little also unblanks the screen.

If it's not a power problem, it's probably not something you can fix yourself. Call your system administrator for help. Some component may have burned out. Stay calm — this does *not* mean that the files stored on your disk are gone. They are probably fine: Disks remember data perfectly well with the power off.

My Mouse Is Acting Glitchy

If you have a computer with a male mouse (a mouse with a ball underneath), dust or crumbs inside it can prevent the ball from rolling smoothly. Most mice with balls have a way to remove the ball for cleaning, usually by turning a plastic ring that surrounds the opening for the ball, or by sliding the ring to the front or side. (We won't begin to suggest appropriate names for that ring.) Turn the mouse over so that the ball falls into your hand and not on the floor, gently wipe off the grit, and snap it all back together. Female mice (optical mice, with no balls) appreciate it if you occasionally wipe off the mouse pad with a tissue. Also, look at the bottom of your female mouse: If it's turned on and working, you should be able to see a little red lamp through one of the openings.

The Network Is Gone

You can't print on the printer down the hall, and you can't run certain programs. The problem may be that your computer is not communicating properly with the network to which it is normally attached.

Most network problems are not for the faint of heart. One thing you can try is to check the cables in the back of your computer. Is the network cable firmly attached to the computer? Try wiggling it a little, even if it looks Okay. Otherwise, it's time to call in the experts.

These Aren't My Files!

Normally, when you log in, you start working in your home directory. If you type the following line, you return to the home directory:

```
cd
```

If cd doesn't get you back home, you may not be who you think you are. Try typing whoami or who am i. If someone else's user name appears, your computer thinks that that's who you are! A coworker may have logged in to your computer to do some work for a moment.

Log out without fouling anything up, and then log in as yourself. Type this line:

```
logout
```

Maybe you have to type exit or just press Ctrl+D. At any rate, when you see the login screen, log in as yourself.

Wrecked X

If you use Motif or another X Window variant, you may find your screen in a peculiar state. You can move the mouse pointer around, but none of the windows change and you can't type in any window. Often you can fix this by restarting the window manager, which controls which window gets what.

Move the mouse pointer outside any window and click and hold the left or right mouse button (which one depends on which window manager you're using) to get the window manager menu. On that menu should be an item such as "Restart mwm." Select it. The borders around all your windows will disappear. After a few seconds, they should reappear. It should be fixed.

It's Not Listening!

The computer is on, and suddenly it doesn't respond to anything you type. The computer is probably fine — a program has frozen. Try these steps:

- ✔ Press Esc a bunch of times.
- ✔ Press Ctrl+C a bunch of times.
- ✔ Press Ctrl+D a bunch of times.
- ✔ Press Ctrl+S and Ctrl+Q several times. (You never know what works.)
- ✔ If you are running Motif, or another X Windows-based system, try using the mouse to select another window so you can type a command or two in a shell window. If you can, you can probably kill the frozen program and start it again (see the paragraph after this list).
- ✔ If your window system is hopeless, try killing the window system and restarting it without restarting your computer (see the next paragraph).

If your computer is networked or has more than one terminal, ask a guru to kill the program. Tell the wizard what happened (in order), which programs were running, and what you did. The wizard will probably kill the process (see Chapter 24). If you have a number of processes running, the wizard may kill one after another until your computer feels better. If you're brave, you can kill it yourself. When you kill a program, you lose any work since the last time you saved data to the disk.

I Give Up....

Sometimes discretion is the better part of valor (whatever that means). If you need to call for help, be sure to do the following:

- ✔ **Don't turn off the computer**. Unless flames are coming out of the screen and threatening to engulf your entire office, this is not a good idea. Even then, you might be better off waiting for it to trip the circuit breaker than facing your wizard, who will surely ask, "Did you turn it off?"
- ✔ **Know the symptoms.** Be ready to tell someone what happened and which actions you took to fix the problem.
- ✔ **Know what has changed recently.** Did you install new software? Did you run something you have never run before? New things are always suspicious. A claim of "I didn't change anything" does not endear you to your wizard. Something, somewhere, *must* have changed.
- ✔ If you call for help by phone, **call from within reach of the computer.** Your savior may want you to try a few maneuvers at the keyboard.

Chapter 23

The Case of the Missing Files

In This Chapter

▶ Four easy ways to lose files

▶ Some ways to get files back

▶ Three almost-as-easy ways not to lose files

S ooner or later, you will delete a file by mistake. Scratch that *later:* Sooner than you think, you will delete a file by mistake. In far too many cases, you are out of luck, but there are a few things you can do to avoid disaster.

How You Clobber Files

Contrary to the usual image of UNIX users being radically technical and without a creative bone in their bodies, we submit that typical UNIX users are immensely creative: They can come up with a zillion inventive ways to avoid the computer altogether, and when they are forced to sit down to stare the computer in the face, they can come up with a dozen more inventive reasons for why things went wrong. UNIX programmers have written thousands of useful freeware and shareware programs, when they should have been getting some work done. There are lots of ways you can make files disappear (either intentionally or accidentally). The following sections list the four main ways you can trash files — although you can probably come up with a dozen new and creative ways to do the vanishing act with your files.

Clobbering files with rm

Because disks are not infinitely large, sooner or later you have to get rid of some files. (Some wag once commented that the only thing standard among UNIX systems is the message-of-the-day reminding users to delete unneeded files.)

The normal way to get rid of files is the rm (for *rem*ove) command. Until (notice that we didn't say *unless*) you screw up, rm removes only what you want it to. Recall that you tell rm the names of the files you want to remove, as follows:

```
rm thisfile thatfile somedir/anotherfile
```

You can remove more than one file at a time, and you can specify files in other directories. (The rm command removes just the file and not the directory.)

This method is usually pretty safe. The tricky part comes when you use wildcards. If you use a word processor that leaves backup files with names ending in .bak, for example, you can get rid of all of them with this command:

```
rm *.bak
```

That's no problem — unless you put in an extra space (**Don't type this line!**), as follows:

```
rm * .bak
```

Note that there is a little, tiny space between the asterisk and the dot. In response to this command, UNIX says this:

```
rm: .bak non-existent
```

Uh-oh. UNIX decided that you wanted to delete two things: * and .bak. Because the asterisk wildcard matches every single filename in the working directory, every single filename in the working directory is deleted. Then UNIX tries to delete a file called .bak, which isn't there. Bad move.

At this point, we recommend that you panic, gnash your teeth, and throw Nerf balls at the computer. After you calm down a little, read the rest of this chapter for some possible ways to get your files back.

You can also make slightly less destructive but still aggravating mistakes when you forget just which files you have. Suppose that you have files called `section01`, `section02`, and so forth up to `section19`. You want to get rid of all of them, so you type this line:

```
rm sec*
```

Now suppose that you forgot you also have a file called `second.version` that you want to keep. Oops. Bye-bye, `second.version`.

The obvious solution is to delete things one at a time. But, unless you are an extremely fast and steady typist, that's not very practical. In the following sections, we make some suggestions about that, too.

Clobbering files with cp, mv, *and* ln

Are you feeling paranoid yet, as though every time you press the R and M keys you're going to blow away a year's worth of work? Wait — it gets worse.

The `cp`, `mv`, and `ln` commands can also clobber files by mistake: If you use one of these programs to copy, rename, or link a file and there is already a file by the new name, the existing file gets clobbered. Suppose that you type the following command:

```
mv elbow armpit
```

If you already had a file called `armpit` — *blam!* It's gone! The same thing happens if you copy or link. (Copying is a *little* different: See the sidebar "Links, copies, moves, truncation, and other details about file destruction" if you care.) Here's an example of the most annoying case of blasting away good files with trash when you use the copy command:

```
cp important.file.save important.file
```

As a responsible and paranoid computer user, you want to save a copy of an important file before you make some changes. But your fingers work a little faster than your brain and you get the two names switched (left-handed users are particularly prone to getting names sdrawkcab) — and *blam!* (again) you've just copied an obsolete saved version over the current version. Fortunately, you can arrange your file-saving habits to make this kind of mistake harmless, or at least mostly harmless.

TECHNICAL STUFF

Links, copies, moves, truncation, and other details about file destruction

Clobber-wise, copying files works a little differently from moving and linking files. More often than not, the practical difference is unimportant, although, in a few cases, it can be worth knowing about.

The cp command does one thing as it clobbers a file; mv and ln do another. The difference is noticeable only if additional names or links were created for that file with ln. (See Chapter 8 for how to create links, or additional names, for files using the ln command.)

Clobbering a file with cp: Suppose that you have two files, first and second. You give second an additional name by using this ln command:

    ln second extra.name

Now suppose that you accidentally (who knows why) type cp first second. (Remember that you already have a file called second.) What happens to the file named second? The cp command replaces the current contents of second with a copy of first. That is, it replaces the text (or whatever) that second contains with whatever the file first contains. This change affects the file named extra.name too, because this is another name for the file second. If you use cat or a text editor to look at either second or extra.name, you see a copy of first. The original contents of second and extra.name are gone with the wind.

Clobbering a file with mv or ln: "So what?" you ask, to cut to the heart of the matter. Here's the interesting part (interesting to us, anyway). If you had used mv or ln rather than cp, the second file would not be gone. The mv and ln commands don't fool with the contents of the file — they just change what filename is

connected with what contents. Suppose that you type the following command:

    mv first second

The mv command disconnects the name second from its current contents. The contents are still linked to the name extra.name, so that file is still safe and sound. The mv command then connects the name second to the contents of first, and finally disconnects the name first from the file. Now there is no file called first.

As a result, the contents of the second file are not clobbered. (You can use the other name for the file to see them.) The ln command works the same way as mv to disconnect filenames and not touch the contents of files.

The message here is that if you have just fouled up an mv or ln command, you may still have hope of retrieving the old file (if it had other links).

Clobbering files with soft links: To add more confusion, the story is a little different if you use soft links rather than regular hard links. (See Chapter 8 to learn how soft links can link files from different file systems.) Because soft links are just aliases for the true filename, if you do something to the original file, all the links refer to the changed file because it has the same name. On the other hand, if you use cp to change one of the links, the cp command replaces the contents of the original file. mv and ln affect just the link.

Confused? The moral is the same with soft links: After a botched mv or ln, you may still be able to find the original file if it had another name. It can't hurt to look.

Creaming files by using redirection

A third popular way to blow away valuable files is by using redirection. If you redirect the output of a command to a file that already exists, whammo! UNIX blows away the existing file and replaces it with your redirected output.

For example, you type the following command:

```
ls -al > dirlist
```

However, you already have a file named `dirlist`. Well, it's gone now, replaced with the new listing.

If you use the BASH shell, you can give this command:

```
noclobber=1
```

If you use the C shell, you can give this incantation:

```
set noclobber
```

Better yet, get a UNIX wizard to help you include it in your `.cshrc` or `.profile` file so that the command is given automatically every time you start the shell. This command tells the shell to *ask* you before clobbering files using redirection.

When you redirect output into a file, you can tell UNIX to add it to the end of an existing file. Instead of typing one >, type two, as follows:

```
ls -al >> dirlist
```

There's little reason not to use >> every time you think of using >.

Wrecking files with text editors

The fourth way you're likely to smash files is in a botched editor session. The problem usually comes up after you have been editing a file for a while and realize that you have completely screwed up: The changes you have made are not what you want, so you decide to leave the editor. On the way out, however, you write the botched changes to the disk and wreck the original file. A similar problem occurs when you use an editor to look at a file: Although you may not intend to change anything, you may make some inadvertent changes anyway. (This can easily happen in emacs, where pretty much anything you type goes straight into the file.) If you're not careful, you can write the changes to the disk by mistake.

If you use vi, you can avoid the accidental-clobber problem by typing view rather than vi. The view editor is the same as the vi editor (vi and view are links to the same program); view works the same as vi except that it doesn't let you write changes to the file. Keep it in mind.

Some versions of emacs can mark files as read-only so that you can't make changes to the files, but the methods of doing this aren't entirely standardized. In GNU Emacs, you press Ctrl+X Ctrl+R in a file window, and Emacs puts an inscrutable %% on the status line at the bottom of the screen. To be even more careful, you can use Ctrl+X Ctrl+R to open a file read-only in the first place.

Ways to Try to Get Files Back

Well, now you've done it: You've clobbered something important, and you really, *really* want it back. Let's see what you can do.

If you're used to other systems, such as Windows 95, in which you can magically get deleted stuff back from the Recycle Bin, we're sorry to tell you that UNIX doesn't let you do that. If it's gone, it's gone. (A version of the Norton Utilities that includes an unerase command is available for some versions of UNIX, but it isn't widely used.)

Copies, copies, everywhere

Maybe you have stashed away in a different directory other copies of the file you deleted. For our important files, we stick copies in a directory called save (or something similar). Also, sometimes you can reconstruct the information from a different form. If you clobber a word processor file, for example, you may have a backup version (the .bak files mentioned earlier in this chapter) that's pretty close to the current version. You may have printed the deleted file to a file (rather than directly to the printer) and can edit the print file back into document form.

If you share your computer with other people or use a network, see whether someone else has a copy. It's a rare file that really exists in only one place.

Call in the backup squad

It's really gone, huh? Now it's time for the final line of defense: backups. You *do* have backups, don't you?

We interrupt this chapter for a stern lecture: *Always make backups.* If your system administrator is on the ball, tape backups are made automatically every night. All you have to do is go to the administrator, with chocolate-chip cookies in hand, and ask very politely for some help getting your valuable file back from the previous night's backups. If no backups exist, it's fair to jump up and down and scream that someone had better get on the ball.

Seriously, backups are a standard part of any administrator's job, either by making the backups personally or by overseeing operators who do the backing up. (After the procedures are set up, making backup tapes is so simple that you can practically train your dog to do it. One reason that it sometimes doesn't get done is that backing up is boring.)

Why you need backups

Making backups is a pain. But the question isn't *whether* you will lose data, it's *when*. Here are some events that have sent us heading for the backup tapes:

✔ The obvious one: We deleted a file by mistake.

✔ Just as we were saving a file, the power failed and scrambled both the old and new versions of the file. Yikes!

✔ One day, while working on the insides of the computer (one of us is a closet nerd), we accidentally dropped a screwdriver on the disk controller. Exciting sparks came out and fried the controller card that attaches the disk to the rest of the computer. We got a new controller card and found that, although the disk was physically fine, the new controller wasn't quite compatible with the old one and we had to reformat the disk and restore everything from tape.

✔ We remembered hearing that we should absolutely, positively run a "disk-head parking" program before moving our hard disk, so we ran one. Unfortunately, it was a version that was incompatible with the hard disk, so it parked the disk head right off the edge of the disk, way out past what you might call the Long-Term Parking Area. We could hear the disk head banging on the side of the hard disk as it tried to get back on. Rats!

✔ Back in the good old days, computers weighed about 15,000 pounds, and you needed a forklift to move one. Now they weigh about 25 pounds, which means that if the cleaning people bump into one with a vacuum cleaner, they can knock it over with a clunk that can put an unreadable ding into the disk. Oops — sorry, lady.

You probably have horror stories of your own, but they all have the same moral: Make those backups.

If your system administrator doesn't make backups, you had better learn how to do it yourself. If you have a tape unit on your machine, the procedure is usually as follows:

1. Put a tape in the tape unit and flip the latch to seat the tape firmly.

2. Give a command to copy files to the tape, usually the tar (*t*ape *ar*chive) or pax (*p*ortable *ar*chive e*x*change) program. On Sun workstations, the program is bar (*b*ackup *ar*chive). The exact things you have to say to the tar program vary from one system to another, mostly because of the peculiarities of different kinds of tape units. You can't use the regular cp command, because tapes aren't logically organized the same way disks are. This can take a while — maybe an hour for a largish disk.

3. Take the tape out of the tape unit.

4. Write the current date on the label so that you know that it is a current backup. (The sensibly paranoid alternate several tapes, in case one of them goes bad. We describe this subject in more detail in the sidebar "Backup strategies.")

5. Put the tape back in its box and put the box back on the shelf.

The usual way to back up stuff on Linux is to use tar. To back up to tape, type this fabulously memorable command:

```
tar cvf /dev/rft0 *
```

The cvf means Create, Verbose Report, to File, and /dev/rft0 is the name of the tape unit. The * means to back up all the files in your directory; if you have a lot, you can list specific files and directories instead.

Some systems don't have tapes; they have diskettes. Diskettes are a major pain for backup use for two reasons: You need a stack of them, and you must format them first.

Before you can use a diskette, you must format it, which means that the computer writes some bookkeeping junk on it to mark where to put the data, and in the process checks to be sure that no bad spots are on the diskette. Fortunately, you only have to do this one time per disk. Formatting diskettes is easy but tedious and, of course (sing along with us as we say this), varies from one system to another. You stick the blank diskette in the computer, type the formatting command, and UNIX does it. If you're stuck with diskette backups, ask your administrator for help setting up the procedure, and while you're feeding all the diskettes into the drive, consider getting a tape drive.

If you back up to diskettes, type this to Linux:

```
tar cvMf /dev/fd0 *
```

The M means Multiple disks, because you can't put much stuff on one diskette. Linux will tell you when to swap disks. Be sure to write the backup date and the diskette number on each disk, so that they don't get out of order.

If you have a lot of files, copying everything to tape can take a while (perhaps an hour or so). You might want to do the backup over lunch. Or do what we do and have your administrator arrange to run the tar program automatically every morning at about 3 a.m. We leave a tape in the tape unit every night. When we come back the next morning, the backup's been done, and we take the tape out and put it away. The tar command creates a report that is e-mailed to us so that we can check to see whether the tape was written correctly.

Thank goodness it's backed up!

Getting stuff back from a tape also involves the use of tar but is somewhat trickier, because you want to restore just the files you clobbered. Ask for help — at least the first time. Generally speaking, you put the tape in the drive the same way you did to make the backup, and then you type a tar or pax command similar to one of these:

```
tar xvf /dev/tape somedir/clobberedfile
pax -rv -f /dev/tape somedir/clobberedfile
```

In the tar command, xvf stands for eXtract Verbosely From. In the pax command, -rv -f similarly means Read Verbosely From. Either way, it's followed by the name of your tape drive (often, /dev/tape, except on Linux, where it's usually /dev/rft0) and the name of the file to look for. The tape spins as tar or pax runs down the tape looking for the file you want. When it finds the file, it reads the file onto the disk, reports that it did so, and stops. If you clobbered a bunch of files, you can use wildcards, as in the following:

```
tar xvf /dev/tape "somedir/*"
pax -rv -f /dev/tape "somedir/*"
```

You have to use quotation marks around the wildcards, because the files to match are on the tape, where tar or pax can find them, not on the disk where the shell (which normally handles wildcards) can find them.

To restore files on Linux, type the following:

```
tar xvf /dev/rft0 "somedir/*"# if it's on tape
tar xvMf /dev/fd0 "somedir/*"# if it's on floppies
```

If you want to see what files are on the tape, but not restore any of them just now, use one of these commands:

```
tar tvf /dev/tape
pax -v -f /dev/tape
```

You should try to run the restore command from the same directory where the program that made the backup tape ran. If it's a system backup, that's probably the root directory /.

Backup strategies

The obvious way to do tape backups is to copy the entire contents of the disk to a tape every night. But here are a couple reasons that it may not be the best approach:

- ✔ The disk may contain too much stuff to fit on a tape. Tape and disk manufacturers continually battle to see who can outstrip the other. The battle is pretty evenly matched — as we write, they're both in the 4 gigabyte (4,000 megabyte) range, although many people are still using 150MB tapes, which are smaller than most disks on UNIX systems.

- ✔ You may not notice for a day or two that you clobbered something important, so a scheme that gives you a few days' grace to get your data back would be nice.

- ✔ Murphy's Law says that the system will fail as it's writing a backup tape, so you had better not depend on one tape.

The best scheme is a combination of rotating and incremental backups. With *rotating backups,* a set of tapes is used in rotation; five

tapes, for example, one written every Monday, one every Tuesday, and so on. Because each tape is written only once a week, if you delete a file by mistake on Tuesday, for example, the file is still on the Monday tape until the following Monday. You then have nearly a week to realize that it's gone and get it back. The number of tapes you use depends on your budget and your paranoia. Some people use as few as two, some as many as seven. (We use four, because we bought a four-pack of tapes.)

With *incremental backups,* you back up only what's changed. Generally, you do a full backup of everything on the disk at infrequent intervals — once a month, for example. This process may take five or six tapes, but because you do it only once a month, it's not that bad a job. For the daily incremental backup, you back up only what has changed since the last full backup (it should fit on a single tape). Any given file then is either on the full backup (if it hasn't changed in a long time) or on the current backup, so there are only two places to look.

If you have a large tape budget, you may want to have two sets of tapes you use alternately for full backups, in case your system fails while it is writing the full backups. Sometimes, full backups are stored off-site in a bank vault or other safe place, but there's a trade-off: the security of the vault versus the inconvenience of going to the bank when you need to recover a file. If you're really paranoid, you can have two full backups, one off-site and one on-site.

Your system administrator should handle all of this, of course. It's useful to understand at least the rudiments of backup theory, however, so that, when the administrator hands you several different tapes that might contain your file, you will understand why.

Three Ways Not to Lose Files

Now you're probably quaking in your boots (or sandals, depending on where you live). You figure that, if you so much as touch the keyboard, you will do horrible, irreparable damage and spend the next week spinning tapes. It's not that bad. The following sections tell you some tricks to avoid deleting files by mistake in the first place.

Are you sure you wanna clobber this one?

When you delete files with rm, use the -i (for *interactive*) switch, as follows:

```
rm -i s*
```

This line tells rm to ask you before it deletes each file, prompting you with the filename and a question mark. You answer Y if you want to delete it, and N to tell UNIX not to delete. (Remember that the question UNIX asks is, "Should I delete this?" and not "Do you want to keep this?")

The main problem with -i is that it can become tedious when you want to delete a lot of files. When you do that, you probably use wildcards. To be safe, check that the wildcards refer to the files you think they do. To make that check, use the ls command with the same wildcard. If you want to delete all the files that start with *section*, for example, and you think that you can get away with typing only *sec* and an asterisk, you had better check what *sec** refers to. First give this command:

```
ls sec*
```

UNIX responds with an appropriate list:

```
second.version   section04   section08   section12   section16
section01        section05   section09   section13   section17
section02        section06   section10   section14   section18
section03        section07   section11   section15   section19
```

Hey, look! There's that file `second.version`. You don't want to delete that, so it looks like you will have to type out `section*` to get the correct files in this case.

Idiot-proofing save files

The best way to make temporary backup copies of files is to make a directory called `save` and put all saved copies of files there, as shown in this example:

```
mkdir save
cp important.file save
```

These commands tell UNIX to make a directory called `save` and then to make a copy of `important.file` to `save/important.file`. If you reverse the order of the names, nothing happens. Suppose that you type this line instead:

```
cp save important.file
```

UNIX makes this observation:

```
cp : <save> directory
```

UNIX is saying that you can copy a file to a directory but that you can't copy a directory to a file. As a result, it doesn't copy anything. To copy a file back from the `save` directory, you have to use its full name: `save/important.file`.

A variation on this is a two-step delete. Suppose that you have a bunch of files you want to get rid of, but there are some good files mixed in the same directory. Make a directory called `trash` and then use `mv` to move to the trash directory the files you plan to delete, as follows:

```
mkdir trash
mv thisfile thatfile these* trash
mv otherfile somefile trash
```

Then use the ls command to check the contents of trash. If there's something in that directory you want, move it back to the current directory by using the following command:

```
mv trash/these.are.still.good .
```

(The dot at the end means to put the file back in the current directory.) After you're sure that there's nothing but trash in trash, you can use rm with the -r option, as follows:

```
rm -r trash
```

This line tells rm to get rid of trash and everything in it.

Don't write on that!

Another thing you can do to avoid damage to important files is to make them read-only. When you make files read-only, you prevent cp and text editors from changing them. You can still delete them, although rm, mv, and ln ask you before doing so. The chmod command changes the "mode" of a file (as explained in the section "If Mom says no, go ask Dad" in Chapter 5). Here's how to use chmod to make a file read-only:

```
chmod -w crucial-file
```

The -w means *not writable*. To make changes to the file later, do another chmod but use +w instead. (This isn't inspired command syntax, but the old syntax was even worse and used octal digits.) After a file is made not writable, editors can't change it. The vi program and some versions of emacs even display a note on-screen that the file is read-only. If you try to delete it, rm, mv, or ln asks you in a uniquely user-hostile way whether that's really what you had in mind. Suppose that you type the following line and crucial-file is a read-only file:

```
rm crucial-file
```

UNIX responds with this line:

```
crucial-file: 444 mode ?
```

The number may not be 444: It may be 440 or 400 (depending on whether your system administrator has set things up so that people can normally see the contents of other people's files). As with rm -i, you type Y if you want to delete the file, or N to say that you don't want to delete this valuable data.

Chapter 24

Some Programs Just Won't Die

ou can almost always get rid of recalcitrant programs without rebooting. In this chapter, we talk about how to figure out which processes you have and how to make unwanted ones go away. Before reading this chapter, be sure that you've read Chapter 13, where we talk about how you can juggle processes yourself and do neat tricks, such as stop one program, run another one, go back to the first one, and pick up exactly where you left off.

Why Killing Is Sometimes Justified

Why kill a process? Don't even the smallest processes deserve to live?

In a word, no. Sometimes a program hangs, and your computer just sits there, inert. Or sometimes a program gets stuck in some kind of loop and never ends. Or sometimes you give the wrong command and realize that you don't want to run that program after all. To stop the process in which the program is running, you kill the process.

Suppose that you're running along, minding your own business, and you find that you have a program that just won't stop. Vell, ve haff vays to make eet stop. First, we discuss the normal ways to kill a process and then we get into some serious artillery.

What Process? (Reprise)

In the Chapter 13 section named "Are There Any Processes in the House?" we told you how to use the ps command to see what processes you've got running. In case you are too weak from struggling with UNIX to turn back to Chapter 13, just type the ps command to see a list of your processes. Note the PID (process ID) of the process that you want to kill. You can identify which process is the one that needs to be offed, because ps shows you the command line that started each process.

50 Ways to Kill Your Process

The usual way to get rid of a process is to press the *interrupt character,* which is usually Ctrl+C, although sometimes it's Delete. In most cases, the rogue program gives up peaceably, and you end up back in the shell. Sometimes, though, the program arranges to handle Ctrl+C itself. If you use the ed editor (if you're a masochist) and you press Ctrl+C, for example, ed returns to command mode rather than give up and throw away any work you have done. To exit ed, you have to use the q command.

If the interrupt character doesn't work, you can up the ante and use the *quit character,* generally Ctrl+\ (a reverse slash or backslash — not the regular forward slash). The quit character not only kills the program but also saves the dead body of the process (this description is awfully morbid, but we didn't invent these terms) in a file called, for arcane historical reasons, core (or maybe *programname*.core). The shell then gives this requiem:

```
Quit (core dumped)
```

This message tells you that the process is dead and that its body has been put on ice with the filename core.

Most programs that catch Ctrl+C give up under the greater onslaught of Ctrl+\. If the program you were running is one written locally, your system administrator may appreciate it if you save the core file, because it includes clues about what was going wrong when you killed the program. Otherwise, delete any core files with rm, because they're a waste of space.

It is possible for a program to immunize itself to Ctrl+\ (ed, for example, just ignores it), so the next possibility is the *stop character* (always Ctrl+Z). The stop character doesn't kill the program; it just puts it to sleep and returns you to the shell. (See Chapter 13 for more information about what Ctrl+Z really does and how it can be useful even with programs you like.) After you're back in the shell, you can apply the stronger medicine described in the next section.

For Ctrl+Z to work, your shell must do some of the work. Many versions of the Bourne shell aren't up to it and ignore Ctrl+Z. The C, BASH, and Korn shells are Ctrl+Z-aware.

Dirty Deeds, Done Dirt Cheap

No more Mister Nice Guy: It's time for merciless slaughter. If you were successful in the preceding section at putting the process to sleep with Ctrl+Z, go ahead and kill it with the procedure in this section.

All the following techniques require that you have a terminal or window in which you can type some commands to do the dirty deeds. If Ctrl+Z didn't work to put the process to sleep, you may not have a shell prompt at which to type the requisite commands. Here are other places you can use to type the commands to kill the process:

- ✔ If you're running X Windows, any window other than the one with the stuck program will do.

- ✔ Otherwise, you may have to find another terminal attached to your computer or go to another computer on the network and use telnet or rlogin to get into your computer.

- ✔ If there's no other terminal or window and no other way into the machine, you're out of luck and probably will have to reboot. Before you reboot, check with your system administrator, who may know some other tricks.

Here is a simple two-step procedure for murdering a rogue process:

1. Find out the rogue process's true name.

2. Utter the true name in an appropriate spell to murder it.

The true name of a process is its PID, one of the things ps reports. First do a ps command to find out the PID of your victim. To find out the PID, follow these steps:

1. If you pressed Ctrl+Z to put the rogue process to sleep and you are using the same terminal to kill it utterly, type a plain ps.

2. Otherwise, you may have to use a different terminal to kill the process, because the amok process has taken over our own terminal. In this case, you have to tell ps which user's processes you want to see. If you use Linux, type the following command:

```
ps -u username
```

Replace *username* with your own login name, so that you see the processes that you are running.

If you use System V, type this command:

```
ps -fu username
```

If you use BSD, type the following:

```
ps -a
```

Suppose that you saw the following listing after typing ps -fu johnl, which lists all the processes for user johnl (the listing is shortened to save space):

```
UID    PID   PPID  C   STIME   TTY   TIME COMMAND

johnl  24806 24799 0   Jan 18  ?     0:39 xclock
```

The PID of the process we want to kill is 24806. You kill it by typing the kill command, as follows:

```
kill 24806
```

The normal kind of kill sends a request to a process: "Please, nice Mr. Process, would you be so kind as to croak?" This method usually works, but occasionally a program won't take the hint. Another kind of kill, the ominously named Number-Nine kill, offers the victim no choice. Type the following command:

```
kill -9 24806
```

If you stopped a particularly uncooperative program with Ctrl+Z, a regular kill may provoke it to retaliate by trying to take over your terminal (something the shell fortunately prevents). Here's a true-life transcript of our attempts to murder our old text editor pal, ed. First we pressed Ctrl+Z, which put it to sleep. Then we tried a regular kill. When ed tried to strike back, we did a Number Nine. Sayonara, Bud.

```
% ed badfile

?badfile

Ctrl-Z

Stopped

% ps

PID    TTY    TIME   COMMAND

12746  ttyp1  0:00   ed

12747  ttyp1  0:00   ps

11643  ttyp1  0:02   -csh

% kill 12746

?

[1]  + Stopped (tty input)    ed badfile

% kill -9 12746

[1]    Killed               ed badfile
```

Resuscitating a terminal

If you blow away a program that reads a character at a time from your terminal, such as vi or emacs, the dead process leaves your terminal in a rather peculiar state that makes it hard to get any work done. The following three-step method usually brings the terminal back:

1. **Press Ctrl+J. The shell may complain about strangely named nonexistent commands. Ignore its whining.**

2. **Type** stty, **a space, and** sane **(as opposed to the insane state your terminal is in). Press Enter. You may not see anything on-screen. Remain calm.**

3. **Press Ctrl+J again. This should put your terminal back into a usable state.**

When X Goes Bad

If you're using X Windows in any of its multiple guises (particularly Motif) and are especially unlucky, X itself may freeze the entire screen. If you can get into your computer through another terminal or a network, you can get rid of X Windows itself. Doing so makes all the programs using X go away, so that you have to log in all over again. The trick is to figure out which program is X Windows. Here's an edited `ps` report from a System V system:

```
UID    PID    PPID  C STIME   TTY   TIME    COMMAND

johnl 24788 19593 0 Jan 18  vt01  0:00    /usr/bin/X11/xinit

johnl 24789 24788 5 Jan 18  ptmx  38:10  Xgp :0
```

In this case, X is called `Xgp`, because the particular computer happened to have a graphics processor running the screen.

Here's the equivalent from a Sun workstation:

```
PID TT STAT TIME    COMMAND

224  co IW    0:00   /bin/sh /usr/openwin/bin/openwin

228  co IW    0:00   /usr/openwin/bin/xinit — /usr/openwin/
                     bin/xnews :0

229  co S    149:23 /usr/openwin/bin/xnews :0 -auth /
                     usr/johnl/.xnews
```

There are two easy ways to know which process is X:

- ✔ The command line has the strange code `:0`, which turns out to be X-ese for "the screen right there on the computer."
- ✔ The amount of computer time used (in the `STAT` column) is large, because X is, computationally speaking, a pig.

After you figure out which process is X, you can give it the old Number-Nine kill and probably be able to log back in.

If you're using an X terminal, the Number-Nine kill doesn't apply, because X itself runs in the terminal and not in the main computer. In this case, you kill X by restarting the X terminal. In the worst case, you turn the terminal off and back on, although your system administrator can probably tell you an easier way.

Chapter 25

My Computer Says It Hates Me

●●●

●●●

Question: You type a command. UNIX says something incomprehensible. What does it mean? And what should you do?

Answer: Look in this chapter for the error message. We tell you what it means and what you can do to fix the problem.

Most error messages start with the name of the command you tried to use. If you want to use the cp command to copy a file, for example, but you spell the name of the file incorrectly, cp can't find a file with the name you typed. So it says something like the following:

```
cp: No such file or directory
```

At the beginning of the line is the name of the command that failed to work. After the colon comes the UNIX error message — UNIX's attempt to explain the problem.

This chapter contains the most common error messages, in alphabetical order. In some of the explanations, we refer to things called *arguments,* not because we are feeling argumentative but because it is the technical name for the information you type on the command line after the command. Suppose that you type this line:

```
cp proof.that.elvis.lives save
```

cp is the command, `proof.that.elvis.lives` is the first argument, and *save* is the second argument. You can have lots of arguments on the line: The number you need depends on the command you use (cp requires two). Type a space between arguments.

There are also things called *options,* which tell the command how you want it to work. Options always start with a hyphen (-). Suppose that you type the following line:

```
ls -l
```

The *-l* tells the `ls` command how you want it to display the files. Options don't count as arguments. If you type the following line,

```
ls -l *
```

the *-l* is an option, and `*` is the first (not the second) argument.

This is really nit-picky stuff, but if UNIX complains about a particular argument or option, it is handy to know exactly which item it doesn't like.

And now (drum roll, please) the error messages!

Arg list too long

Meaning: The list of arguments (stuff on the command line after the name of the command) is too long.

Probable cause: When you type a wildcard character as part of a filename or pathname, UNIX replaces it with the list of filenames and then calls the command. If you go wild with the asterisks, the result is a very long list. The list can be more than 5,000 characters long, so it is unlikely that you typed too long a list of filenames unless you are an unusually fast typist.

Example: You are in the root directory (/) and you type this line:

```
ls */*
```

If there are a lot of files in the root directory and its subdirectories, `*/*` turns into a really long list.

Solution: Check the wildcards you used in the command and use fewer of them.

Newer versions of UNIX allow much longer argument lists than older ones did. If you're using a modern system, such as Linux or BSD/OS, and get this message, something strange is probably going on.

Broken pipe

Meaning: You are running two programs connected by a pipe, and the program at the receiving end of the pipe exited before it received all its data (see Chapter 7).

Probable cause: You get this error occasionally when you use a pipe (|) to redirect the output of a program into the more program and then type **q** to cancel the more program before you see all the output. The program has no place to put its output because you canceled the more program, so you get this error. In this case, it's harmless.

Example: You type this line:

```
man furgle | more
```

The man program (which displays frequently incomprehensible UNIX manual pages) gives you screen after screen of boring information. You type **q** to cancel the more program, but the man program gives you the error message.

Solution: Nothing to do — it's not really an error!

Cannot access

See the message No such file or directory.

Cross-device link

See the message Different file system.

Device or resource busy

Meaning: A device, such as a terminal or printer, is in use by another program.

Probable cause: Sometimes you see this message when you try to use cu or tip to access a terminal that's already in use by another program or user (see Chapter 21).

Example: You type the following line:

```
cu somesystem
```

Solution: Wait until the other user finishes.

Different file system

Meaning: You are using the ln command to create a link to a file in a different file system (a different disk or a disk on a different computer).

Probable cause: If your system can't do soft links (see Chapter 7), you can't create a link from one file system to another. The file you want to link to is probably in a different file system from the directory in which you want to make the link (usually the working directory).

Solution: Use the df command to find out which disks your computer has and which directories are on which disk. (See Chapter 21 to figure out what file systems you are dealing with.)

If your version of UNIX can't do soft links, you are out of luck. The only solution may be to make a copy of the file rather than create a link to it.

File exists

Meaning: A file already exists by that name.

Probable cause: When UNIX expected the name of the file you want to create, you typed the name of a file that already exists.

Solution: This message is rarely seen, because most UNIX commands blow away an existing file when they want to create a new one by the same name (which is not always what you want).

File table overflow

Meaning: The system is way too busy and can't juggle as many files simultaneously as all the users have asked it to.

Probable cause: The system isn't configured correctly, or someone is doing way too much work.

Solution: Complain to the system administrator.

File too large

Meaning: You are trying to make a file that is too big.

Probable cause: There is a maximum file size, set by your system administrator. Maximum file sizes prevent a messed-up program from making a file that uses up the entire disk by mistake. It is unlikely that you really want to make a file this big. Usually it happens when you use >> to add a copy of a file to itself, so you end up copying the file over and over until it passes the preset size limit.

Example: You type the line shown here:

```
pr myfile >> myfile
```

Solution: Check the command and make sure that you are saying what you mean. If you are sure that you want to make a really big file, talk your system administrator into upping your file-size limit.

Illegal option

Meaning: You typed an option that doesn't work with this command. (*Options* are things that tell the command how you want it to work. They begin with a hyphen.)

Probable cause: You typed a hyphen in front of a filename or you typed the wrong option.

Example: You type the following line:

```
ls -j
```

There is no -j option for the ls command, so you get an error message. Frequently, after the illegal option message, UNIX also prints a line about usage, which is its cryptic way of reminding you about which options *do* work with the command. (*See also* Usage.)

Solution: Check your typing. Look up the command in this book to make sure that you know which option you want. Alternatively, use the man command to display an exhaustive and exhausting list of every option the command might possibly understand.

Insufficient arguments

Meaning: You left out some information.

Probable cause: The command you are using needs more arguments than the ones you typed. UNIX may also print a usage message in its attempt to tell you which arguments you should have typed. (*See also* Usage.)

Example: The cp command needs two arguments: The first one tells it what to copy from, and the second one tells it what to copy to. You can't leave out either one.

Solution: Check your typing. If it is a command you don't use very often, check to make sure that you have the correct arguments and options.

I/O error

Meaning: *I/O* is computerese for *i*nput and *o*utput. There has been some physical problem reading or writing information on a disk, tape, screen, or wherever your information lives.

Probable cause: Broken disk drive.

Solution: Tell your system administrator. You may have big trouble ahead.

Is a directory

Meaning: You typed the name of a directory when UNIX wanted a filename.

Probable cause: The command you typed is trying to do something to a directory rather than to a file. You can look at a directory by using a text editor, but it looks like binary junk with filenames mixed in. You can't change a directory by editing it.

Note that `emacs` has a special mode for "editing" directories (called `dired` mode). But `emacs` has its own special way to create, rename, and delete files, too.

Solution: Make sure that you type a filename, not the name of a directory.

Login incorrect

Meaning: You are trying to log in and didn't enter a correct user name or corresponding password.

Probable cause: There are two possibilities: One is that you typed your password incorrectly, and the other is that you typed your user name incorrectly.

Solution: Type very slowly and deliberately, especially when you type your password and can't see what you are doing. If you have trouble remembering your password, use the `passwd` command to change it to something more memorable (see Chapter 2).

No process can be found

See the message `No such process`.

No such file or directory

Meaning: UNIX can't find a file or directory with the name you typed.

Probable cause: You spelled a filename or pathname wrong. This happens to most of us ten times a day. If you typed a pathname, you may have misspelled any of the directory names it contains. You may also have capitalized something incorrectly.

Example: You typed the following line:

```
cp june.bugdet save
```

But the file isn't called `june.bugdet` — it's `june.budget`.

Solution: Check your spelling and capitalization. Use the `ls` command to see how the file and directory names are spelled and whether there are any uppercase letters. For pathnames, check to see whether it should begin with a slash (which means that it is an absolute pathname that describes the path from the root directory) or not (which means that it is a relative pathname that describes the path from the current working directory). See Chapter 5 for more information about pathnames.

No such process

Meaning: UNIX can't find the process you are referring to.

Probable cause: You have given a command that talks about processes, probably a `kill` command to stop a runaway process. (See Chapter 24 for what a process is and why you may want to kill the poor thing.)

Solution: The process may already have gone away, in which case there's no problem. You may have mistyped the PID that specifies which process to do in. Check your typing and use the `ps` command to check the PID.

No more processes

Meaning: Your system can't create any more new processes.

Probable cause: This message appears when you tell UNIX to create a new process, and UNIX can't do it. See Chapter 24 for information about processes.

Possible reasons for this message are that the system doesn't have any more space for this kind of thing. Occasionally you get this message on very busy systems when you try to run something, or if you start dozens of background processes (see Chapter 13).

Solution: Wait a minute and try the command again. If you have lots of background processes, get rid of some of them. If you see this message very often, complain to your system administrator.

No space left on device

Meaning: The disk is full.

Probable cause: Either your files take up too much space or someone else's do.

Solution: Delete something to make space. If you don't think you can or you don't have any large files, talk to your system administrator, who has probably already gotten the same message and is checking to see who is taking up all the space.

Not a directory

Meaning: UNIX needed the name of a directory, but you typed a filename or the name of something else.

Probable cause: Either you spelled a directory name incorrectly or you forgot to create a new directory.

Example: You type the following line:

```
cd /gillian
```

But there is no directory called /gillian.

Solution: If you are referring to a new directory you planned to make, make it first by using the mkdir command. If you are referring to an existing directory, get the spelling right. Use the ls command to see how it is spelled.

Not enough space

Meaning: The system has run out of space in memory (not on disk).

Probable cause: Things are much too busy in your computer system. You probably caught UNIX at a bad moment when it was in the middle of getting itself organized.

Solution: Wait a minute and try the command again. If you see this message very often, complain to your system administrator.

Permission denied

Meaning: You don't have permission to do whatever the last command you issued tried to do.

Probable cause: You are trying to change, move, or delete a file you don't own.

Example: You type the following line:

```
rm /usr/bill/resignation.letter
```

But you are not Bill. You don't have permission to delete this file, so UNIX doesn't let you.

Solution: Use the `ls -l` command to find out who owns the file and what its permissions are. (See Chapter 5 for information about permissions.) If you think that you ought to be able to mess with the file, make your own copy of it or talk to the owner of the file or your system administrator.

RE error

Meaning: You are using the `grep` program, and it doesn't understand what you are searching for. (*RE* stands for *regular expression*.)

Probable cause: You probably have to use backslashes before a character that is a wildcard in `grep`.

Example: You type this line:

```
grep '[x' myfile
```

Solution: Put a backslash before any character that has a special wildcard meaning in `grep` (`grep` wildcards include periods, asterisks, square brackets, dollar signs, and carets). If you are searching for text that contains special characters, put single quotation marks around the text to match.

Read-only file system

Meaning: You are trying to change a file that UNIX is not allowed to change.

Probable cause: Some disks, particularly NFS remote disks, are marked read-only so that you can't create, delete, or change files on them. It doesn't matter what the permissions are for the individual files: The entire file system can't be changed.

Solution: Talk to your system administrator. Alternatively, make a copy of the file you want to change and change the copy.

Too many links

Meaning: You are trying to make so many links to a file that you have exceeded the maximum number of links to a file.

Probable cause: The maximum number of links to a file is 1,000. You must be a heck of a typist to get this message. Because the parent directory is linked to each of its subdirectories, you also get this message if you try to make more than 1,000 subdirectories in one directory.

Solution: Stop making links.

Usage

Meaning: UNIX doesn't like the number or types of arguments you typed after the command. It is telling you (in its own cryptic way) the correct way to use the command.

Probable cause: UNIX usually displays this message with another, more specific, message. Check out the other message to see what the real problem was. The usage message is UNIX's reminder about how to use the command. After usage, you see the command, followed by the options and arguments you can use with the command. Unfortunately, there's no clue about what the options do.

Example: You type this line:

```
kill abc
```

UNIX responds with the following message:

```
usage: kill [ -signo ] pid
```

This line means that the correct way to use the `kill` command is to type **kill**, a space, (optionally) the type of signal you want to send to the process, another space, and then the process ID. Not that this is entirely clear from the message!

Solution: Check your typing, as always. Make sure that there are spaces between things on the line (between filenames or between a filename and an option, for example). If this is a command you don't use very often, check to make sure that you have the correct arguments (filenames and so on) and options (things that begin with a dash, such as the *-l* in `ls  -l`). Look up the command in this book or consult the UNIX manual page about it. (See Chapter 27 for instructions on how to display manual pages.)

444 mode? (or some other three-digit number)

Meaning: You don't have permission to change this file, but you have told UNIX to delete it.

Probable cause: You are using `rm`, `mv`, or `ln` to remove or replace a read-only protected file or a file that belongs to someone else. (See Chapter 5 for information about permissions.) Rather than refuse outright to do what you asked, UNIX asks you whether you really want to do this.

Example: You used the `chmod` command to make a really important file read-only. Then you decide to delete it by typing this line:

```
rm important.file
```

UNIX asks whether you really want to delete it, even though the file is read-only.

Solution: The question mark at the end of this message indicates that UNIX is asking you a question. By divine intuition, you are supposed to guess that UNIX is asking whether you want to go ahead and do the command anyway. Press Y if you want to go ahead and do the command. Press N if you want to cancel it (for this file, anyway).

If you own the file, you can change its permissions by typing the following line:

```
chmod 644 filename
```

Rather than `filename`, type the real filename. This command has the result of allowing anyone to read or write to the file.

Part VI
The Part of Tens

In this part . . .

*U*NIX includes a lot of commands, programs, options, and other stuff — much more than we can pack into this book. The real, official manuals for a UNIX system take up about three feet of shelf space. (For cost savings, all the pages of these manuals are blank because no one ever reads them, but if you don't tell, neither will we.)

In this part of the book, we organize facts into neat lists of ten so they'll be easier to remember. Astute readers may claim that none of these lists contains exactly ten items. Well, we were using mixed radix arithmetic (survivors of New Math in school may remember some of this from fourth grade), so a chapter with eight items has ten items counting in base 8, a chapter with twelve items has ten items counting in base 12, a chapter — what? You say we can't bamboozle you with such nonsense? Truth is, we can't count.

Read on — there's good stuff here, regardless of the numbers.

Chapter 26
Ten Common Mistakes

● ●

In This Chapter

▶ Mistyping commands

▶ Believing that it will be easy

▶ Pressing Enter or not pressing Enter

▶ Working in the wrong directory

▶ Not keeping backup copies

▶ Not keeping files organized

▶ Turning off your computer

▶ Writing your password on a note next to the computer

▶ Sending angry electronic mail (flaming)

● ●

*H*ere are ten (or so) of the most common user mistakes we have run into. Although you will probably invent some new ones yourself, at least avoid the ones on this list.

Believing That It Will Be Easy

UNIX was designed a long, long time ago in computer time (computer years are similar to dog years, except that 50 computer years equal a human year). Software design has made a lot of progress since 1972. UNIX has not. If you are used to a Macintosh or a PC with Windows, or even a PC with DOS, UNIX is not going to be easy to use.

On the other hand, UNIX has a certain cachet and glamour; it takes a macho person (of either gender) to face it. You should give yourself major kudos, and maybe even one or two of those cookies you made to bribe your UNIX wizard, every time you get UNIX to do something useful.

Mistyping Commands

If you type a command the UNIX shell doesn't understand, it says that it can't find it. The reason is that it looks high and low for a file with the name you just typed, hoping to find the program you want to run. And then it says:

```
eatmylunch: Command not found.
```

Or perhaps it says:

```
eatmylunch: not found
```

The exact wording varies from shell to shell (we bet you already guessed that).

- ✔ Check your spelling (as always). You may have typed a correctly spelled English word rather than the garbled set of letters that comprise the name of the program.

- ✔ Check your capitalization. Capital and small letters count as completely different things in filenames and, therefore, in commands too. Nearly every command uses only small letters.

- ✔ Change directories (maybe). You may have given the right command, but UNIX may not know where to look for the file containing the program. If you know where the program file is, move to that directory and give the command again. If you don't know where the file is, either look for it (see Chapter 23) or give up and ask your system administrator or local wizard.

To Press Enter, Or Not to Press Enter

Depending on which program you are using, sometimes you must press Enter (or Return) after a command, and sometimes you don't. In the UNIX shell, you *always* have to press Enter or Return before UNIX performs the command. If you don't, UNIX waits forever for you to do so.

In other programs, particularly in text editors like emacs and vi, as soon as you press the command (Ctrl+K to delete a line in emacs, for example), the program does it right away. If you press Enter or Return after the command, emacs sticks a new line in your file and vi moves down to the next line.

When you use a program you are not familiar with, hesitate a moment before pressing Enter or Return to see whether the computer might already be performing the command. If nothing is happening, press Enter or Return.

Working in the Wrong Directory

If you use separate directories to organize your files, make sure that you are in the proper directory when you begin working. Otherwise, UNIX won't find the files you want to work on.

To find out which directory you are in, type pwd. Remember that this command stands for *p*rint *w*orking *d*irectory.

If you are really lost, you can type whoami. This command tells you your user name.

To move back to your home directory, type cd.

Not Keeping Backup Copies

Sooner or later, it happens. You give an rm command to delete a file, and UNIX deletes the wrong file or it deletes everything in the directory. Chances are, you typed an extra space or spelled a filename wrong, but the point is — what now?

See Chapter 23 for how to proceed if you delete something important. The best approach is to keep extra copies of important files: in another directory, on a floppy disk, or on a backup tape that either you or your system administrator makes. If you haven't talked to your system administrator about backups, now is a good time to find out whether your files are backed up automatically; you can also tell him which of your directories contain files you want to have backed up.

Not Keeping Files Organized

Unless you do all your work on one or two files, you will run into trouble if you don't do the following:

- ✔ Make directories for the groups of files you use (see Chapter 6 for how to do this). Directories help you separate your files into groups of files you use together.
- ✔ Use filenames that mean something. UNIX lets you name your files with nice long names, so take advantage of it (up to a point, anyway). Filenames should tell you what's inside the file rather than make you guess.

Turning Off the Computer

Leaving the computer on all the time is better than turning it off at the wrong time. Chapter 1 talks about this subject in detail. UNIX can get messed up if you turn off the computer (kick the plug out by mistake, for example) without warning it that you are going to do so.

If you use UNIX from a terminal rather than directly with a workstation, it may make sense to turn off the terminal (not the computer) at night. Check with your system administrator.

Writing Your Password on a Sticky Note

Okay, maybe this doesn't apply if you work at home, live alone, and don't have any friends, cleaning people, or burglars. But, otherwise, you should keep your password to yourself. Not that anyone has malicious intent — let's not get paranoid — but people can get curious around computers. And you never know when an inquisitive 14-year-old will appear on the scene who knows more about UNIX than you do. If you can't remember your password, choose a new one that is more memorable. See Chapter 1 for hints.

Sending Angry Electronic Mail (Flaming)

Electronic mail can bring out your insidious side. There you are, sitting alone in your cubicle with your computer, and you get ticked off at something, usually some stupid message sent by a coworker. Before you know it, you have composed and sent a tactless, not to say downright rude, response.

It is easy to say things in e-mail that you would never say in person, or even write in a memo. But e-mail has an off-the-cuff, spontaneous style in most organizations, and it can get you into trouble.

Sarcasm seldom works in e-mail — instead, you just sound mean. Gentle suggestions can turn into strident demands just because they appear in ugly computer type on a computer screen. There is even a special name for rude mouthing off via e-mail — *flaming*. A message full of tactless, pointless complaints is referred to as a *flame*. A series of flames between two or more people is called a *flame war*. You get the idea.

Recipients of your mail can easily forward copies of it to anyone else, so imagine that everyone in the office might read your missives. Think twice before sending e-mail containing negative remarks! Then don't send it.

Chapter 27

Ten Times More Information than You Want about UNIX

• •

In This Chapter

▶ How to use the man command for on-line help

▶ What's on a manual page

▶ Other books about UNIX

▶ Finding UNIX information on the Internet

• •

*W*e wish that this book contained every single thing that you might ever want to know about UNIX. We considered writing the book that way, but our publisher frowned on printing a book with 25,000 pages. (Books like that are hard to bind, not to mention hard to pick up off the floor.) So, we tried to include just the information that new UNIX users really need to know. But what about the more advanced facts that you, a seasoned UNIX veteran, now need?

Let's Hear It from the man

You thought that UNIX was completely unhelpful. For the most part, you are absolutely right. But a standard UNIX command called man (for *man*ual) can give you on-line help.

Sound good? Well, yes and no. The information is there, all right, but it is written in a rather nerdy style and can be difficult to decipher. Of course, each part of the on-line manual is written on the assumption that you have read all the other parts and know what all the commands are called. The man command is definitely worth knowing about, though, when you just can't remember the options for a command or what to type where on the command line after the command name.

The man's on-line manual contains *manual pages* for every UNIX command, and other pages about internal functions that programmers use, formats for various system file types, descriptions of some of the hardware that can be attached to your UNIX system, and other odds and ends. When you type the man command, you indicate which page or pages you want.

All manual pages have a standard format. Figure 27-1 shows part of the manual page for dcheck, a program a system administrator might use to deal with people whose files take up too much space on the disk.

The parts of the manual page include the following:

✔ The title of the manual page is the first line. It includes the name and page number of the manual page at the left and right ends of the line. Centered on the line may be the name of the system of which the command is a part. In this example, the dcheck command is part of the diskhog **system.**

✔ NAME: The one-line name of the manual page. The name is usually the command or commands the page is about, as well as a brief description.

✔ SYNOPSIS: What you type when you give the command, with a terse and cryptic example of every option available. This often makes no sense until you read the description that follows. Sometimes it still makes no sense.

Figure 27-1:
A section
of the man
page for
dcheck, a
truly arcane
command.

```
DCHECK()                    Diskhog                    DCHECK(1)
NAME
    dcheck - send mail to potential disk hogs
SYNOPSIS
    dcheck
DESCRIPTION
    dcheck is normally run from the crons procedure to check
    if users are taking up too much space. It creates a tag
    file for such users, will send them warning mail, and
    also sends mail to the system administrator about what
    it's done.
SEE ALSO
    diskhog(1).
FILES
    $DQUOTAS/hogs/$LOGNAME  -   tag file indicating that
                                diskhog should be run
WARNINGS
    Should know about multiple file systems.
BUGS
    None.
```

✔ DESCRIPTION: A few paragraphs about the command. For commands with a lot of options, the description can run for a few pages. There is usually a list of the options with an explanation of every one. Sometimes there are examples, although not often enough.

✔ SEE ALSO: This section lists names of related manual pages, if any.

✔ WARNINGS and BUGS: If the command has known bugs or common problems, they may be listed here. Then again, they may not be.

✔ FILES: A list of the files this command uses. The elm and mail commands, for example, use your Mail directory, the central list of mailboxes, and other files. (These files usually are set up by your system administrator and rarely are things you want to fool with yourself.) The manual pages for elm and mail mention these files.

Reading manual pages

To see a manual page, type the following line:

```
man unixcommand
```

Except, of course, you substitute for unixcommand the name of the UNIX command you are interested in. Some versions of man present the manual page a screen at a time. Other versions just whip the page by at maximum speed, assuming that you can read 150,000 words per minute. If that happens (and you can't read that fast), you can use the usual more command to show you the manual page a screen at a time by typing the following command:

```
man unixcommand | more
```

On the other hand, if you're on a system that normally presents manual pages a screen at a time, and you want it to whip by at full speed because you just finished a speed reading course — so you *can* read 150,000 words per minute (or, more likely, because your terminal is a PC and you're capturing the terminal output to a file) — type the following line (the dash tells UNIX you're a fast reader):

```
man - unixcommand
```

Printing manual pages

You can also print the manual pages for later perusal. To print the manual pages, type this line:

```
man unixcommand | lpr
```

Remember to use `lp`, if that is the command you use to print. It might be better to put the manual pages in a file first, remove the information you don't want, and print the result. You could type the following line, for example (remember to substitute for `filename` the name of the file you want the information in):

```
man unixcommand > filename
```

Then edit the file with a text editor (see Chapter 10) and print it (see Chapter 9). Before you print the file, however, keep in mind that the on-line manual pages are generally identical to the printed manual pages in the dusty UNIX manuals on the shelf, except that the printed manual pages are typeset so that they're easier to read. Rather than print the on-line page, it's often better to look it up in the paper manual. (Bet you didn't think we would *ever* tell you to do that!)

If you have a laser printer, it's often possible to print out the manual pages with nice fonts and italics and such rather than the typewriter-like version you see on the screen. Ask your local guru for advice. Usually, you use `troff` or `groff` typesetting programs.

Finding the manual page you want

If you use the `man` command, there is no good way to find out which manual pages are available. Sometimes it can be difficult to find the one you want. Suppose that you type the following line:

```
man ln | more
```

UNIX shows you this message:

```
man: ln not found
```

The `ln` command has no separate manual page. Instead, it shares a set of pages with `cp` and `mv`. You get information about `ln` by typing the line shown here:

```
man cp | more
```

(Typical UNIX ease of use!) If `man` doesn't display anything about the command you want, try some similar commands. BSD UNIX systems have an `apropos` command that suggests manual pages relevant to a particular topic, so you can type `apropos ln` to see what it has to say.

In addition to manual pages about commands, there are lots of pages about other topics. You can type this line, for example:

```
man ascii
```

If necessary, you can type the following line:

```
man ascii | more
```

This command shows you a table of the ASCII-character codes for all the characters text files can contain. You probably aren't interested in them, but it does look impressively technoid.

It's a bird, it's a plane, it's xman!

If you use X Windows or Motif, you can use the xman command to look at manual pages. The nice thing about xman is that it displays a list of the available manual pages. When you run xman, it pops up a little box with three buttons, one of which is labeled Manual Page. If you click on it, a larger window then displays a manual page describing xman. Select Display Directory from the Options menu on that page, or press Ctrl+D as a short-cut, to see a screen of all of the manual pages it has — probably more than 100 of them. Click on the one you want to see, and xman switches to that page. Press Ctrl+D again to return to the directory of manual pages. Read the initial description of xman for other tricks you can get xman to do, such as show you two or three different pages at a time, or search for keywords in manual-page titles.

Scanning the Networks

If your system is connected to the Internet, or if you have dial-up access to an Internet provider, you can connect to Usenet, a gigantic distributed on-line bulletin board described in Chapter 19. Most of the systems on Usenet are running on UNIX systems, so there's a lot of discussion of UNIX issues and questions.

Your basic UNIX news

Usenet discussions are loosely organized into about 10,000 topic areas, or *newsgroups*. Table 27-1 lists some of the newsgroups that discuss UNIX topics.

Table 27-1	UNIX-Related Newsgroups
Group	*Description*
comp.unix.admin	UNIX system administration.
comp.unix.advocacy	Arguments about how wonderful UNIX is.
comp.unix.aix	AIX, IBM's version of UNIX.
comp.unix.amiga	UNIX on the Commodore Amiga.
comp.unix.aux	Apple's AUX for the Macintosh.
comp.unix.bsd.386bsd.announce	Announcements about the 386BSD version of UNIX.
comp.unix.bsd.386bsd.misc	Discussions about the 386BSD operating system.
comp.unix.bsd.bsdi.announce	Announcements about BSD/OS.
comp.unix.bsd.bsdi.misc	Discussions of BSD/OS.
comp.unix.bsd.freebsd.announce	Announcements about the FreeBSD version of UNIX.
comp.unix.bsd.freebsd.misc	Discussions of FreeBSD.
comp.unix.bsd.misc	Various BSD versions of UNIX.
comp.unix.bsd.netbsd.announce	Announcements about the NetBSD version of UNIX.
comp.unix.bsd.netbsd.misc	Discussions of NetBSD.
comp.unix.bsd.openbsd.announce	Announcements about the OpenBSD version of UNIX.
comp.unix.bsd.openbsd.misc	Discussions of OpenBSD.
comp.unix.cde	The Common Desktop Environment.
comp.unix.cray	UNIX on Cray supercomputers.
comp.unix.dos-under-unix	Running MS-DOS programs under UNIX.
comp.unix.internals	Technical internals of UNIX.
comp.unix.large	UNIX on large systems.
comp.unix.misc	Random UNIX discussions.
comp.unix.osf.misc	Discussions of the OSF/1 version of UNIX.
comp.unix.osf.osf1	OSF/1 version of UNIX.
comp.unix.pc-clone.16bit	UNIX on 16-bit IBM PC compatibles.
comp.unix.pc-clone.32bit	UNIX on 32-bit IBM PC compatibles.

Group	Description
comp.unix.programmer	Programming on UNIX.
comp.unix.questions	Questions about UNIX. The best place to ask questions. Look at articles first to see if someone has just asked the same question.
comp.unix.shell	UNIX shells.
comp.unix.solaris	Sun's Solaris version of UNIX.
comp.unix.sys5.r3	SVR3 version of UNIX.
comp.unix.sys5.r4	SVR4 version of UNIX.
comp.unix.ultrix	Digital's Ultrix version of UNIX.
comp.unix.unixware.announce	Announcements about Novell UNIXWARE.
comp.unix.unixware.misc	Discussions about Novell UNIXWARE.
comp.unix.user-friendly	An oxymoron.
comp.unix.wizards	Technical discussions among UNIX wizards.
comp.unix.xenix.misc	Miscellaneous versions of Xenix.
comp.unix.xenix.sco	SCO Xenix, a old, popular UNIX for IBM PC clones.
comp.security.unix	UNIX security issues.

Just for Linux

Since Linux is so popular, Table 27-2 lists a whole bunch of discussion groups of its own.

Table 27-2	Linux-Related Newsgroups
Group	**Description**
comp.os.linux.admin	Linux system administration.
comp.os.linux.advocacy	Discussions of how great Linux is.
comp.os.linux.announce	Announcements of new versions of Linux.
comp.os.linux.answers	Answers to frequently asked questions; a good place to look.

(continued)

Table 27-2 *(continued)*

Group	Description
comp.os.linux.development.apps	Development of application programs.
comp.os.linux.development.system	Development of the underlying Linux system.
comp.os.linux.hardware	Making Linux work with various kinds of hardware.
comp.os.linux.misc	Linux discussions that don't fit anywhere else.
comp.os.linux.networking	Networking issues.
comp.os.linux.setup	Setting up Linux.
comp.os.linux.x	X Windows on Linux.

Other Sources of Information

Your system administrator or nearby UNIX users probably have copies of UNIX manuals lying around. The advantage of the printed manual is that an index is in the front (or the back). It is usually a permuted or KWIC index (an overly clever abbreviation for *key word in context*), which means that you can find an entry by looking under any of the words in the title except for boring ones, such as *the*. Then again, it's not a bad idea to try typing help, just to see what happens. Someone may have installed some kind of help system — you never know.

UNIX is used widely enough that a growing industry of UNIX books, magazines, user groups, and conferences has sprung up. Any of them can provide additional help and information.

Read a magazine

Several weekly or monthly magazines cover UNIX. Most of them include in their titles either the name UNIX or the code phrase Open Systems (for systems that act like UNIX but haven't licensed the UNIX trademark). The major brands of workstations (Sun, Hewlett-Packard, and IBM) also have magazines that specifically cover those product lines.

If you use Linux, take a look at the *Linux Journal.* Linux (P.O. Box 55549, Seattle, WA 98155-0549 USA, phone 206-782-7733, e-mail `linux@ssc.com`).

Read a book

Yeah, we know, you just read a book. Here are a few more you might like:

- Levine and Young, *UNIX For Dummies Quick Reference,* 3rd edition, IDG Books. (Equally big surprise.) Essential information from this book squashed down into a smaller, less expensive, pocket-sized form.

- Daniel Gilly, *UNIX in a Nutshell,* O'Reilly. A very complete UNIX reference, the one we turn to when memory fails. Comes in various editions for different versions of UNIX. Intended for more advanced users than our *Dummies Quick Reference.*

- Welsh and Kaufman, *Running LINUX,* O'Reilly. All about installing and using Linux. Medium technical, but quite informative.

- Naba Barkakati, *Linux Secrets,* IDG Books. A wide range of topics, from hardware debugging to using Linux in your business.

- *The Linux Bible,* Yggdrasil Computing. The on-line Linux documents neatly printed and bound — all 1200 pages of them.

Join a user group

There are two major UNIX user groups. The older one is called *Usenix,* which dates back to about 1976; it is traditionally for technical users. The other is *Uniforum,* formerly */usr/group,* which is more for business users. There are also local and regional UNIX user groups; you tend to find out about these groups from notes posted on physical or electronic bulletin boards.

Index